The London Conference and the Albanian Question (1912-1914)

The Dispatches of Sir Edward Grey

Edited by Bejtullah Destani and Robert Elsie

Centre for Albanian Studies, London

Publisher's Cataloging-in-Publication data

Names: Grey of Fallodon, Edward Grey, Viscount, 1862-1933, author. | Destani, Bejtullah D., editor. | Elsie, Robert, 1950-, editor.
Title: The London Conference and the Albanian question (1912-1914) : the dispatches of Sir Edward Grey / edited by Bejtullah Destani and Robert Elsie.
Series: Albanian Studies.
Description: London, UK: Centre for Albanian Studies, 2016.
Identifiers: ISBN 978-1535304726.
Subjects: LCSH Grey of Fallodon, Edward Grey, Viscount, 1862-1933. | Conference of Ambassadors (1912-1913 : London, England). | Eastern question (Balkan). | Balkan Peninsula--History--War of 1912-1913--Diplomatic history. | Balkan Peninsula--History--War of 1912-1913--Territorial questions--Albania. | Albania--History--1912-1944.
Classification: LCC DR46.9 .G 2016 | DDC 949.65/02

Albanian Studies, Vol. 27
ISBN 978-1535304726
2016

Cover photo: Albanian lad among the Balkan refugees camped out near Salonica (Thessaloniki), having fled the Balkan Wars (photo: Stéphane Passet, early September 1913, Musée Albert Kahn, Boulogne-Billancourt).

Table of Contents

Introduction 5

The Dispatches of Sir Edward Grey 11

Resolution of the London Conference on the Independence of Albania 349

Biographical Notes 351

Map of Albania, by Ismail Gagica (Prishtina).

Introduction

It was by no means evident in the early years of the twentieth century that Albania in southeastern Europe would become an independent country and would join the family of European nations. After five centuries as a part of the Ottoman Empire, the country was hardly noticed by the other peoples of Europe. This was to change at the time of the Balkan Wars (1912-1913) and the London Conference, at which Albania played a central role and where its fate was decided.

In the last decade of the nineteenth century and the first decade of the twentieth, the thought of political autonomy or indeed of independence had placed Albanian leaders in a dilemma. They were well aware of the possible boomerang effect that independence for the little Balkan country might have. As part of the Ottoman Empire, flagging though it was, the Albanians were at least protected from the expansionist designs of the neighbouring Christian states. Despite the sorry level of corruption and incompetence of the Ottoman administration under which Albanians suffered in the last decades of imperial rule, many Albanian leaders appreciated the tactical advantage of being governed from the distant Bosporus rather than from Belgrade or Athens, or from Cetinje, the nearby mountain capital of the expanding Kingdom of Montenegro, and confined themselves to strengthening national awareness and identity rather than to inciting direct political confrontation with the Sublime Porte.

In a memorandum sent by the Albanians of Monastir (Bitola) to the Great Powers in October 1896, Muslim and Christian Albanians alike protested that the Serbs, Bulgarians and Greeks enjoyed the support and protection of the Great

Powers, whereas the Albanians had no support at all. They were not looking for privileges nor did they desire full independence from Turkey. All they wanted was to be able to live their lives as Albanians. To this end, they demanded the unification of their five vilayets (Kosovo, Monastir, Salonika, Janina and Shkodra) into one administrative unit with its capital at Monastir, a bilingual (Turkish/Albanian) government administration, an assembly of representatives, Albanian-language schools, full religious and linguistic freedoms, and the restriction of compulsory military service to duties in the European part of the Empire. But the Porte showed no willingness to compromise on the issue of Albanian autonomy. As a result, popular uprisings against Turkish rule continued in this period with an almost predictable regularity, in particular in northern Albania and Kosovo. Guerrilla bands throughout the country added to the general confusion and insecurity, destroying what remnants of economic order existed and poisoning inter-ethnic relations in the region.

Many Albanian nationalists initially held great faith in the movement of the Young Turks, which was to lead to revolution in July 1908 and to the overthrow of Sultan Abdul Hamid II (r. 1876-1909) the following year. Mid'hat bey Frashëri (1880-1949) called upon Albanian leaders to give their full support to the Young Turks, who had their headquarters in his hometown of Salonica. Indeed, the Albanians played a major role in the Young Turk revolution, which precipitated the demise of this age of stagnation, and which gave the empire a constitution and a semblance of equality among citizens regardless of faith. Yet the hopes that the Albanians had stored in the Young Turks were soon dashed when it became apparent that the new administration was just as centralistic as the old one, or even more so. As the survival of the Ottoman Empire became more and more questionable, the Albanian uprisings continued: 1910 in Kosovo and the northern Albanian highlands, 1911 in the Catholic Mirdita region and the northern highlands, and 1912 in Skopje, Dibra and Vlora (Valona).

In October 1912, the final demise of Turkey-in-Europe was signaled by the outbreak of the First Balkan War in which the Greeks, Serbs, Montenegrins and Bulgarians united to drive the Turks out of the Balkans and back to the Bosporus. Within two months, virtually all of Albania was occupied by the neighbouring Balkan states, which, in their anti-Turkish and to a large extent anti-Muslim campaigns, had no intentions of recognizing the waking aspirations of the Albanian people.

Amidst the chaos and confusion created by the swift defeat of the Turks, the Albanian political figure, Ismail Qemal bey Vlora (1844-1919), assured of Austro-Hungarian support, convoked a national congress of Albanian leaders at Vlora on the southern Albanian coast. It was attended by thirty-seven delegates, primarily from southern and central Albania. At this meeting on 28 November 1912, Albania was declared independent, and centuries of Turkish rule were brought to an inglorious end.

Albania's declaration of independence was one thing, but the international recognition thereof was quite another. This occurred in London eight months later.

The London Conference (1912-1913), also known as the Conference of the Ambassadors, was a gathering of representatives of the six Great Powers (Great Britain, France, Germany, Austria-Hungary, Russia and Italy) who met in an attempt to resolve the problems in the Balkans that had arisen as a result of the collapse of the Ottoman Empire. It began its work on 17 December 1912 under the direction of the British Foreign Secretary, Sir Edward Grey (1862-1933), in the wake of the First Balkan War. On 30 May 1913 an agreement was reached under which Turkey would give up all territory west of the Enos-Midia line, i.e. virtually all of the Balkans.

With regard to Albania, the Ambassadors had initially decided that the country would be recognized as an autonomous state under the sovereignty of the sultan. After much discussion, however, they came to the formal decision that Albania, though to be deprived of much of its ethnic territory, would be a sovereign state independent of the Ottoman Empire. This decision was reached at the fifty-fourth meeting of the Conference on 29 July 1913 and provided the basis for the international recognition of Albanian independence.

Two major problems remained, however. Albania had no government with control over the whole country, nor did it have fixed and recognized borders. An international border commission was thus set up, charged with the awesome task of delineating the frontiers of the new state.

Though independence had been obtained and at least temporarily secured at the international level, enthusiasm among the Albanians was soon dampened. More than half of Albanian-settled territory and about thirty percent of the total Albanian population were left out of the new state. Most tragic of all, Kosovo, which had been brutally "liberated" by the Serbian army, was given to the Kingdom of Serbia, an error that haunted the Balkans right to the end of the twentieth century.

The new provisional government of Albania, whose sphere of influence hardly extended beyond the town of Vlora, had been formed with Ismail Qemal bey Vlora as prime minister and with a senate composed of eighteen members. Central Albania, i.e. Durrës (Durazzo) and Tirana, remained under the sway of landowner Essad Pasha Toptani (1863-1920), and it was not until 22 April 1913 that the citadel of Shkodra (Scutari) in the north, the last Turkish stronghold in the Balkans, was abandoned by Ottoman forces to the Montenegrins and was then handed over to the International Control Commission. There were initially thus three administrations in Albania with which the Great Powers had to contend. In addition to domestic chaos and intrigue created by conflicts of interest amongst the various feudal landowners, tribes and religious groups within the country, neighbouring Greece, Serbia and Montenegro all strove to exert as much influence – and grab as much land – in Albania as they could.

The choice of a head of state for the new Balkan nation recognised at the London Conference fell upon Prince Wilhelm zu Wied (1876-1945). The well-meaning German prince, a compromise solution, arrived in the port of Durrës on 7 March 1914 and was welcomed to the boom of cannons, but in the months to follow, he was unable to gain control of much more than the port city itself. With the outbreak of World War I, Prince Wilhelm lost all semblance of international support and was forced to leave Albania on 3 September 1914, after a mere six months of inglorious reign. During the ensuing 'Great War,' Albania was occupied by a succession of Italian, Greek, Serbian, Bulgarian, Montenegrin, Austro-Hungarian and French troops. The first seven years of Albanian independence were more of an empty formality than anything else, yet the country survived.

The present volume brings together British Foreign Office documents focusing on Albania from 1912 to 1914. Among them are the dispatches and private correspondence of the British Foreign Secretary, Sir Edward Grey, who chaired the London Conference and endeavoured to keep peace in Europe at an age when the Great Powers were unwaveringly gravitating towards war and conflagration. He was thus a pivotal figure in Balkan affairs at the time.

As a word of conclusion, we would like to express our gratitude to the National Archives in Kew near London, without whose support this volume could not have been published.

Robert Elsie
Berlin, July 2016

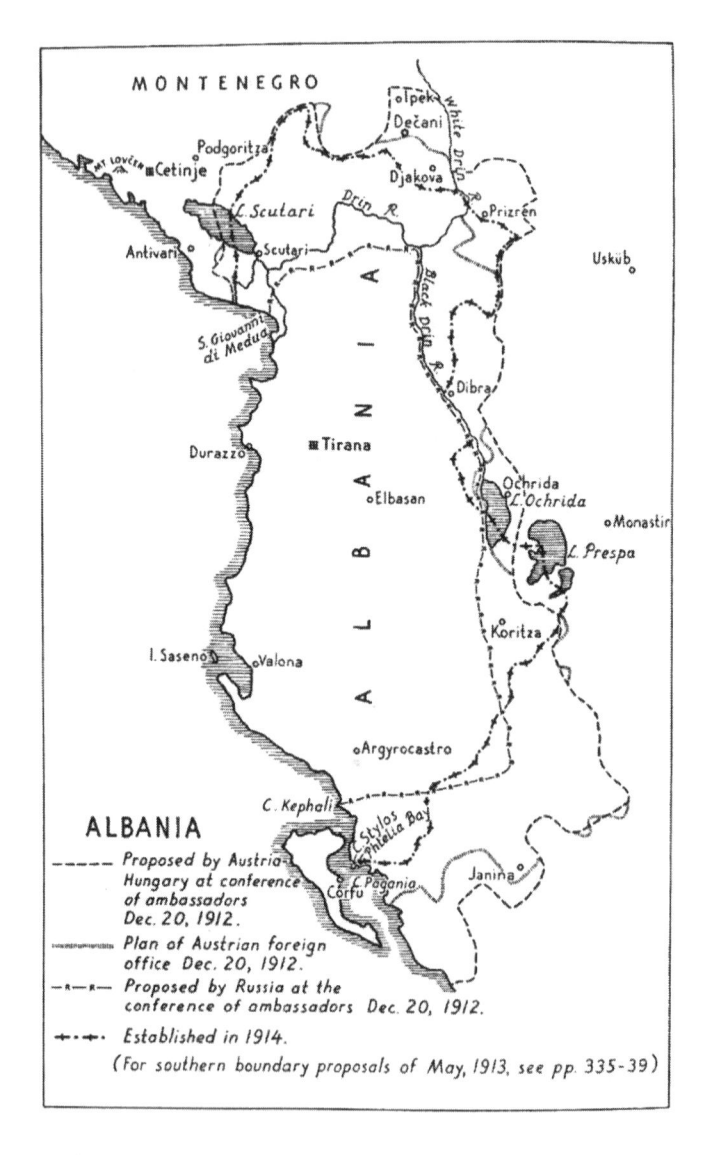

Propositions for the borders of Albania (taken from Ernest Christian Helmreich: *The Diplomacy of the Balkan Wars, 1912-1913* (Cambridge MA 1938).

The Dispatches of Sir Edward Grey

SIR EDWARD GREY.

[FO 45603/42842/12/44]

Sir Edward Grey to Sir E. Goschen
Foreign Office, October 25, 1912

Sir,
    The German Chargé d'Affaires informed me to-day that he had sent reports of previous conversations to his Government, and he now had instructions to say that, in the view of Herr von Bethmann-Hollweg, England and Germany ought to keep closely in touch and proceed "pari passu," if they could, in the present Balkan crisis. He would therefore be glad to have my views, and was ready to express certain views of his own.
    I said that I quite agreed that we should keep closely in touch, and I would gladly know what Herr von Bethmann-Hollweg's view was.
    In reply the Chargé d'Affaires said that, in the first place, Russia and Austria should be allowed to lead the Concert of Europe, as they were the parties most interested. In the next place, the present "status quo" should be maintained as far as possible. I observed that I presumed this meant the territorial "status quo," for there must be change of the "status quo" in Macedonia in the shape of reform.
    Herr von Kühlmann said it was the territorial "status quo" that he meant, and he added that if Turkey had the best of the war, it would be comparatively easy to secure this second condition.
    I agreed that this was so, as it had become an axiom of European politics that Turkey was not to reoccupy Christian territory from which she had withdrawn.
    The Chargé d'Affaires went on to say that the Chancellor thought that it would be more difficult to preserve

the territorial "status quo" if the Coalition met with success. He would be interested to know what I thought with regard to this.

I said that, if the Coalition met with success, everything would depend upon Russia and Austria: they, with Roumania, could stop the war, and prevent any disturbance of the territorial "status quo." But, if there was complete success for the Allies, so that they practically occupied Macedonia and Albania and right up to Constantinople, I did not see how any of the other Powers, except Russia and Austria and Roumania, were to turn them out.

I then told the Chargé d'Affaires that I welcomed both the fact that the Chancellor had made this communication and the substance of it. As far as it went, I was in entire agreement. I thought that the Powers ought to be ready for an opportune moment of mediation, and for this they must be agreed as to what form the settlement should take. An essential condition for such an agreement between the Powers was that Austria and Russia should come to an agreement. I had already put this view before M. Sazonoff, and had suggested that Russia should make up her own mind as to the settlement which she would consider satisfactory, and that she should then come to an agreement with Austria about it, if possible. I also showed Herr von Kühlmann the record of my conversation of the 24th instant with Count Mensdorff, and pointed out that I had brought the same point to the notice of the latter, so that everything I had done this week had been in the direction to which Herr von Bethmann-Hollweg's communication pointed.

I went on to say that, since the news of the Turkish reverses, I had been reflecting on the possibility that, if the Bulgarians won a big engagement at Adrianople, the whole Turkish Army might become disorganised; there might be a complete "débâcle"; and this would be followed by all sorts of unpleasant consequences. In this event, the present Turkish Government, if they were not swept away, might make a sudden appeal to the Powers for mediation. Such an appeal would, I thought, be of no use in enabling the Powers to stop the war, unless it was accompanied by an intimation that the Turks put the settlement unreservedly in the hands of the Great Powers. I thought that they should do this, if they appealed as the beaten party. This hypothesis was, however, an extreme one: and I did not mention it except as such; the result of the fighting during the next two or three days might be quite different from the result hitherto.

The Chargé d'Affaires asked me whether, in the event of such a collapse on the part of the Turks, we would disinterest ourselves in the question of Constantinople?

I replied that I did not think any Power could say that. I understood the Russian view to be that Russia could not allow Bulgaria to go to Constantinople, and that if the Turks were turned out of it she could not stand seeing anyone else there, except herself. What she contemplated was that the Turks should remain there.

In conclusion, Herr von Kühlmann said that the Chancellor felt it would exert a great moral force if it were known that England and Germany were acting together, and I asked him to come again on Monday that we might discuss any further developments that had taken place in the situation by then.

I observed that France and Italy remained, the former was politically disinterested, as we were, in a Balkan settlement.

Herr von Kühlmann said that he did not suppose that the French view would differ from the one which we had been discussing, and that Italy did not appear as yet to have settled what her policy was to be.

I am, &c.,
E. Grey

[FO 45378/38672/12/44]

Sir F. Cartwright to Sir Edward Grey
Vienna, October 26, 1912

I saw Austrian Minister for Foreign Affairs this morning on his return from Italy.

He declared that he was very satisfied with his visit there, but he assumed attitude that nothing definite had been mentioned with regard to Balkan matters. He admitted, however, that the Albanian question had been discussed. From his language I gathered that he did not reject idea of creating under certain circumstances a principality of Albania either great or small under the suzerainty of the Sultan. He observed that both Greece and Montenegro would, however, stand out for a rectification of frontier at the cost of Albania at the end of the war. I could get no definite reply as to his Excellency's views as to the annexation of Scutari by Montenegro. With regard to sanjak, I enquired if he would object to its being merged into an Albanian principality. His reply was vague.

The Minister for Foreign Affairs said to me that he thought the moment for mediation was rapidly approaching. On my enquiring whether he thought that Bulgaria would accept an armistice before the Turks evacuated Adrianople, he replied in the negative, but from his language I gather that he looks upon an evacuation as likely to occur at any moment. Minister for Foreign Affairs declared that all the Powers still clung to the principle of maintenance of status quo at the end of the war. When I pressed him, however, he seemed to admit that it would be somewhat difficult to make the Balkan League entirely give up their conquests, and that they would probably insist on some rectification of their frontiers. He appeared to me also to have doubts whether Balkan League would accept mere reforms in

Macedonia under surveillance of Ambassadors at Constantinople.

[FO 45372/33672/12/44]

Sir R. Paget to Sir Edward Grey
Belgrade, October 27, 1912

Austrian Minister informs me that he learns that Balkan States now look upon the result of war as certain. In the partition of Turkey in Europe which is to follow, Servia is to take the sanjak, Old Servia, and port of Medua on the Adriatic; Montenegro is to have Scutari, the surrounding territory, and a strip of littoral, Greece receives Epirus, Thessaly, and the rest goes to Bulgaria. The four States are to enter into offensive and defensive alliances for fifty years.

I could not ascertain from whom Austrian Minister had this information, but he assured me that his informant was absolutely reliable and it came from an official source. In any case it reflects the tone noticeable here at present.

[FO 45926/33672/12/44]

Sir Edward Grey to Sir E. Goschen
Foreign Office, October 28, 1912

Sir,
  I told Herr von Kühlmann again to-day that I was anxious to keep in touch with the German Government with regard to the Balkan war, as the German Chancellor desired. Herr von Kiderlen had also approached France and had told Sir E. Goschen that he thought France, Germany and England should keep in touch. The news of Balkan successes still continued. As the Chancellor had said, Austria and Russia must lead the Concert of Europe. They could not lead unless they were in agreement, and it would be desirable that they should make up their minds, on the assumption that the Balkan States were going to win, what was the maximum disturbance in the territorial "status quo" that Austria and Russia would regard as reconcilable with their interests.
  Herr von Kühlmann suggested that it might be possible to invite the Balkan States to say what was the minimum which they would accept.
  I observed that this might be a very useful suggestion, and if the Balkan States had a great victory in Thrace and the Turks were completely beaten, Austria and Russia might follow up the step which they had taken together before the war by asking the Balkan States to formulate their minimum demands. This was however all on the assumption that the Balkan States would be victorious, everything would be changed if the Turks won a big battle.
  Herr von Kühlmann asked me about our attitude.
  I said that I was sure that British public opinion would not be a party to any attempt to turn the Balkan States by force

out of territory which they actually conquered by their own arms, and we had not sufficient political interest to insist upon interfering in the results of the war. Austria and Russia might feel differently, and that was why it was essential to promote agreement between them.

Herr von Kühlmann asked me whether what I had said about our attitude would apply even to a conquest of Constantinople.

I replied in the negative, saying that a change in the ownership of Constantinople would be a large European question.

I concluded by remarking that this was all I could say at the moment. There might still be Turkish successes which would give the problem quite a different complexion. All we could do for the present was to discuss possibilities, and I was giving him my views as a contribution towards keeping in touch with each other.

In the course of the conversation Herr von Kühlmann said that Austria would probably want to make some reserves about the Sandjak and about the way to Salonica not being completely closed; Albania too could hardly be absorbed: Albanians both Christian and Moslem would combine against Serbs, but Albania might become an autonomous unit of some sort. This would still leave a great deal of Macedonia for Bulgaria and Servia. He asked me whether we should object to Bulgaria getting to the Mediterranean.

I said I saw no reason why we should, as far as ourselves were concerned, make any reserves.

Herr von Kühlmann made it clear that in these suggestions respecting the settlement he was speaking his own personal opinion only, and I said that I was doing the same as I had not consulted my colleagues on these points.

I am, &c.,
E. Grey

Sir Edward Grey to Sir F. Bertie
Foreign Office, October 30, 1912
Private

My dear Bertie,
    Your letter of the 28th, giving an account of your conversation with Poincaré and Iswolsky, is interesting.
    You will see by the records that my path in the conversations with Germany was made smooth by the fact that the German Chancellor put in the forefront of his views that Austria and Russia should lead the Concert. I have stuck to this as a text, and therefore no question arose in my conversations with Kühlmann as to leaving Russia out.
    Poincaré continually talks of mediation, but mediation will be of no use unless the Powers are agreed upon the settlement. If Turkey were to win, an agreement would be easy. The prospect of a Turkish "débâcle" and the complete victory of the Balkan States makes things more difficult. Public opinion here will be dead against turning the Balkan States out of what they may show their ability to conquer by their own forces. If Russia and Austria do agree upon a settlement, public opinion here will not push its own views and force the Government to assert them. But if Austria were to attack the Balkan States, and Russia said "Hands off," it would be impossible for a British Government, even if it desired, to side diplomatically with Austria against Russia. I propose to work for agreement between Russia and Austria, but it will have to be with the limitation that Austria is reasonable.
    I think it is rather a good idea that, when the time for mediation comes, assuming that the Balkan States have Turkey at their mercy, mediation should take the form of a proposal by Austria and Russia to the Balkan States of a settlement to which Austria and Russia would agree, and which might content

Bulgaria. The Balkan States will not claim to keep every thing if they find that their extreme demands would entail war with Austria. I do not suppose that Russia would insist that Austria must not make any reserves, and that the Balkan States must have every thing. But they will have to get a good deal; and whatever they do not get, as far as Macedonia and Albania are concerned, will have to be reserved as some sort of autonomous units.

Unforeseen developments of the war may upset these calculations, and they contain very uncertain factors. But they are as definite as I can make them at present.

Yours sincerely,
E. Grey

[FO 47311/42842/12/44]

Sir Edward Grey to Sir F. Cartwright
Foreign Office, November 4, 1912, 9.30 p.m.

Austrian Ambassador having come to the Foreign Office to-day I observed that as his Gov[ernmen]t gave him no instructions to tell me their views or ask for mine, I thought they might perhaps not wish to be sounded. I therefore left it to his discretion whether to report anything I said to his Gov[ernmen]t and I observed that if it were known what reserves Austria and Russia had to make, we should have some ground upon which to go. Ambassador could only discuss matter on his own personal opinion, but thought there would be difficulty in giving Servia San Juan di Medua the country behind was too hilly for a railway and part of it was Mahommedan. I observed that the first objection was the risk of Servia alone. Ambassador thought there would be no difficulty in Servia having outlet through a Montenegrin Port. I observed that this would involve question of the Sanjak. Ambassador said it was a barren place and he did not think there would be difficulty on this point.

I urged upon Ambassador that there was opportunity for a great settlement of Balkan question that would secure peace there for generations; that difficulty appeared to be how to secure for Servia an outlet to Adriatic, and that it was worth some effort to overcome this difficulty.

[FO 47362/42842/12/44]

Sir Edward Grey to Sir F. Cartwright
Foreign Office, November 5, 1912

Sir,
     The Austro-Hungarian Ambassador informed me today that he was instructed to make the following communication to me, not as a cut and dried scheme, but as the general conditions necessary to secure Austro-Hungarian interests in a Balkan settlement. Austria-Hungary must fix certain points which, if a formal partition of European Turkey or an extension of neighbouring countries took place, must be the basis of future Austro-Hungarian policy, to safeguard the most vital interests of the Monarchy —

(1)   The assent of Austria-Hungary to the extension of the power and territory of a neighbouring State must be conditional upon guarantees that the State would not pursue a policy directly hostile to Austria-Hungary. Guarantees would be required that Servia would maintain friendly and neighbourly relations. Fine words and promises only would not be enough: there must be closer economic connection. This would bring many advantages to Servia, and would create a community of interests that would secure for a long time to come a peaceful existence side by side. The closer this connection was, the more could Servia count upon Austro-Hungarian sympathy with plans of aggrandisement.

     I observed that this suggested a reflection which of course was not serious; that the closest connection of all was annexation, when both countries were aggrandised together.

     Count Mensdorff replied that, of course, nothing of this sort was meant.

He added that the stipulations as to Montenegro were the same as those for Servia.

(2) A Servian claim to the addition of territory as far as the Adriatic, and covering Albania proper, would have to be rejected "ad limine." Such a claim would be a proof that Servia did not contemplate relations of friendship and confidence with Austria-Hungary, and did not intend to avail herself of the latter's friendly dispositions in economic questions. If Servia based herself upon the principle of nationality, she could have no right to take purely Albanian territory, and to do so would be an unjustified injury to legitimate Albanian claims.

(3) Albania must be allowed to develop freely. This meant that there must be created an independent body large enough to live; if it was too small, it would have no safeguard for its continued existence.

(4) Such desires of Roumania as were just must be satisfied.

(5) The Austro-Hungarian frontier must be rectified, but only on a small scale.— This, said Count Mensdorff, probably referred to some small rectification of the frontier on the Sandjak.

(6) Parts of Turkey-in-Europe that had up to now formed important markets for Austro-Hungarian industry must not be totally lost in a commercial sense when absorbed by one or other of the Balkan States.

(7) There were also several other Austro-Hungarian economic interests in the Balkans that would have to be safeguarded, such as the importance of Salonica and of a railway line to this port. Austria-Hungary could view with equanimity the withdrawal of Turkish sovereignty from Salonica, and the passing of this port into other hands, only if Austro-Hungarian interests were fully secured: as might be done by making Salonica a free port, with sufficient safeguards for Austria-Hungary, besides giving by means of a convention a very complete safeguard for railway communication with that port.

I thanked Count Mensdorff cordially for this communication, and said that as it was confidential I supposed that I must not make any use of it with others.

He thought, though he was not sure, that the same communication was being made to other Powers. But I should soon be able to ascertain whether this was the case.

I said that, in any case, it was very useful to have the information which he had given me. Proposals were being made every day, and it was only by knowing what everyone wished that one could see where to steer with the best prospect of helping a solution.

I am, &c.,
E. Grey

[FO 47561/42842/12/44]

Sir Edward Grey to Sir E. Goschen
Foreign Office, November 6, 1912

Sir,
 I told Herr von Kühlmann to-day that the Austrian Ambassador had communicated to me yesterday the terms of his Government with regard to a Balkan settlement.
 Herr von Kühlmann said that he thought this communication had been a circular one. There had been an idea that Austria might make her views known through Germany; but this might not have been convenient, as Germany might not have wished to endorse all the Austrian views.
 I remarked that it was a great relief to find that Austria was putting forward no territorial claims: this put one great difficulty out of the way. That Salonica should be a free port commended itself, I thought, to everyone. So far as I could see, the point on which there would be the greatest difficulty would be the determination of the limits of an autonomous Albania; or, to state this in another way, the question whether Servia should have access to the Adriatic. The Servian Chargé d'Affaires had just come to see me, and had said that this access was a matter of life and death to Servia. Nothing was worth anything to her without the economic independence for which a port on the Adriatic was essential, and the Servians would fight to the end to obtain such a port.
 Herr von Kühlmann suggested that, if economic independence was what Servia wished to have, then surely, just as Austria desired to arrange for a railway to Salonica for her economic advantage, so a railway to the Adriatic might be arranged for Servia on economic terms.

I said that if, as seemed possible, this point turned out to be the only outstanding difficulty in the way of a Balkan settlement, then the fact that there was agreement as to the whole of the great field of European Turkey, except with regard to this one point, would be a great make-weight in favour of peace and of finding some solution of the difficulty.

I am, &c.,
E. Grey

[FO 47559/42842/12/44]

Sir Edward Grey to Sir R. Paget
Foreign Office, November 6, 1912

Sir,
    The Servian Chargé d'Affaires informed me to-day that, as a result of the Balkan war, Servia would claim Old Servia, which included the Vilayet of Kossovo, the Sandjak of Novi-Bazar, and the north-west part of the Vilayet of Scutari, including the Old Servian ports of Durazzo, San Juan di Medua, and Alessio. Servia, owing to her geographical position, could not escape, and did not wish to escape, special economic relations with Austria; but she could not submit to being made dependent upon Austria economically. During the past ten years Austria had, as a matter of fact, treated Servia much worse commercially than Servia had treated her. Servian exports to Austria, and even the transit of Servian produce through Austria, had sometimes been prohibited. Servia had had great difficulty in finding other markets at such times. A port on the Adriatic was therefore essential to her. Otherwise, she would be shut off from the sea, and could have no economic independence. To suggest that she might have a port on the Ægean was only to try to make difficulties between her and other States, and she did not wish to have a port on the Ægean. It was alleged that there must be Albanian autonomy, because of Albanian national feeling. There was really no Albanian national feeling. There were Servians in the north of Albania, they had been oppressed before, and the danger of their being oppressed again was a reason against Albanian autonomy. The Albanians themselves were divided, especially in the northern part. Servia hoped that we would see that what she asked was just, and a matter of life and death to her. A port on the Adriatic

meant to her all or nothing. She must make every effort, and use all her force to secure it.

I asked what Montenegro was to have, if Servia had all this which was claimed.

The Servian Chargé d'Affaires could not say exactly; but he was sure that the matter had been settled so that the Servian demands would not give rise to difficulties between Servia and Montenegro.

In reply to some questions as to Albanian nationality, he made it clear that his remarks on that point applied more especially to the northern part of Albania.

I told him that I was very glad to have the views of his Government. Our public opinion would not side with any attempt to deprive the victors of the fruits of their victories. We ourselves had no reserves to make, but we wished to promote a settlement peaceably. The settlement of practically the whole of the European dominions of Turkey was a very large affair. The first step was to learn the views of all the parties who were most interested. We could then see what divergencies there were between all the parties interested and how these could be reconciled.

I am, &c.
E. Grey

[FO 47409/42842/12/44]

Sir E. Goschen to Sir Edward Grey
Berlin, November 7, 1912

Secretary of State for Foreign Affairs sent for me this evening to tell me of his conversation with Servian chargé d'affaires. His account corresponded with that which I have already reported. He added, however, that on his explaining to Servian chargé d'affaires that both Austria and Italy were against Servian access to Adriatic because it would divide Albania, Servian chargé d'affaires had replied that Servia desired the whole of Albania. On the Secretary of State pointing out that this was mad, Servian chargé d'affaires replied that their plans for settlement had been submitted to Russia, who had approved them. Secretary of State said to me that he presumed that in this case "Russia" meant Russian representative at Belgrade. His Excellency added that this attitude on the part of Servia was bad, but that what disquieted him most was that Russian Ambassador in Paris had held somewhat similar language to that of the Servian chargé d'affaires to Baron Schoen at Paris, and had said that if Servia failed to get access to Adriatic owing to opposition of Austria it would mean fresh humiliation of Russia. Secretary of State for Foreign Affairs said that he did not believe that Russian Ambassador was speaking in name of Russian Government, but it was very dangerous language, and he was instructing the German Ambassador to St. Petersburgh to report to Russian Minister for Foreign Affairs and ask him what were the real views of Russian Government. He was of opinion that if war was to be avoided it would be advisable for Russian Minister for Foreign Affairs to instruct Russian representatives at Paris and Belgrade to moderate their tone. He intended to give Russian Minister for

Foreign Affairs discreet hint to this effect, and thought it would be very useful if England and France could do the same, as the matter seemed really serious. He held similar language to my French colleague.

[FO 49178/42842/12/44]

Sir G. Buchanan to Sir Edward Grey
St. Petersburgh, November 18, 1912

From conversations which he had with Austrian and German Ambassadors to-day, my French colleague gathers that Austria's chief objection to granting Servia a commercial port, such as Russian Minister for Foreign Affairs proposes, is that, judging by past experience, States in the end always fortify such ports, despite their treaty engagements to the contrary. Were Servia in a few years' time to adopt this course, and were Austria then to try to force her to observe her treaty obligations, Russia would certainly intervene on the ground that she could not allow a Slav State to be crushed by Austria.

On French Ambassador repeating this to Minister for Foreign Affairs, latter said that to accept this contention as valid would be to say that it was useless to make any treaty in the future for fear of its being broken. His Excellency's language was, however, calmer than that which he held to me on Saturday. He seemed to be under the impression that Austria is anxious to find a way out of the difficulty. Austrian solution would be a neutral or international port, and Minister for Foreign Affairs even went so far as to say that if only Servia would be contented with this he would not make difficulties. His Excellency added, however, that he could not answer for Russian public opinion.

As far as I can ascertain, public opinion at present is distinctly bellicose. It is generally believed that Italy will not support Austria, that Germany wants peace, and that Austria will have difficulties with her Slav population. The moment is therefore considered favourable for Russia, and it is contended that if Russian Government are only firm Austria will have to yield.

[FO 49284/42842/12/44]

Sir Edward Grey to Sir G. Buchanan
Foreign Office, November 18, 1912, 5.45 p.m.

  I entirely agree that to get all six Powers into line is most desirable. But to induce Austria to agree to let Servia have San Giovanni di Medua as proposed by M[inister for] F[oreign] A[ffairs] it will be necessary to give Austria firm assurance that no Power including Russia will support Servia in asking for anything more than this in the Adriatic and that principle of an autonomous Albania of reasonable size will be supported by all the Powers. I do not see why Russian Gov[ernmen]t should not sound Austrian M[inister for] F[oreign] Affairs direct. If France or ourselves were to make the proposal suggested by M[inister for] F[oreign] A[ffairs] at Vienna, we should, if Austria were prepared to entertain it which is doubtful, be asked what assurance there was that if Servia refused it or continued to press her claims in Albania, she would receive no support from Russia. It is essential that Russian Gov[ernmen]t should be explicit on this point if there is to be any chance of further concession from Austria.

[FO 48632/42842/12/44]

Sir Edward Grey to Sir G. Buchanan
Foreign Office, November 18, 1912

Sir,
 The Russian Amb[assado]r called at this Office on the 12th inst[ant] and left the enclosed copies of telegrams from his Gov[ernmen]t relative to the question of Servian access to the Adriatic and Austria's objection to the acquisition by Servia of a port on the Adriatic coast.
 I have informed Count Benckendorff and M. Cambon that I agree to the preliminary discussion suggested in the penultimate paragraph] of the tel[egram] dated Nov[ember] 12.
 When C[oun]t Benckendorff drew my attention to the last para[graph], I said that it was true, but that Servia first provoked the discussion, and Austria would no doubt retort by calling attention to the published interview given by M. Hartwig.

I am, &c.,
E. Grey

Enclosures in No. 228.
(1.)
Très confidentiel.
 Nous pensons que Sir Edward Grey partage notre point de vue sur le danger d'une action armée Autrichienne contre la Serbie, au sujet d'une question dont la solution n'appartient pas à cette dernière sans sanction internationale. D'autre part, nous estimerions extrêmement utile que les Cabinets de Londres et

de Paris donnent à Belgrade des conseils de modération et de raison.

Nous pensons que la décision prise par l'Autriche-Hongrie de ne pas laisser pénétrer la Serbie sur le littoral Adriatique est ferme. L'Autriche-Hongrie est soutenue par ses alliés. Cette solidarité de la Triple Alliance rend pour nous extrêmement important de savoir quelle attitude prendraient la France et l'Angleterre pour le cas où les efforts d'empêcher une intervention armée de l'Autriche-Hongrie resteraient sans résultats.

Le Comte de Thurn, étant venu chez moi hier, je me suis efforcé de le convaincre des inconvénients et des dangers d'une action qui ne serait pas justifiée par une nécessité absolue. J'ai prié l'Ambassadeur de s'informer par télégraphe si le Cab[ine]t de Vienne ne consentirait pas à accorder à la Serbie, sur l'Adriatique, un port qui aurait un caractère exclusivement commercial. Le C[om]te de Thurn ne me cacha pas qu'il doutait fort que la question puisse être ainsi posée. D'un autre côté il me signala que le Gouv[erneme]nt Imp[éri]al et Royal serait disposé à accorder à la Serbie, pour la garantie de ses intérêts économiques et du transit de ses produits par chemin de fer sur Salonique et l'Adriatique, des conditions tout à fait semblables à celles qui garantiraient les siens.

Nous pensons que le moment approche où il s'agira d'établir l'équilibre entre la situation que l'Autriche-Hongrie compte s'assurer et les intérêts tant politiques qu'économiques de la Serbie. Il nous semblerait indiqué de resserer dans les limites du possible le territoire Albanais, et aussi d'établir certaines garanties dans son organisation future.

Toutes ces questions peuvent faire l'objet d'un échange d'idées préliminaire, tandis qu'une décision définitive ne saurait être prise que par les Puissances collectivement et d'après un examen des intérêts réciproques engagés.

C'est pourquoi la façon Autrichienne de forcer la question de la pénétration de la Serbie sur l'Adriatique, comme décision catégoriquement prise, ne nous semble pas régulière.

Le 12 Novembre 1912.

(2.)

      Je télégraphe à Belgrade

      La décision prise par l'Autriche de s'opposer à l'acquisition par la Serbie d'un port sur l'Adriatique est irrévocable et approuvée par ses Alliés. La France et l'Angleterre ne sont nullement disposés d'entrer pour cette cause en conflit avec les Puissances de la Triple Alliance. De notre côté nous déclarons catégoriquement à la Serbie que nous ne nous laisserons pas entraîner par elle. Nous ne ferons pas la guerre aux trois Puissances pour un port Serbe sur l'Adriatique.

      Si vraiment les Alliés balkaniques ont pris la décision de partager entre eux la Turquie d'Europe intégralement, sans tenir nul compte des intérêts de l'Autriche et de l'Italie, nous tenons à les mettre en garde contre une politique aussi irréflechie. Elle lui aliénera tout d'abord les sympathies de l'Angleterre et la France. On oublie en Serbie le danger de ne pas compter sur les circonstances. Elles rendent inévitable la création d'une Albanie littorale.

      Plus la Serbie montrera d'esprit de sagesse, plus il deviendra possible d'obtenir, lorsqu'il s'agira d'établir les limites et de créer une administration pour l'Albanie, des conditions avantageuses pour elle au point de vue économique. Mais plus elle manifestera d'obstruction, plus augmenteront pour elle les dangers d'un complet isolement.

      Veuillez sans le moindre retard vous expliquer avec M. Paschitsch surtout ce qui précède et le prevenir contre une occupation de Durazzo. La Serbie ne doit pas nous obliger à renoncer hautement à toute solidarité avec elle sur une question ou nous considerons qu'elle se laisse guider par pur entrainement.

[FO 48136/42842/12/44]

Sir Edward Grey to Sir G. Buchanan
Foreign Office, November 18, 1912

Sir,
	The Russian Amb[assado]r called on the 10th inst[ant] and comm[unicate]d the enclosed copy of a tel[egram] sent by the Russian Gov[ernmen]t to their Representative at Belgrade, indicating the extent to which Russia is prepared to support Servia, and denying the truth of the statements made by the Servian Representative at Berlin as to Servia being able to rely on Russian help.

I am, &c.,
E. Grey

Enclosure in No. 229.
	Je télégraphie à Belgrade:
	La question de l'accès de la Serbie à l'Adriatique a pris ces derniers jours une tournure qui ne laisse pas de nous causer de sérieuses inquiétudes.
	Nous sommes disposés à prêter à la Serbie,—conjointement avec l'Angleterre et la France,—un appui diplomatique des plus actifs. D'après des renseignements sérieux nous ne pouvons pas mettre en doute que l'Allemagne et l'Italie sont, ainsi que l'Autriche, préparées à s'opposer à une expansion territoriale de la Serbie sur la côte de l'Adriatique.
	Il n'est guère admissible d'accentuer,—pour cette question,—le conflit, au point de risquer le danger d'une guerre européenne. L'attitude de certains Représentants Serbes à l'étranger nous parait, pour cette raison, d'autant plus préjudiciable.

Nous apprenons que le Représentant serbe à Berlin aurait déclaré à Monsieur de Kiederlen-Wachter que les Alliés avaient partagé le littoral Adriatique et que l'appui, non seulement de la Bulgarie, mais même de la Russie, avait été accordé à la Serbie. Nous considérons inadmissible pareille déclaration faite en notre nom.

La Convention de l'Alliance Balcanique ne permet guère à la Serbie de compter sur le concours armé de la Bulgarie pour faciliter son accès vers l'Adriatique. Les pertes subies par la Serbie et la Bulgarie pendant cette guerre prédestinent d'avance leur insuccès dans un conflit avec l'Autriche.

L'envoi de détachements serbes dans la direction de Dourazzo, à l'occupation duquel l'Autriche ne manquera certainement pas de s'opposer, démontre jusqu'à quelles conséquences dangereuses peut amener pareille détermination irréfléchie.

Veuillez attirer l'attention de Monsieur Pachich sur l'intérêt qu'auraient les Serbes de ne pas nous rendre plus difficile notre tâche de défendre leur cause.

Nous faisons, dans la question de l'accès de la Serbie à la mer Adriatique, une distinction entre le but et les moyens d'y aboutir.

Le but consiste en l'établissement de l'indépendance économique de ce pays :

Les moyens—en l'accès vers l'Adriatique soit par voie d'acquisitions territoriales sur le littoral,—soit en garanties spéciales en vue du ralliement de la Serbie avec tel ou outre part, par une ligne ferrée, dans des conditions identiques à celles qu'obtiendrait l'Autriche pour le transit de ses marchandises sur Salonique.

Une concession faite par la Serbie dans la question d'acquisition d'un port Adriatique faciliterait les démarches en faveur d'autres compensations, telles qu'expansion territoriale vers le Sud ainsi qu'une certaine limitation du territoire Albanais.

Si l'Autriche ne se rend pas compte de l'intérêt qu'il y aurait à établir une paix durable dans les Balcans,—la Serbie devrait, semble-t-il, comprendre qu'à force de prétentions exagérées elle ne pourrait que compromettre le résultat final d'une guerre qui lui apporte des avantages inespérés. Il est dans l'intérêt de la Serbie de ne pas formuler des demandes exagérés, dont le rejet porterait atteinte à son amour-propre.

[FO 49802/42842/12/44]

Sir Edward Grey to Sir E. Goschen
Foreign Office, November 21, 1912, 10 p.m.

German Ambassador has informed me that German Gov[ernmen]t think the Great Powers should now come to an agreement on the main points of the Balkan settlement. He mentioned Albania, Servian access to Adriatic, Constantinople, Adrianople, and Mount Athos.

I said that the points on which agreement between Great Powers was required appeared to be three.

1. Whether there should be an autonomous Albania, and, if this was in principle agreed to, what the limits of it should be.
2. By what method and under what conditions should Servia be given access to the Adriatic.
3. The question of the Islands.

I thought it would be desirable that the Powers should if possible come to an agreement on these points, but any discussion should be as informal as possible; it would not be desirable yet to formulate definite proposals for acceptance or rejection.

As far as I was aware, difficulties were not likely to arise now between Russia and Bulgaria about Constantinople, Adrianople, or Mount Athos. Bulgaria was not claiming Constantinople in any of her terms; and unless Russia wished to raise these points, I did not suppose any other Great Power would wish to do so.

[FO 50219/42842/12/44]

Sir Edward Grey to Sir F. Bertie
Foreign Office, November 21, 1912

Sir,
The French Ambassador informed me to-day of the communication which Herr von Kiderlen had made to the French Ambassador in Berlin, suggesting that the Powers should come to an agreement as to (1) the points which they would leave the Balkan States to settle for themselves, and (2) the points on which the Great Powers must have their say. These last were the questions of Albania, Constantinople, Adrianople, Mount Athos, the Roumanian demands, and the Ægean Islands.

I told M. Cambon that the German Ambassador had not mentioned Roumania or the Islands to me. I would suggest the Islands to him as a subject which interested the Great Powers; but I would make no mention of Roumania, as I thought it preferable that the Roumanian claims should, if possible, be settled direct with Bulgaria.

M. Cambon told me further what the Italian Ambassador in Paris had suggested. It showed, amongst other things, the importance which Italy attached to the economic independence of Servia, and her desire that Albania should be internationalised under the guarantee of the Powers. The Austrian Ambassador, in conversation with M. Poincaré, had not excluded the idea of a strip of Servian territory to San Giovanni di Medua: and, though it was not clear whether this was the opinion of his Government, or only his own personal opinion. M. Cambon regarded it as a very favourable indication. It appeared that Montenegro was now claiming San Giovanni di Medua.

I agreed with M. Cambon that the impression derived from the Austrian Ambassador in Paris was a very favourable indication. If confirmed by his Government, it might reduce the question of Servian access to the Adriatic to a dispute between Servia and Montenegro for the possession of the particular port in question. M. Cambon also told me that M. Sazonoff objected to an autonomous Albania believing that the Albanians were not homogeneous, and that the autonomy of their country would lead to endless trouble, but, out of deference to the opinion of others, he was prepared to waive his objection.

I am, &c.,
E. Grey

[FO 50589/42842/12/44]

Sir Edward Grey to Sir F. Cartwright
Foreign Office, November 25, 1912

Sir,
The Austrian Ambassador informed me to-day that Count Berchtold gathered from various quarters that there was an impression that San Giovanni di Medua might be made the object of a transaction, so that it might be severed from Albania at a later period and made a Servian port; and that Austria could be reconciled to this. The Ambassador was instructed to say that this was not the case, and did not correspond to Austrian intentions. The Italian Minister for Foreign Affairs had also expressed himself against the territorial possession of a port by Servia, though all manner of economic outlets would be agreed to. There seemed to be some misunderstanding too as to Austria's economic views. She did not wish to hinder the economic independence of Servia; all she wished was not to lose markets which she had had before, and she must have rights of transit for her trade.

I said that there had been a suggestion that there might be for Servia a narrow strip of territory neutralised to a port also neutralised.

Count Mensdorff said that it would be difficult to work this. Austria was afraid that Albania would disturb the neutralised strip, and that the Servians would then make this a pretext for asking for more. A commercial port would become a military port, and he did not think that Austria could agree to this. He referred to the communication from M. Pasitch in "The Times" of to-day.

I said that I did not think it a fortunate communication, and I supposed that Count Mensdorff had seen what the leading article in the "Times" said about it.

He replied that he thought the leading article excellent.

I observed that no doubt M. Pasitch was asking for a good deal more than he really expected, in order to get sympathy and support for something less.

Count Mensdorff said that he hoped we would work for peace.

I replied that we would do so, and I hoped that Austria would not shut the door prematurely at this stage upon possible solutions.

I am, &c.,
E. Grey

[FO 50679/42842/12/44]

Sir Edward Grey to Sir G. Buchanan
Foreign Office, November 28, 1912, midnight

Russian Ambassador has urged me to take initiative in proposing a Conference. I prefer to call it a consultation of six Ambassadors and am sounding the German Government in first instance.

I wish Russian M[inister for] F[oreign] A[ffairs] could see his way to propose at such consultation that, on condition of Servia and Montenegro acquiring the Sandjak and Servia getting the other territory except Albania, that the allies' terms of peace may give her, the question of Servian access to Adriatic should be settled as suggested by Russian M[inister for] F[oreign] A[ffairs] in your telegram No. 449.

It must be remembered that in 1909 the desire of Servia and Montenegro was the Sandjak in return for Austrian annexation of Bosnia. If there was any humiliation then it was solely that Servia and Montenegro were kept out of the Sandjak. Russian public opinion should surely regard it as some success if the main thing desired by Servia in 1909, which till a few weeks ago it was thought that Austria would never concede is gained now. And if as regards access to an Adriatic port Servia gets commercial terms at least as good as Austria gets respecting Salonica there will be no real humiliation in such a settlement. I have urged this on Russian Ambassador, who received it favourably. I can only put it to M[inister for] F[oreign] A[ffairs] as a suggestion, for Russian interest is so much more directly concerned than ours, but I think it is worth considering. If Russia made this proposal my expectation is that she would get the credit of having made the settlement that preserved the peace of Europe and secured the Balkan Allies their other gains, which may all be endangered if there is European war about a Servian port.

[FO 50769/42842/12/44]

Sir Edward Grey to Sir F. Bertie
Foreign Office, November 28, 1912

Sir,
Sir A. Nicolson noticed in conversation on Nov[ember] 25 with the Italian, Russian and French Ambas[sado]rs considerable uneasiness in respect to the immediate future and grave doubts whether we were not marching towards a most serious situation. The Russian Ambas[sado]r feared that there was a possibility that Austria-Hungary and Germany would be prepared to face a conflict, and he considered that if Germany felt more or less assured that we should stand aside, she would consider a serious, and possibly dangerous, factor—our Navy—could be written off and that her hands were free. C[oun]t Benckendorff argued that so long as uncertainty existed as to whether we should or should not range ourselves alongside of France and Russia, Germany was to a certain extent, held in check. Once she considered that we should not take part she would be relieved of anxiety.

C[oun]t Benckendorff also said that it would be impossible to restrain Russian public opinion if it were thought that Austria and Germany were thinking of preventing the Balkan Allies from keeping what they had won.

M. Cambon had news from Rome, the source being the Italian Min[iste]r of Marine, that Austria-Hungary was making mobilization preparations both by sea and land, and from Berlin that the visit of Field-Marshal Schemua was to complete details as to military co-operation.

Ferid Pasha, Albanian and ex-Grand Vizier, is reported to have arranged with the Khedive (whose daughter married his son) that he should be head of an autonomous Albania, that he should arrange this with the Porte, and at the same time propose that Syria should be united to Egypt. This latter transaction, if seriously meant, would hardly be acceptable to the Porte.

All the Ambassadors, for one reason or another, deplored M. Pasitch's manifesto, which they consider most inopportune and most foolish and dangerous.

Sir A. Nicolson gathered an impression is existing that Germany and Austria-Hungary are encouraging Turkey to resist.

I am, &c.,
E. Grey

[FO 50627/42842/12/44]

Sir Edward Grey to Sir G. Buchanan
Foreign Office, November 28, 1912

Sir,

M. de Etter called on Nov[ember] 22 and told Sir A. N[icolson] that the Servian Gov[ernmen]t had enquired what reply they should give, supposing the Austro-Hungarian Gov[ernmen]t were not satisfied with the answers already sent and of which M. Grouitch had spoken to me on the day before. M. Sazonow had informed M. Passich that if Austria-Hungary asked for a more definite statement, the Servian Gov[ernmen]t should answer that the object of Servia was to obtain an outlet to the sea in order to develop her economic and national interests. In case Austria-Hungary were not even then satisfied, Servia should reply that the question might be submitted to the deliberation of the Powers.

M. Sazonow enquired if we had been approached by Servia. Sir A. N[icolson] said we had been informed of the Servian reply already sent, and that I had told M. Grouitch that it was a proper reply if it implied that everything done during the war should be regarded as provisional. Servia had not consulted us as to the nature of future replies which she might have to give. M. de Etter said that M. Sazonow hoped that if she did, we would give the same advice as he had done.

C[oun]t Mensdorff mentioned to Sir A. N[icolson] on the same afternoon that it was all very well for Servia to say that the question should be discussed when the war was over, but in the meantime she was effecting accomplished facts, which it might require serious measures to rectify later. Sir A. Nicolson observed that he understood that all that was being done was provisional and in the nature of military acts during the course of a war. C[oun]t Mensdorff remarked that he was unaware that Servia had definitely stated that occupation of Alessio, &c., was provisional.

I am, &c.,
E. Grey

[FO 52635/42842/12/44]

Sir Edward Grey to Sir R. Rodd
Foreign Office, December 5, 1912, 10 p.m.

Italian Ambassador informs me that M[inister for] F[oreign] A[ffairs] regards suggestion of consultation of Ambassadors with sympathy and is consulting Vienna. He wished to tell me for my private information that Italy agreed with Austria that they could not consent to discuss Durazzo or Vallona or any part of the coast between these points being under Servian, Greek or Montenegrin sovereignty. He did not include points north of Durazzo in this statement and was favourable to guaranteed railway access for Servia to a neutralized port.

I deprecated any prohibition of discussion being made a condition, especially a public condition, of accepting consultation or conference. This would appear as if meeting of Ambassadors was from beginning a victory for Austria and Italy, whereas any agreement should be a compromise, the result of mutual concessions made in the Conference. I could not say that Russia would accept solution of an international railway to a neutral port for Servia but she had never said that this was an impossible solution. If however Italy and Austria were to state in advance that they would only accept a consultation on understanding that a Servian port was not discussed, Russia might very well say that she would not accept a consultation with such a limitation. The better course would be for Italy and Austria, to instruct their Ambassadors that they could not give way on this point if it was raised, but not to make conditions about it beforehand.

You should inform M[inister for] F[oreign] A[ffairs].

[FO 52335/42842/12/44]

Sir Edward Grey to Sir G. Buchanan
Foreign Office, December 9, 1912, 10.30 p.m.

 I entirely agree with what M[inister for] F[oreign] A[ffairs] says about Albania both as to the place it should occupy in discussion and how the settlement of it may precede and prepare the way to a settlement of the Servian difficulty by means of a railway, international I presume, to a neutralized Albanian port.
 It is very desirable that conversations of Ambassadors should begin as soon as possible. Once they have begun there will be less risk of an incident between Austria and Servia, if such does occur, being fatal to peace.
 There is an impression in Paris that Russian Gov[ernmen]t are insisting on Paris being place of meeting. I have explained to French Ambassador in accordance with your telegrams No. 473 and No. 480 that this does not agree with my information. It is clear from views received from Berlin and Vienna and generally that for various reasons Paris is not regarded as very suitable for these informal and non-committal conversations. I have suggested that if formal conference is arranged later it might be held at Paris: there is no desire to have that in London.
 You should inform M[inister for] F[oreign] A[ffairs] and ask whether he thinks it possible for Ambassadors to begin conversations here before detailed statement of his views arrives.
 We might agree this week (1) that Great Powers do not desire to interfere with settlement of terms between belligerents except on certain points on which reserves must be made, (2) these points might be enumerated: Albania will certainly be one

of them and Ambassadors would then be able to enter upon discussion of that, after Russian M[inister for] F[oreign] A[ffair]s' detailed views had arrived. It seems desirable to constitute informal reunion of Ambassadors as soon as possible for reason given above, but conversations once begun need not be hurried.

[FO 53444/42842/12/44]

Sir Edward Grey to Sir G. Buchanan
Foreign Office, December 11, 1912

Sir,
Count Benckendorff gave me to-day the accompanying sketch respecting Albania and Servian access to the Adriatic.

I said that it seemed to me excellent. The geographical details respecting the limits of Albania I should have to study on a map before I could say anything about them, but the general lines of the sketch seemed to me an excellent way of discussing the question.

Count Benckendorff said that, with this in his possession, he thought that he ought to be in a position to enter into the discussions with the Ambassadors at any time. It seemed to him to be on lines with which Austria had indicated agreement.

I remarked that I did not see how Austria could possibly refuse an agreement on these lines without going back upon what she had said in Belgrade some time ago, respecting communication by the Danube-Adriatic railway to an Albanian or Montenegrin port.

I am, &c.,
E. Grey

Enclosure in No. 374
Communication from Count Benckendorff
London, December 11, 1912
Confidentiel

Un échange d'idées avec les Cabinets de Paris et de Londres pour établir un accord le plus complet possible, sur les questions qui seront soumises à la Conférence des Ambassadeurs nous semble urgent.

Nous plaçons en première ligne la question de l'Albanie et celle de l'accès de la Serbie à la mer Adriatique.

Il est notoire que notre but fondamental est de garantir l'indépendance politique et économique de la Serbie.

Mais en même temps le Gouvernement Impérial désire affranchir ces questions autant qu'il sera possible du caractère de conflit Austro-Serbe, à plus forte raison de conflit Austro-Russe, que l'opinion publique très à tort lui a donné.

Gardant en vue ce but et cette difficulté nous sommes d'opinion qu'il importerait de poser tout d'abord à la Conférence la question de l'organisation de l'Albanie, remettant en seconde ligne celle concernant la délimitation des frontières de cette province.

Sans entrer dès aujourd'hui dans les détails de la question, l'Albanie devrait dans l'opinion du Gouvernement Impérial constituer une province autonome sous la Souveraineté du Sultan avec le droit pour la Turquie d'y maintenir une garnison militaire restreinte dont les proportions seraient à définir plus tard.

Nous portons en outre un intérêt principiel [sic] spécial à ce que soit stipulée la neutralisation de l'Albanie et de son litt[o]ral, de manière à exclure toute prédominance spéciale d'aucune Puissance.

Le Gouvernement Impérial attache le même intérêt à la reconnaissance au profit de la Serbie d'un droit d'accès à la mer libre et exempt de toute perception de droits de douane, à travers le territoire Albanais par les chemins de fer qui relieront la Serbie aux ports Albanais. Le droit d'importation de munitions de guerre devra être garanti à la Serbie.

Toute jonction entre les chemins de fer Serbes et les ports du littoral Albanais qui pourra être effectuée au moyen d'un syndicat international devra être soumise à des conditions donnant toute garantie au fonctionnement régulier et de la sécurité du mouvement de transit à travers l'Albanie.

Dans la pensée que le degré des bonnes dispositions de l'Autriche Hongrie à faire droit aux intérêts légitimes de la Serbie sera conditionnée surtout par le cours des négociations au sujet de la délimitation des frontières Albanaises, le Gouvernement Impérial est d'avis que les frontières naturelles de l'Albanie devraient être déterminées à peu près de la façon suivante:

Au Nord de l'Adriatique le long de la rivière Drine jusqu'au point de son conflux avec le Drine Blanc; à l'est—à partir de ce point en suivant le Drine jusqu'au lac d'Okhrida en suivant la rive Ouest de ce lac la continuation de la frontière vers le sud un peu plus vers l'est dans la direction d'Onnisé, d'où la frontière méridionale suivrait en ligne directe vers la mer jusqu'à Delvine.

Le Gouvernement Impérial aime à espérer que la communication des principes qui précèdent concourra efficacement à l'établissement d'un point de vue commun entre les trois Cabinets.

[FO 54360/42842/12/44]

Sir Edward Grey to Sir F. Cartwright
Foreign Office, December 17, 1912

At the meeting of the Ambassadors this afternoon it was agreed that our proceedings should be kept secret, in the sense that no "communiqué" should be made to the Press until we judged it opportune to make an agreed "communiqué," and that meanwhile each Representative should regard our proceedings as conversations of which he would make his own report to his Government, putting on record such points as had been definitely agreed upon.

After some conversation, it was agreed to discuss the Albanian question first.

The Austrian Ambassador stated that the view of his Government was that Albania should be autonomous, and "viable": that is to say large enough to have a separate existence.

The Russian Ambassador added that the autonomous Albania should be guaranteed and controlled exclusively by the six Powers under the sovereignty of the Sultan.

The word "exclusively" was suggested by the Italian Ambassador.

It was left undecided whether "sovereignty" or "suzerainty" should be the word finally selected.

After some general discussion as to whether there should be any Turkish troops allowed in Albania, it was agreed that the Governments of Austria and Italy should be invited to indicate their general views on the organisation of Albania.

It was then agreed that the autonomous Albania should be neutralised.

The next step was to discuss the limits of Albania. On this it was agreed: "que les frontières de l'Albanie autonome et du Monténégro au nord et de la Grèce au sud seront en tout cas limitrophes." We were unable to be more definite, as the Austrian Ambassador contended that the frontiers of Albania and Montenegro must remain as they are at present, Austria considering that no territory inhabited exclusively by Albanians should be detached from the future Albania, and urging that the territory now called Albanian on the north came emphatically within this category.

The Russian Ambassador declared that he could not associate himself with this point of view: seeing that it implied "une ingérence" in the negotiation of Montenegro and Turkey. He would, therefore, bring it to the cognisance of his Government.

Finally we proceeded to discuss the question of Servian access to the Adriatic. It was obvious that, whether the frontiers of Montenegro and Servia were to be varied or not, so long as they remained limitrophe there could be no territorial access for Servia to the Adriatic. This point, therefore, was not discussed, and no mention was made of it. It was agreed that: "un accès commercial sera réservé à la Serbie à un port albanais libre et neutre, desservi par un chemin de fer international sous un contrôle européen et sous la garde d'une force spéciale internationale, avec liberté de transit pour toute la marchandise, y compris les munitions de guerre."

It is apparent that Austria objects to allowing Montenegro to have Scutari and that Russia would support the Montenegrin claim in this respect. The German and Italian Ambassadors did not commit themselves on this point. The Servian difficulty, on the other hand has completely disappeared as far as access to the Adriatic is concerned.

I am, &c.,
E. Grey

[FO 54513/42842/12/44]

Sir Edward Grey to Sir F. Cartwright
Foreign Office, December 18, 1912

Sir,
 To-day the Ambassadors again met in the Foreign Office, and discussed in the first instance what should be the eastern limits of Albania.

The Austrian Ambassador indicated that if other points as regards the littoral were satisfactorily settled, Prizrend might go to Servia; and there appeared to be general agreement that, further south, Lake Ochrida should be the boundary of Albania. But the instructions of the Austrian Ambassador were too vague to enable a line to be drawn, even approximately, on any map. He was therefore requested to obtain a map, if possible, with a line traced upon it that would show the view of his Government as to what the boundary should be.

We then passed to the question of the Ægean islands.

The Russian Ambassador said that his instructions were that Lemnos, Tenedos, Imbros, and Samothrace should not be in the possession of any power except Turkey. Autonomous institutions in these islands would, however, be indispensable for the guarantee of the population.

I said that, while I raised no objection in principle, one or two questions occurred to me: for instance, if the first use which these islands made of their autonomy was to declare their annexation to Greece, what would happen?

The Russian Ambassador replied that he assumed that there would have to be some Turkish troops in the islands to maintain the Turkish flag.

I observed that there might be a revolt against the flag, the Turkish troops might attack the islanders, who were Greek;

and I asked what would happen then? If the Powers were to interfere, they would reproduce a Cretan question.

The Russian Ambassador said that he would refer these points to his Government.

I suggested that, without prejudice to the Russian proposition, we might record some unanimous decision about the neutralisation of the Islands, and the following decision was agreed to:—

"Quel que soit le statu futur des îles de la Mer Egée, nous sommes d'avis qu'elles doivent être neutralisées sous la garantie des Puissances.

The French Ambassador said that he was instructed to raise no objection to the cession of all the Islands to Greece, and he observed that the object of Russia in wishing to reserve four islands near the mouth of the Straits for Turkey would be accomplished by their neutralisation, even if they went to Greece. The Russian Ambassador doubted if this would be sufficient protection against blocking exit from the Straits.

It was understood that this part of our conversations did not apply to Crete, which would go in full sovereignty unconditionally to Greece.

The question of Salonica was raised. None of the Ambassadors had any territorial conditions to make.

The Austrian Ambassador said that he was instructed:—

"que les conditions du port de Salonique et du chemin de fer y conduisant soit réglées à manière de garantir nos intérêts commerciaux."

He explained that freedom of commercial access would be a common interest, and no one made any objection to his stipulation.

The French Ambassador said that he was instructed that:—

"A ce qui concerne Constantinople, nous sommes fermement attachés au maintien du statu quo. Cette ville devrait donc demeurer en possession de l'Empire Ottoman. La Turquie devra en outre conserver en Europe un territoire longeant la Mer de Marmara et les Dardanelles."

The Russian Ambassador said that, though this was not mentioned in his instructions, he knew that it represented the view of his Government also.
No one raised any question or objection on this.
I observed at the end of our sitting that, if we adjourned on Friday (the 20th instant) without making any "communiqué" to the Press, it would be supposed that we had come to a deadlock, or at least had made no progress. This would produce a very bad impression. I suggested, therefore, that the Ambassadors should ask their Governments to authorize some such "communiqué" as the following:—

"Que nous avons recommandé unanimement à nos Gouvernements respectifs le principe de l'autonomie de l'Albanie et une proposition garantissant l'accès commercial à la Serbie à l'Adriatique. Les six Puissances sont tombées d'accord sur ces principes."

The Ambassadors all agreed to do this.

I am, &c.,
E. Grey

[FO 54361/42842/12/44]

Sir Edward Grey to Sir H. Bax-Ironside
Foreign Office, December 18, 1912

Sir,
    Dr. Daneff came to see me to-day. He showed me the demands which the Allies thought of making "en bloc" on Turkey. They included the cession of all the Turkish dominions in Europe west of a line from the Black Sea to the Ægean that would leave Adrianople to Bulgaria. This meant the cession of Albania, the independence and organisation of which would subsequently be arranged between the Balkan States and the Great Powers. It meant also a cession of the Ægean Islands, and the removal of the last vestiges of Turkish authority in Crete. He said that he showed me these terms in case I could give any advice as to how they might be viewed by the Great Powers.
    I said that the Great Powers would certainly require to decide the "status," the organisation, and the limits of Albania.
    Dr. Daneff thereupon said that he would propose to modify the terms by making a reserve that, when the Turkish territory was ceded, the limits and organisation of Albania should be left to the decision of the Great Powers.
    I told him that this would be much preferable to his first alternative, and would avoid arousing difficulties with the Powers about Albania.
    As he pressed me about the Ægean Islands, I said that I did not know what difficulties some of the Powers might raise; Dr. Daneff himself had pointed out that certain of the islands commanded the Turkish coast, and that Turkey would be defenceless if they were ceded. The only solution which occurred to me at the moment was that the Islands should in some form be neutralised under the guarantee of the Powers, so

that, whoever administered them, they should not be made into a place of arms, or fortified or used for ships of war or for other warlike purposes.

Dr. Daneff asked me whether, if the Turks refused the terms of peace, I would exercise influence with them in favour of their yielding.

I said that, especially as London had been chosen as the place for the peace negotiations, I must be neutral. I could not be a partizan of one party or the other. If I had to say anything to the Turks, it could only be that, if they broke off the negotiations and continued the war, and got the worst of it, they must not expect the Powers to intervene in their favour. The Turks might, however, have hopes of doing better if they resumed the war; and, if so, what I said would not influence them. All I could do would be to impress on them that, if they lost in the fighting, there could be no intervention in their favour.

Dr. Daneff said that, if the peace negotiations were broken off and the war continued, the terms now proposed by the Allies would be increased, and the question of the Straits would be raised. He was content that it should be made clear to the Turks that, if they went on fighting, they did so at their own risk.

I told him that this was the position which I should take up if need be. It was one which applied also to Bulgaria.

Dr. Daneff readily admitted this, but he seemed confident that the Turks could not make headway if the war was resumed, and he appeared to think that Nazim Pasha himself knew that they could not make headway, for it was he who had wished to discuss terms of peace and an armistice.

I am, &c.,
E. Grey

[FO 54893/42842/12/44]

Sir Edward Grey to Sir F. Cartwright
Foreign Office, December 20, 1912

Sir,
    At the meeting of Ambassadors to-day I was authorised to make the following "communiqué" to the Press:—
    (See paper herewith A.)
    I was further authorised to make the following communication confidentially to the Servian Chargé D'affaires for the information of his Government:—
    (See paper herewith B.)
    Both these communications were authorised in consequence of instructions received by the Ambassadors from their respective Governments since our last meeting.
    The Russian Ambassador made the following stipulation respecting the decision come to about Servian access to the Adriatic
    (See paper herewith C.)
    I expressed the opinion, in which I understood the Ambassadors generally, certainly the French and Italian Ambassadors, to agree, that there was nothing in the Russian Ambassador's stipulation that was at all inconsistent with the decision to which we had come.
    Finally, it was resolved that:—

"Sir E. Grey et les Ambassadeurs de l'Allemagne, de la France et de l'Italie ne soulèvent pas d'objection à la proposition du Comte Benckendorff, et se réservent de la soumettre à leurs Gouvernements respectifs. L'Ambassadeur de l'Autriche-Hongrie ne se prononce pas, et soumettra cette proposition à son Gouvernement."

We had some discussion as regards the eastern frontier of Albania. It was apparent that no settlement could be made simply in principle, the ethnographical principle being so vague, and the Russian and Austrian Ambassadors were therefore asked to produce maps at the next meeting, each with a line showing the views of their respective Governments.

We had now reached the maximum of agreement that the instructions and information in the possession of the Ambassadors rendered possible, and we had come to a unanimous decision in principle about Servian access to the Adriatic and the autonomy of Albania. It was, therefore, felt that we could do no further work until the respective Governments had had time to digest what we had put before them, and to consider the points, which still remained.

I expressed the opinion that it was very desirable that this "réunion" of Ambassadors should not be dissolved as long as any difficulties remained. I thought that this week had shown that we provided a most excellent medium in which difficulties could be discussed.

This opinion seemed to be shared unanimously, and we agreed provisionally to meet again on January 2nd next.

I am, &c.,
E. Grey

Enclosure 1 in No. 403

A.	ALBANIE

"Les Ambassadeurs ont recommandé à leurs Gouvernements qui les ont acceptés le principe de l'autonomie albanaise avec une proposition garantissant à la Serbie un accès commercial à l'Adriatique. Les six Gouvernements sont tombés d'accord en principe sur ces deux points."

Enclosure 2 in No. 403

B "Autonomie albanaise garantie et contrôlée exclusivement par les six Puissances sous la souveraineté ou la suzeraineté du Sultan.

"Un accès commercial sera réservé à la Serbie par un port albanais libre et neutre desservi par un chemin de fer international sous le contrôle européen et sous la garde d'une force spéciale internationale avec liberté de transit et franchise de droit pour toutes les marchandises y compris les munitions de guerre."

Enclosure 3 in No. 403

C. Reconnaissance à la Serbie du choix de la direction du chemin de fer et du port terminal.

Toute garantie au Gouvernement Serbe pour la liberté des Etudes nécessaires pour établir son choix et pour celles du tracé de chemin de fer contre les difficultés qui pourraient éventuellement être créées par le futur Gouvernement Albanais.

Droit pour la Serbie de participer au contrôle international de la ligne et du port.

[FO 54892/42842/12/44]

Sir Edward Grey to Sir R. Paget
Foreign Office, December 20, 1912

Sir,
    The Servian Chargé d'Affaires was instructed to make to me the communication of which he gave me to-day the following "aide-mémoire":—
    (See paper herewith A.)
    In return, I informed him that the Ambassadors had unanimously made a recommendation to their respective Governments, which all the six Governments had now approved. I was authorised on their behalf to give him confidentially, for the information of his Government, the following statement.—
    (See paper herewith B.)
    After reading it, he asked me whether it meant that Servian commerce would be free from Customs duties.
    I replied that it was clearly intended that Customs duties should not be levied at the Adriatic port on goods in transit for Servia.
    The Chargé d'Affaires then asked me confidentially for my personal opinion whether, in view of this decision, it would or would not be desirable for Servia to stipulate, in the terms of peace with Turkey, for any territory giving access for Servia to the Adriatic.
    I answered that my advice would be that, in the terms of peace, which I understood were to be presented "en bloc" by the Allies to Turkey, Turkey should be asked to cede the territory to the west of a certain line, with the exception of Albania, of which the future "status," organisation, and limits would be settled by the Powers. If I had given this advice before

the Great Powers had come to the decision of which I had just told him, he might fairly have asked me how Servia was to be sure of any commercial access to the Adriatic; but, as Servia was now in possession of the unanimous decision of the Great Powers, she would safely leave the question of Albania to them, as far as commercial access to the Adriatic is concerned. By making the conditions of peace as I had suggested, she would avoid any interference with the Great Powers in the actual terms of peace.

I am, &c.,
E. Grey

Enclosure 1 in No. 404
A.

La Serbie est entrée en guerre avec la Turquie pour délivrer ses conationaux et pour assurer une paix durable sur ses frontières, ainsi que son indépendance politique et économique. Après d'énormes sacrifices en vies et en argent, la Serbie, grâce à ses succès militaires, a délivré ses frères et a regagné les territoires sur la mer Adriatique que la Turquie lui avait enlevés.

Mais comme l'Autriche-Hongrie a déclaré qu'elle ne pourrait pas permettre que la Serbie conservât les territoires bordant sur la mer que son armée a occupés, le Gouvernement Serbe, tenant sérieusement compte de cette déclaration et désirant vivre en paix et en amitié avec son puissant voisin, considère que le moment est arrivé—maintenant que les Ambassadeurs des Grandes Puissances se sont réunis à Londres pour un échange d'idées sur les questions litigieuses soulevées par la guerre—de remettre entre les mains des Grandes Puissances la question de l'accès de la Serbie à la mer, par territoire serbe, et de les prier en même temps de prendre en considération, lors de la solution de cette question, les sacrifices que la Serbie a supportés pour obtenir son indépendance économique et politique.

20 Décembre 1912.

Enclosure 2 in No. 404
B.
"Autonomie Albanaise garantie et contrôlée exclusivement par les six puissances sous la souveraineté ou la suzeraineté du Sultan.

"Un accès commercial sera réservé à la Serbie par un port Albanais libre et neutre desservi par un chemin de fer international sous le contrôle Européen et sous la garde d'une force spéciale internationale avec liberté de transit et franchise de droit pour toutes les marchandises y compris les munitions de guerre.''

[FO 172/1/13/44]

Sir Edward Grey to Sir G. Buchanan
Foreign Office, December 30, 1912

Sir,
 Count Benckendorff asked me to-day to go through with him the four points which he had been instructed to submit to me confidentially, and on which he was to ask my support.
 I then discussed textually his communication of the 28th.
 On the first point, I said that I had already promised support about Scutari. If Germany and Italy used their influence at Vienna, I hoped that some arrangement might be come to, perhaps with some condition that, if Montenegro ever parted with Scutari, it should be joined to Albania under the same conditions as the rest of Albania.
 Count Benckendorff saw no objection to this.
 As to the Catholic difficulty, he said that Montenegro was the only Orthodox country that had a Concordat with the Pope; the Catholics under Montenegrin rule were therefore particularly well off and had a Bishop in Montenegro. Some conditions might be made as to privileges for Catholic schools in the Scutari district.
 On the second point, I said that I had assumed that Prizrend, Ipek, and Djakova would eventually not be in Albania. But subject to this I thought that there must be room for give and take, and we could not draw a hard and fast line on the map, and might have to refer the details to a Frontier Commission.
 The third point I agreed to, on the understanding that it meant, not that Servia should have a share equal by itself to that of all the other Powers interested, but that her share in the

control of the line and the port should be equal to that of any one Great Power.

On the fourth point, I said that it was covered by the resolution already come to by the Ambassadors, and it was not for me to raise the point. But I foresaw that Austria would contend that a neutralised Albanian port, if available for Servia in time of war, would give her advantages which no territorial port could have given, for instance, if Servia had a territorial port, and the Austrian Fleet was stronger than that of Servia and of any Power helping Servia, Austria could either take the port or blockade it, if she was at war with Servia. But in the case of a neutralised port, the Austrian Fleet, however superior, would not be able to blockade the port. The Austrian rights would be limited to seizing contraband before it reached the port, and as all goods would presumably be consigned nominally to Albania it might be difficult for the Austrians to prevent even contraband of war from reaching Servia. They would also be quite helpless to stop Servian commerce, as they could have stopped it in the case of a blockaded territorial port. I thought that M. Sazonoff had to consider how these arguments were to be met if Austria put them forward; but we must of course wait till she did so.

For convenience of reference, I add a copy of Count Benckendorff's communication of the 28th.

I am, &c.,
E. Grey

[FO 252/1/13/44]

Sir Edward Grey to Sir R. Rodd
Foreign Office, December 31, 1912

THE Italian Ambassador told me to-day that, according to his information, the Servians attached the greatest importance to getting Prizrend and Ipek. They would be resigned to letting Dibra be included in Albania, and Russia would not press the point of Dibra. Gjakova had not the same importance for Servia as Prizrend and Ipek; and, though Russia would put the suggestion forward, he personally thought that one possible arrangement in the end would be that, if Austria gave way about Scutari, Russia should give way about Djakova. He told me also that Austria wished very much to get Mount Lofchen, which dominated Cattaro, and made the Austrian fortifications there useless. But, if Austria got Mount Lofchen, she would dominate Cettinjé, and the independence of Montenegro would be gone,

I said that all these points and possibilities would have to be borne in mind. At present, what seemed to me most important was to press Turkey to conclude peace. I heard that the Roumanian mobilisation was becoming serious, and this was a most unfavourable piece of news.

The Ambassador asked me if I was quite sure that Bulgaria would insist on having Adrianople.

I replied that she had shown no sign whatever since the peace negotiations began of giving way on that point.

The Ambassador thought it was possible that Bulgaria would leave Adrianople to Turkey if the fortifications were razed, and if she could be quite sure of getting Salonica.

I remarked that it would be a somewhat invidious task for the Powers to intervene between Greece and Bulgaria about

Salonica. In any case, I did not see that we could do anything until we were approached either by Turkey or Bulgaria.

The Ambassador expressed apprehension of the new points which Austria was raising. He was afraid that she might not interpret the resolution that Albania should be controlled by the six Powers in a way which really meant control by all the Powers, and he developed to me a scheme for carrying out this control.

I observed that his scheme was certainly one way of effecting control by the six Powers, and it seemed to me a scheme in accordance with the resolution of the Ambassadors. Other schemes might be suggested, and all I could say was that in my opinion the resolution come to by the Ambassadors meant control by the six Powers, and not a privileged position for two Powers, and still less for one Power in Albania.

With this the Ambassador was satisfied.

He expressed the opinion that the Servian participation in the international line to the neutral port should not be limited solely by the Servian financial contribution, but should be on a footing equal to that of any one of the other Powers represented in the control of the railway.

To this I agreed.

The Ambassador had also heard that Austria would object to Servia having the right to import munitions of war in war-time.

I observed that, in time of war, the Austrian fleet could, by seizing contraband at sea, prevent munitions of war from reaching the port.

He expressed considerable apprehension less Austria, as intimated in her press, might claim to have some compensation for recognising the terms of peace. Such a claim would start every Power on the same quest, and he suggested that some resolution might be adopted to provide against this.

I replied that the suggestion came very near to a formula of "désintéressement," such as had already caused some trouble, and I doubted the advisability of complicating the conversations of the Ambassadors by proposing this.

The Ambassador also remarked on the campaign which was being carried on in France about Syria, and suggested that this question might have to be discussed.

I said that all I had done was to deny that we were carrying on the intrigues or had the designs attributed to us. I had no reason to think that France was meditating any "coup." Of course, if the Syrian question was raised, other Powers would wish to raise their own questions about Asia Minor. I thought that there was no need to discuss Syria.

The Ambassador was very anxious that the questions of Scutari and the frontiers of Albania should not be brought on prematurely at the meetings of Ambassadors.

I said that I had no intention of bringing them forward until, by ascertaining the views of the different Powers, I could see my way to a settlement.

I am, &c.,
E. Grey

[FO 448/135/13/44]

Sir R. Paget to Sir Edward Grey
Belgrade, December 31, 1912

Sir,
    Monsieur Pashitch called upon me on the morning of the 28th instant evidently somewhat perturbed in his mind. He had received news from London,—I gather from the peace delegates—that the Austrian Government intended to press for a frontier of Albania including Lake Ochrida and Prizrend, Djakova and Ipek. His Excellency protested that Servia could never submit to such a frontier. He had proved his good disposition by giving way about Durazzo and the coast—a concession which was already creating sufficient discontent in the country—but the Servian nation would never tolerate such a frontier as proposed by Austria, it would be an injustice to the Serbs whom Servia freed from the Turkish rule to subject them now to Albania and if the Austrian Government persisted in its view, Servia would have no option but to resist by force. He added that in so far as he was concerned himself he could always resign, but this would not solve the difficulty as no one would be found to take office under such conditions. He therefore requested me to telegraph and urgently beg your intervention on behalf of Servia when the delimitation came to be discussed.
    I have since ascertained that Monsieur Pashitch the same day visited all my Colleagues and similarly requested them to ask the good offices of their respective Governments. To the Austrian Minister, however, he simply expressed the hope that the Servian claims would receive due consideration. As His Excellency also telephoned to the Servian Minister in Sofia to ask Sir H. Bax Ironside to telegraph to you in the same

sense and the same request was possibly made also to other foreign Representatives there, it seems as though he had been seriously alarmed and had determined to spare no effort to enlist the Powers on his side.

I have the honour to enclose translation of an Article on this subject which appeared in the "Samouprava" of the 28th instant.

I have, &c.,
Ralph Paget

[FO 36/1/13/44]

Sir Edward Grey to Sir R. Rodd
Foreign Office, January 1, 1913

The Italian Ambass[ado]r called on Dec[ember] 27. As to Scutari he said that Italian M[inister for] F[oreign] Affairs] trusted that the discussion on that question would be postponed till a later date, when the atmosphere was clearer, and when an agreement had been practically reached on other questions. It would then be easier to obtain a settlement of the Scutari problem. M[arqu]is Imperiali added that Italy was in a delicate position as she was, on the one hand, bound by her agreements of 1897 and 1900 with Austria Hungary and moreover it could not be denied that Scutari was Albanian, or, as he put it, was "l'ame de l'Albanie": and on the other hand there was the supreme necessity of maintaining agreement among the Powers and, if possible, also of avoiding any danger to the dynasty in Montenegro.

M[arqu]is Imperiali was a little troubled as to the islands. Russia might maintain (tho[ugh] this view is not shared by the French Ch[argé] d'Aff[aires]) her desire that the four islands near the Straits should remain Turkish, and the Germans might require that Mitylene and Scio, commanding the entrance to the Gulf of Smyrna should also be under Turkish sovereignty.

M[arqu]is Imperiali mentioned that he thought of proposing at the next Ambassadorial meeting that at the termination of each sitting the Ambassadors should agree on an identic telegram to be despatched to their respective Gov[ernmen]ts, summarising what had passed at the sitting. This was the course adopted at Ambassadorial sittings at Constantinople, and would not be of so formal a character as a procès-verbal, while having the advantages of that species of record.

I am, &c.,
E. Grey

Sir Edward Grey to Sir F. Cartwright
Foreign Office, January 2, 1913

The Ambassadors met me this afternoon.

I expressed my keen regret, which I was sure was shared by them all, at the death of Herr von Kiderlen, and also the very sincere sympathy which we all felt.

The Ambassadors individually joined in this.

The German Ambassador thanked us, and said that he would tell his Government of the expression of our sympathy.

I then said that, with regard to the question of Albania, there were some points of minute detail and other points too important to be called points of detail that still remained unsettled. I had gathered that some of the Governments were still considering these points, and that we were not all fully instructed respecting them.

This being confirmed by one or two of the Ambassadors, it was unanimously agreed not to discuss the question of Albania to-day.

The Russian Ambassador said that he had a further declaration to make about the Ægean Islands. He made it in the following terms:—

"La Russie ne s'oppose pas à la réunion de toutes les îles de la Mer Egée à la Grèce sous la réserve pour les quatre îles voisines des Dardanelles d'une neutralisation [...]portant les dispositions suivantes:

"1. Engagement de la part de la Grèce de raser les fortifications existantes, tant militaires que navales.
"2. Engagement de ne jamais ériger de nouvelles fortifications ou autre construction de défense.

"3.   Engagement de ne pas utiliser les îles pour des opérations militaires ou dans des buts stratégiques, quelle que soit la Puissance avec laquelle la Grèce serait en guerre.
"4.   Engagement de ne céder à aucune autre Puissance les droits de possession, exploitation, ou d'autres droits qu'obtiendra la Grèce par le fait de la réunion des îles au royaume."

The German Ambassador "fait observer que son Gouvernement n'a qu'un intérêt secondaire dans ces îles, et qu'il adhérera, pense-t-il, à toute décision des Puissances à ce sujet; mais dans le cas où toutes ces îles seraient attribuées à la Grèce il lui dit qu'elles devraient être neutralisés dans les mêmes conditions que celles qui sont voisines des Dardanelles."

On this, the French Ambassador and I declared, on behalf of our Governments, "Nous ne nous opposons pas à l'annexion de toutes les îles à la Grèce sur conditions à déterminer."

The Ambassadors of Germany, Austria-Hungary, and Italy "se réservent de dire à leurs Gouvernements la déclaration russe actuelle."

The French Ambassador asked if the Island of Thasos should not be given to Bulgaria because of its proximity to the Coast; which will became Bulgarian by terms of peace.

The Russian Ambassador "ne fait pas d'objection à l'attribution de Thasos à la Bulgarie."

The French Ambassador said that he made an identic declaration.

I said that I thought the Greeks and Bulgarians must be left to arrange this point between them.

With regard to Crete, I said that we were disposed to propose that Crete should be given to Greece. I understood that in the peace negotiations, the Turks had made some question of their inability to dispose of Crete, because it was en dépôt with the four Powers. It might therefore be opportune that we should declare our readiness to hand Crete to Greece.

The French and Russian Ambassadors said "que leurs Gouvernements étaient dans la même disposition."

The Italian Ambassador said "que son Gouvernement était dans la même disposition, mais qu'il s'attendait à ce que la Grèce modère ses prétentions au sud de l'Albanie."

The German and Austro-Hungarian Ambassadors did not anticipate that their Governments would make any objection, but said that they must refer the matter to them.

We had some general discussion respecting the progress of the peace negotiations. We understood that, at yesterday's meeting of the delegates, the question of Adrianople was left acute, but nearly everything else except the islands was disposed of. It was possible that some compromise might be arranged between the Bulgarians and Turks about Adrianople, and an agreement reached tomorrow; or the Bulgarians or the Turks, or both, might appeal to us. In view of the possibility of this happening, it was felt that we ought to make no delay in referring to our Governments. Even if no appeal was made to us, and the question of Adrianople still remained acute and the rupture of the peace negotiations was thereby threatened, we felt that the question whether the Great Powers should make representations in some quarter to avert a recommencement of the war should be considered by us the day after to-morrow (the 4th instant).

We agreed, therefore, to meet in any case on Saturday next at 11 o'clock in the morning, to consider the information which we might then have respecting the meeting of the peace delegates to-morrow.

I am, &c.,
E. Grey

[FO 250/1/13/44]

Sir Edward Grey to Sir G. Buchanan
Foreign Office, January 2, 1913

The Russian Ambassador called on Sir A. N[icolson] on Dec[ember] 28. As H[is] E[xcellency] had the telegram with him, Sir A. N[icolson] asked him to read again the telegram from M. de Giers at Vienna recording his conversation with C[oun]t Berchtold, and of which M. de Etter had read to Sir A. N[icolson] a summary on Dec[ember] 27. Sir A. N[icolson] found that his record of yesterday was on the whole accurate, though there were some addenda which M. de Etter had not given. Firstly C[oun]t Berchtold had said that no one should doubt the pacific intentions of Austria-Hungary. The military measures had been taken two months ago and no additional ones had been adopted. They were simply defensive and not aggressive. Secondly Austria-Hungary might be able to disarm in 10 or 15 days. C[oun]t Berchtold hoped that during that period the serious questions now before the ambassadorial meetings, and the negotiations with Servia would be concluded, and, if so, he would then disarm. Servia had been obstinate: and it had been necessary to make military preparations. Thirdly Russia had 500,000 reservists under arms—far more than Austria-Hungary. Would Russia be prepared to send them home?

It may be noted that there was no mention as to the "guarantee" Austria-Hungary required, as mentioned in the French version of the interview.

C[oun]t Benckendorff then read to Sir A. N[icolson] the reply of M. Sazonoff to C[oun]t Berchtold. The substance was as follows—

M. de Giers was to tell C[oun]t Berchtold that M. Sazonoff was not convinced by C[oun]t Berchtold's arguments as to the necessity of maintaining the military preparations. M. Sazonow further did not understand how Servia's alleged "obstinacy" could be adduced as a reason, as Servia had been most subservient. M. Sazonow would like to know what were the negotiations with Servia to which C[oun]t Berchtold alluded. As to the necessity of maintaining military preparations during the discussion of the Ambassadors of serious questions, this was not an argument which Russia could in consonance with her dignity as a Great Power admit. M. Sazonow did not understand the allusion to the danger in Galicia, nor could he admit that Austro-Hungarian military preparations were solely defensive. The whole number of Russian reservists under arms in European and Asiatic Russia did not exceed 350,000 [men]. If Austria-Hungary would reduce her military preparations, Russia would send her reservists home. M. de Giers was to explain to C[oun]t Berchtold how desirable it was that the question of armaments should be promptly solved on account of the impression which was being produced on Russian public opinion and the effect it produced on good neighbourly relations.

In another telegram M. Sazonow desired C[oun]t Benckendorff to point out to me the reference of C[oun]t Berchtold to the necessity of maintaining military preparations during the Ambassadorial conversations. M. Sazonow was also disquieted by what C[oun]t Berchtold had said as to Servian obstinacy. The Vienna Cabinet might be wishing to impose on Servia the grant of some special privileges, even if they were only economic. Russia maintained her point of view that no Great Power should endeavour to obtain special privileges, and M. Sazonow hoped that H[is] M[ajesty's] Gov[ernmen]t held the same opinion. Russia did not wish to exacerbate the present situation, and was ready to make every allowance for the amour-propre of Austria-Hungary. M. Sazonow would, therefore, be quite satisfied if the recall of the military measures were taken at Austria-Hungary's own initiative, without any pressure.

M. Sazonow was of opinion that the limits of Albania should not be discussed at the Ambassadorial meetings till the Powers were assured that Austria-Hungary was disarming. Perhaps Sir E. Grey might devise some reason for postponing that question—as for instance proposing that further local information is needed. By the time further information is obtained, the question of Austro-Hungarian armaments may have been decided in a satisfactory way, or it may be in such a position as would require that the three Powers should consult together.

Sir A. N[icolson] told C[oun]t Benckendorff he would report the above to me. So far as Sir A. N[icolson] could see, C[oun]t Berchtold said that he would put away his revolver when all questions as to Albania &c. had been solved, and M. Sazonow said that he did not want to discuss Albania till the revolver had been put away. C[oun]t Benckendorff said that this was shortly the position.

C[oun]t Benckendorff also told Sir A. N[icolson] confidentially that Russia under certain conditions would be ready to hand over the four islands near the Dardanelles to Greece. M. Venizelos had accepted 3 out of the 4 conditions at once, and had referred the 4th to his Gov[ernmen]t. Russia in return expected Greece to abandon her sovereignty over M[oun]t Athos.

I am, &c.,
E. Grey

[FO 639/1/13/44]

Sir Edward Grey to Sir F. Bertie
Foreign Office, January 3, 1913

M. Cambon told me to-day that the Austrian Ambassador in St. Petersburg had explained that the number of men in an Army company in Austria had hitherto been far less than in the Russian and German Armies, and that to maintain a corresponding military strength, the number had now been raised to 130, and must be kept so as regards troops near the Russian frontier. On the Servian frontier, the strength had been raised to 200, but that would be diminished after Servia evacuated the Adriatic littoral, and the frontiers of Albania were settled. As, however, Count Berchtold realised the difficulty of making public opinion understand the real meaning of the Austrian increase, he would, if Russia retained her reservists with the colours, accept this as inevitable, and if need be explain it. This had made M. Sazonoff desire to hurry on the discussion of the Albanian question at the meetings of Ambassadors. M. Cambon considered it quite unnecessary to take this alarmist view, and thought that we should proceed at leisure, undisturbed by what Austria was doing. In fact, we might say presently that we could not discuss the Albanian question if Austria maintained this form of pressure.

I said that the Servian Officers in Durazzo were talking childishly of staying there; but of course they would evacuate the Adriatic littoral after peace was made. I did not propose to bring on the Albanian question at the meetings of Ambassadors till we saw our way to a settlement. I proposed also to tell the Italian Ambassador, whose Government were discussing the question with the Austrian Government, that Italy and Austria must find some way of satisfying Montenegro. I assumed that

Russia would not be more Montenegrin than Montenegro, and that if Montenegro was satisfied it would not matter to Russia how this was effected. Once the Montenegrin question was settled, we could discuss the eastern frontier of Albania, for we knew that Austria would yield as regards Prizrend and Ipek, and possibly about Djakova.

  M. Cambon agreed to this procedure.

I am, &c.,
E. Grey

[FO 757/1/13/44]

Sir Edward Grey to Sir G. Buchanan
Foreign Office, January 3, 1913, 11 p.m.

    Russian Ambassador has communicated to me substance of Austrian Ambassador's communications to Russian M[inister for] F[oreign] A[ffairs] respecting Austrian military measures. As Austrian M[inister for] F[oreign] A[ffairs] will accept Russian retention of reserves and explain it as natural under the circumstances, I do not anticipate any unfavourable developments in near future. Servian officers at Durazzo talk childishly of refusing to withdraw, but no doubt they will withdraw from Adriatic littoral after peace with Turkey is concluded in accordance with declaration of Servian Gov[ernmen]t that Servia will accept decision of Powers. Austria will then slacken her preparations on Servian frontier.
    Meanwhile it would be very undesirable to bring on Albanian question at meeting of Ambassadors before we see our way to a settlement. The important point seems to be to find some means of satisfying Montenegro. I understand that Austria and Italy are discussing Albanian question and that German Ambassador has instructions to support them when they have come to an agreement. I propose to tell Italian Ambassador that some means must be found of satisfying Montenegro respecting Scutari and that Italy and Austria must find it, before we resume discussion, though I cannot postpone discussion indefinitely.
    An agreement once reached on this point we can safely proceed to discuss Eastern frontier of Albania for we practically know for certain that Austria will give way about Prizrend and Ipek and probably on some other points.
    You should inform M[inister for] F[oreign] A[ffairs].

I am, &c.,
E. Grey

[FO 546/1/13/44]

Sir G. Buchanan to Sir Edward Grey
St. Petersburgh, January 4, 1913

I have communicated to the Russian Minister for Foreign Affairs substance of your telegrams Nos. 1 of Jan[uary] 1, and 5 of Jan[uary] 3.

In the course of conversation I expressed the hope that His Excellency would not commit himself too far on the question of Scutari, as it was not of sufficient importance to form the subject of a European war, while it was one on which you could not promise him more than diplomatic support. His Excellency replied that it was a matter, no doubt, of secondary importance, but that Russia was always having to support Montenegro or Servia on questions in which she herself had no direct interest. He quite agreed that we must wait until we knew the views of the German and Italian Governments, but it was always possible that Austria might suddenly raise the question. From conversation with the Austrian Ambassador he gathered that the object was to make Scutari the capital of Albania, so as to make it easier for her to exercise a predominant influence by means of her protectorate over the Catholics. He had called the attention of the Italian chargé d'affaires to this probable move on the part of Austria, and had pointed out that it would not be to Italy's interest to see the centre of government in the extreme north of Albania. He had further urged in the interest of the dynasty that Italy should insist on Scutari being given to Montenegro.

I do not think that there is any danger of his pressing the matter too far. He would, he said, think it over and telegraph his views to the Russian Ambassador in London. The one point, however, on which he insisted was that some material satisfaction must be given to Montenegro. He spoke of the possibility of her retaining San Giovanni di Medua, or of her being given the two banks of the Boyana with some of the adjacent territory, but begged that you would keep what he had said to yourself until he had had more time to reflect on what it was best to do.

[FO 973/1/13/44]

Sir Edward Grey to Sir R. Rodd
Foreign Office, January 4, 1913, 11.30 p.m.

It is most important that Italy and Austria should find some means of getting over difficulty about Montenegro. If this is done I can bring on question of Albania at meetings of Ambassadors with every hope of a settlement that will remove last serious difficulty between Great Powers. But until some means are found of satisfying Montenegro by some compromise about Scutari, in which perhaps railway or commercial concessions might play a part, we are faced with possibility of a deadlock and consequent breakdown of meetings of Ambassadors. I am convinced that Russia cannot throw Montenegro over, if latter appeals for support. What Russian Gov[ernmen]t can do in interest of peace has been exhausted over Servian access to Adriatic, and if other questions become acute I cannot press that Russia should be the Power to urge or make further concessions, and must give her support at meetings of Ambassadors. I suppose that Italy would regret as much as any Power a rupture over Montenegro and I hope that Italian Gov[ernmen]t who have intimate relations with Montenegro will devise some settlement that will satisfy Montenegro and that Austria will accept.

Till this is done I can make no further progress with Albanian question here and everything depends upon it. I have spoken in this sense to Italian Ambassador. You should speak privately to M[inister for] F[oreign] A[ffairs].

[FO 666/1/13/44]

Sir R. Rodd to Sir Edward Grey
Rome, January 5, 1913, 8.15 p.m.

The M[inister for] F[oreign] A[ffairs] fully appreciates the gravity and difficulty of the question with Montenegro. He had urged upon the Austrian Gov[ernmen]t the withdrawal of their opposition to Scutari becoming Montenegrin in general interests, though somewhat against his own instincts because, the town of Scutari being wholly Albanian he foresees difficulty in a small state being saddled with the future focus of Albanian Irredentism. Hitherto, however, he has not been able to move the Austrian Gov[ernmen]t. Montenegro is equally persistent in maintaining the claim to Scutari. He is continuing to work for a compromise in the sense of ceding a portion of the plain of Scutari, while leaving the town to Albania and offering commercial and railway facilities. I urged the necessity of arriving without delay at some concrete proposal, which the Powers could reasonably press the acceptance of on Montenegro. He admitted that public opinion here was favourable to Montenegro receiving adequate satisfaction, and for that reason he may be counted on to do his best to advance a solution. Should such a compromise, to which he has reason to hope Austria-Hungary will not be indisposed, be submitted, he feels that Russia would have most influence in inducing the King of Montenegro to agree, as he is financed by Russia. He said that the Austrian Gov[ernmen]t were now indisposed to leave the issue of Scutari to the end, and were anxious that it should be settled forthwith. Their position was very difficult, because they had imposed such sacrifices on the country that they were compelled to have tangible results to show for them. Italy's agreement with Austria regarding Albania precluded her from going further in resisting Austrian opposition to the surrender of Scutari, as it was of essential interest to Italy that that agreement should be recognized as binding on both parties.

[FO 1209/1/13/44]

Sir Edward Grey to Sir F. Cartwright
Foreign Office, January 7, 1913

Sir,
    The Austrian Ambassador impressed upon me to-day the impossibility of giving Scutari to Montenegro. The inhabitants of Scutari had neither in race nor in religion any affinity to Montenegro. They were Catholics, and Austrian sentiment would be mortally offended by Catholics being merged in, not a great State, but a quite small State, where they would find no affinity of race or religion. It was not for Austria a question of acquiring power or influence, but a question of sentiment; and Count Berchtold's position would be untenable if he gave way.

    I said that on the Russian side too it was a matter of sentiment. Russian public opinion accused M. Sazonoff of having thrown over Servia about access to the Adriatic. If Montenegro was thrown over, it would be said that M. Sazonoff had given way all along the line, and his position would become untenable.

    The Ambassador said that Austria had given way, for instance, about the Sanjak, which a short time ago everyone assumed that she would claim and occupy. He then went on to say to me privately that, though Scutari could not be given to Montenegro, there was rich land in the plain of Ipek that might be conceded to Montenegro, and the Russians might propose that the stream of the Boyana should be regulated so as to lower the level of the Lake of Scutari and thereby place new land, which would be very fertile, at the disposal of Montenegro on the Montenegrin side. If the Montenegrin difficulty could be overcome, the Ambassador thought that the eastern frontier of Albania could be arranged.

I said that this was just the point which made it so much worth while trying to find some compromise which would satisfy Montenegro. If this were done, the way would be clear for a settlement of the eastern frontier of Albania, and every serious and dangerous point of difficulty between the Great Powers would be removed. But, if I were to ask the meeting of Ambassadors to discuss the question of Scutari before we saw our way to a settlement, there would be a deadlock; the whole meeting of the Ambassadors might break down on this point; and then everything would be in confusion, and none of us would know where we were. I took note of what the Ambassador had suggested to me, about the plain of Ipek and the Boyana, as a contribution in feeling our way to a compromise; but I could not say more without knowing the views of the others concerned in the matter. I suggested that Italy might be very useful in getting the King of Montenegro to express himself favourably about whatever settlement was possible.

The Ambassador feared that the Italians were almost more Montenegrin than the Montenegrins themselves.

I observed that it would be most disagreeable to Italy if the negotiations broke down on a difference between Austria and Russia about Montenegro, and it must therefore be to the interests of the Italian Government to avert such a contingency.

I am, &c.,
E. Grey

[FO 11186/185/13/44]

Sir Edward Grey to Sir G. Buchanan.
Foreign Office, March 8, 1913, 7.20 p.m.

After resolutions come to at meeting with Ambassadors on Thursday, it seems urgent to make some communication that will stop useless bloodshed at Scutari, and indeed all along the Albanian frontier. Very ugly reports reach me from time to time through British consuls of massacres in districts in Servian occupation, though it is difficult to be sure how much is authentic. All this would cease if a firm intimation could be made both to Montenegro and Servia that the destiny of places of chief importance on the frontier has been settled by the Powers and will not be affected by anything that Servia and Montenegro may do.

The meeting with Ambassadors on Thursday suggested that the previous communication, "Les Puissances considèrent que la Serbie sera tenue d'évacuer le littoral et le territoire de l'Albanie après sa délimitation par les Puissances, dès que lesdites Puissances lui auront notifié leur décision," should be repeated to Servia and made also to Montenegro.

You should ask Minister for Foreign Affairs whether he would agree, if Austrian Government will also agree, to add to this a notification that the Powers have practically come to an agreement that will exclude Ipek, Prisrend, and Dibra from Albania, but will give Scutari to Albania, and that the question of Djakova remains for the moment in suspense.

It would not be necessary to discuss in this connection smaller outstanding points such as the banks of the Boyana.

I am aware that agreement of Russia as regards Scutari was dependent upon concession of both Djakova and Dibra to Servia, and that agreement of Austria respecting Dibra was dependent on concession to Albania not only of Scutari, but of whole of the rest of Austrian line, but it seems very desirable not to let this point of form stand in the way of an intimation at once to Servia and Montenegro that Powers are practically agreed about all the populous centres on north and north-east frontier of Albania except Djakova. It seems really of great importance that this intimation should be made.

[FO 2265/1/18/44]

Sir Edward Grey to Sir G. Buchanan
Foreign Office, January 14, 1913

Sir,
     Count Benckendorff and M. Cambon came to see me together to-day.
     Count Benckendorff spoke with much emphasis about the Albanian question. He suggested that the discussion at the meeting of Ambassadors should follow the lines on which the question had been discussed between the Governments of St. Petersburg and Vienna. These Governments were agreed on certain points of detail about the international railway to the Adriatic, and we might come to a settlement on those points. The only point not yet settled was the question of Servia's right to import munitions of war in time of war. Then we should discuss the question of Scutari, on which there would be difference of opinion. Russia might possibly give way at the end about Scutari, but in that case would have to adopt practically the Servian line for the eastern frontier of Albania, and say that her offer was there to take or to leave.
     I said that Austria would probably say, when the question of Scutari was discussed, that she was prepared to make sacrifices as regards the eastern frontier of Albania; but by this she would mean giving up Ipek and Prizrend and possibly Dibra, and I feared that this would not go far enough to meet the Russian view.
     Count Benckendorff said that it certainly would not.
     I observed that the British sources of information at my disposal all said that it was unreasonable that Montenegro should have the town of Scutari, which was purely Albanian.

Count Benckendorff agreed to this on its merits, but said that, if Russia gave way about Scutari, she must have complete satisfaction for Servia about the eastern frontier of Albania.

I pointed out that some places, such as Djakova, claimed by the Servians, were really Albanian.

Count Benckendorff said that there were, in fact, four races in the district of Albania: there were true Servians and true Albanians, and false Servians and false Albanians. Numbers of people who were called Albanians were not really Albanians, and at places like Djakova the language used was Servian.

As he spoke very seriously of the feeling of public opinion in Russia about the Servian question, I said that it was really most unreasonable that there should be a great war on the question of whether Servia was to get at the present moment so many square kilometres, more or less. It was now absolutely certain that, at the close of the present war, there would be a great Bulgaria and a Servia larger than before. In a few years, especially after the death of the Emperor of Austria, the Slav position would be enormously stronger, and the future developments of the present change would not be affected in the least by whether Servia got a little more or a little less at this moment. Count Benckendorff had said that, if there was not a good settlement now, there would be constant fighting and trouble, and war would come a year or two hence. I urged that, if it was to be so, let the war be later rather than sooner. From the Russian point of view it seemed to me that the whole of time in the next few years was on the side of the Slavs in that part of Europe.

Count Benckendorff did not contest all this, but said that feeling was so strong in Russia that she could not give way about Scutari without complete satisfaction for Servia in the eastern hinterland of Albania.

M. Cambon said that Germany and Italy would have to be used to overcome the difference in Vienna as to the eastern boundary of Servia. Germany and the Emperor, he was sure, were bent upon avoiding war.

I said that no doubt all this must be tried; but even should it all fail and should there be a complete deadlock between Austria and Russia, could not the matter be referred to some international Commission, which would enquire into the ethnographical and geographical conditions on the spot, and make a report?

Count Benckendorff did not exclude this possibility.

I also urged upon Count Benckendorff that, if I were a Russian journalist, I should find it much easier, instead of writing articles to show that Russian policy had been defeated, to write articles pointing out how, by Austria's giving up of the Sanjak to Servia and Montenegro, and by her allowing them to join hands and cut her off for ever from territorial access to Salonika, the Austrian policy as it was understood in Count Aehrenthal's time, four years ago, had been defeated and humiliated.

Count Benckendorff said rather significantly that there were still ways in which Austria might get territorial access to Salonica. I said I did not see how this could happen unless the Austrian Slavs united with Bulgaria in Servia, in which case it would be as if Austria or part of it were annexed by Bulgaria and Servia.

I am, &c.,
E. Grey

[FO 3038/185/13/44]

Sir Edward Grey to Sir E. Goschen
Foreign Office, January 17, 1913

Sir,
  I asked the German Ambassador to-day whether he had had any conversation with Count Benckendorff about the Albanian question.
  He told me that he had had some conversation and had found him very firm about Scutari. But, on the other hand, Austria was prepared to fight rather than let Scutari go to Montenegro. Prince Lichnowsky's impression was that the question might be settled by concessions on the eastern frontier of Albania. He thought that this could be arranged. Austria was prepared to give up Ipek and Prizrend.
  I said that no doubt the eastern frontier of Albania could be settled easily if Scutari went to Montenegro. But, if Scutari was retained by Albania, I feared that the settlement of the eastern frontier of Albania would be very difficult. The concession of Ipek and Prizrend to Servia would not be enough. I feared that we had a very difficult task ahead of us, that would require very hard work on our part.

I am, &c.,
E. Grey

[FO 3522/135/18/44]

Sir Edward Grey to Sir R. Paget
Foreign Office, January 21, 1913

Sir,
    The Servian Delegate to the Peace Conference gave me to-day the accompanying paper, which was being communicated to the Ambassadors also this afternoon.
    I said that he must not think me unsympathetic if I did not make promises. The matter was one to be discussed between all the Powers, and it would be undesirable to push to the point of war the question of whether Albania was to be a little bigger or a little smaller. Servia was sure, in present circumstances, of a large accession of territory, and whether she got rather more or rather less at the present moment seemed less important than the risk of losing, as the result of a European war, what was at present assured to her. If war took place between the Great Powers, the frontiers of Albania would be settled, not by ethnographical, historical, or geographical considerations, but simply by the result of the war.
    M. Vesnitch argued the importance of arranging something now that would be a final settlement.

[FO 4625/1/18/44]

Sir Edward Grey to Count de Salis
Foreign Office, January 28, 1913

Sir,
      The first two Montenegrin Delegates asked to see me to-day, and impressed upon me the impossibility for the King of Montenegro of giving way about Scutari. It was absolutely essential that he should get the town.
      I said that unfortunately the language of Austria was equally strong in this sense on the subject of Scutari.
      The Delegates said that, if Austria marched against Montenegro, Russian opinion would be very strongly moved.
      I observed that this meant that, if Austria marched against Montenegro, Russia would march against Austria; Germany would then march against Russia, and France would march against Germany: all this on account of Scutari. It would be intolerable.
      The Montenegrins laughed a good deal in a way which showed that they appreciated the situation.
Finally, I said that the question of Scutari was a bomb which might set the whole of Europe on fire, and we must prevent it from bursting. I know very well how strong Montenegrin feeling was about it. But others also had strong feelings, and we must find some way of reconciling the various people who were interested. Montenegro would gain a considerable amount of territory in any case, and it would be a pity for her to press the question of Scutari to the point of a European war.
      The Montenegrin Delegates said that their country would not gain so very much without Scutari. The Montenegrins would take nothing in the Sandjak because it was valueless. All they would get would be Ipek and Djakova.

I asked whether they had an arrangement with Servia that they were to get these places.

They replied that they had no special arrangement, but these places were occupied by them, and it was understood that they would keep them.

I am, &c.,
E. Grey

[FO 6128/135/13/44]

Sir Edward Grey to Sir G. Buchanan
Foreign Office, February 6, 1913, 10.45 p.m.

The utmost concessions that we have been able to obtain from Austria were described at the meeting of Ambassadors to-day, and Russian Ambassador is presumably telegraphing them to St. Petersburgh. The German Government and especially the German Ambassador here have exerted considerable pressure to induce Austria to consent to some of these modifications of the Austrian line originally proposed. Russian Ambassador does not consider them sufficient compensation for abandonment of Scutari.

On the other hand, I am informed by such independent information as I can obtain from people who know the country, that the town of Scutari is undoubtedly Albanian and would be an unmanageable possession for Montenegro; also that Djakova is practically a purely Albanian town.

It appears to me that the information is so conflicting as to ethnographical and geographical conditions and the habits of the tribes &c. that I doubt whether a decision could be arrived at on all disputed points without an enquiry on the spot by some international commission. I think this suggestion is worth considering in case it is found impossible to arrive at a complete agreement by any other means.

I have pointed out to German Ambassador the difficulty of expecting Russia to give way on all points—Adriatic port, Scutari, Djakova and Dibra—and M[inister for] F[oreign] A[ffairs] will therefore see that I have put forward Russian standpoint. German Ambassador on the other hand urges that Austria made a great concession in giving way about Sandjak, which it was assumed a few months ago she would not allow

Servia and Montenegro to take, and thereby to bar all territorial access for Austria to Salonica; also that Ipek and Prizrend are concessions as they might reasonably have been claimed, especially Ipek, as Albanian: and he says concession as to certain tribes near Lake Scutari has only been obtained with great difficulty from Austria.

I shall be glad to know view of M[inister for] F[oreign] A[ffairs] as to further discussion or as to any proposal that he wishes to make.

[FO 6120/135/13/44]

Sir Edward Grey to Sir F. Bertie
Foreign Office, February 10, 1913

Sir,
    The following is the record of what passed at the meeting of Ambassadors on Feb[ruary] 6:
    "Sir Edward Grey informe la réunion d'une proposition qui lui a été communiquée par le prince Lichnowski pour la délimitation de l'Albanie au Nord et à l'Est. La frontière à partir de l'Adriatique suivrait le cours de la Bojana jusqu'à un point situé entre Ruskuli et Samric, puis elle se dirigerait vers le lac de Scutari en laissant Tarabosch à l'Albanie, elle traverserait le lac jusqu'à la baie Liceni Hotit et laisserait au Monténégro les Hotis et les Groudas et à l'Albanie les Castratis, les Clémentis et les Screnes. Plava, Goussigné, Ipek et le monastère Visokivetcheni resteraient en dehors de l'Albanie ainsi que Prizrend à l'exclusion du territoire de Luma. Diakovo, Dibra seraient à l'Albanie, la frontière passerait ensuite sur la rive gauche du Drin sur une certaine longueur jusqu'au lac d'Ochrida.
    Le Prince Lichnowski dit qu'il est à la connaissance de son Gouvernement qu'à Vienne comme à Pétersbourg les dispositions sont des plus conciliantes et qu'avec l'Ambassadeur d'Autriche-Hongrie il a étudié ce tracé à titre de compromis. Le Comte Mensdorff dit que c'est en s'inspirant du désir d'arriver à une solution transactionnelle qu'il s'est, non sans peine, rallié à ce projet. Il fait observer que le Monténégro pourra gagner des terrains fertiles grâce aux travaux de dessèchement et d'irrigation dont il a déjà été question dans une réunion précédente et qui pourraient être opérés par une société internationale.

L'Ambassadeur d'Italie appuie avec plaisir la solution proposée qui répond aux vues de son Gouvernement.

Les Ambassadeurs de France et de Russie se réservent de consulter leurs Gouvernements respectifs.
Sir E. Grey dit qu'en présence des difficultés provenant pour certains districts de leurs diversités ethnographiques, géographiques et des usages des tribus qui les habitent, on peut douter de la possibilité d'arriver à une décision sur les points en litige sans une enquête locale confiée à une commission internationale. Cette suggestion lui semble devoir être prise en considération dans le cas où l'on reconnaîtrait l'impossibilité d'arriver à une entente par d'autres moyens."

I am, &c.
E. Grey

[FO 6484/135/13/44]

Sir Edward Grey to Mr. Barclay
Foreign Office, February 12, 1913, 4.45 p.m.

Servian public opinion seems to take no account of the great gains that are already practically assured to her: these include the Sandjak, which till a few months ago it was assumed that Austria would never allow to pass into any other hands than her own. Servia will also gain largely by conquests in Macedonia. Prizrend and Ipek can probably also be obtained and I suppose Servia and Montenegro will both benefit by this. We have given and shall continue to give diplomatic support, but if these very substantial gains are assured and it becomes evident that Djakova and Dibra cannot be obtained except by resort to force, it would be out of the question that H[is] M[ajesty's] Gov[ernmen]t should consider these two places a casus belli or sufficient justification for a European war.

I understand the desire of Servia to possess Djakova and Dibra, but it seems to me that it would be little short of madness to risk in a war to obtain these all that Servia has gained and may still gain by diplomatic support. Servia will emerge from the war with Turkey not only with large present gains but with the prospect of a still more prosperous future. All this and even her present existence may be menaced if she forces war with Austria. You should speak in this sense to the Prime Minister, making it clear that I do so as a friend.

[FO 7688/135/13/44]

Sir Edward Grey to Sir G. Buchanan
Foreign Office, February 15, 1913, 5 p.m.

I have communicated privately to Austrian, German and Italian Ambassadors the line proposed by Russian M[inister for] F[oreign] A[ffairs] for Albanian frontier. This was the procedure desired by Russian Ambassador.

Austrian Ambassador expressed greatest disappointment that Russian line differed so widely from last Austrian proposal which he reaffirmed was put forward as making greatest concessions that Austria could yield on frontier originally proposed by her. I was pressed to say whether the line now put forward was Russia's last word. I said I could not be the medium for saying it was the last word, but it was the utmost I had been able to ascertain that Russia would concede and that I regarded it as impossible that Russia should give way on all three points of Scutari, Djakova and Dibra.

I foresee that the strongest objection will be taken to giving Tarabosh to Montenegro as it dominates town of Scutari, which it is said cannot be held apart from Tarabosh: there will also be great objection to excluding plain of Luma from Albania.

My personal impression is that Austria will be ready to concede Djakova or Dibra but not both towns (though I am urging on German Gov[ernmen]t that both should be conceded) and that Austria will insist on Tarabosh and Luma being included in Albania.

I have said to [the] three Ambassadors that there appear to me to be only two courses left: either to find some compromise between Russian line now proposed and the Austrian line, which was said to be Austria's last word, but on which I think she would concede either Djakova or Dibra: or else to propose an international Commission d'Enquête. Austrian and Italian Ambassadors are not favourable to a Commission saying that it would involve delay and lead to massacres, but I have said that if deadlock occurs I shall propose a Commission.

Austrian Ambassador agreed to refer the Russian line to his Government though he said it was impossible they should accept it. I urged that they should not simply say the line was impossible but should state their criticisms upon it; I would pass these on to Russian Ambassador, but hoped they would be as few as possible.

You should inform M[inister for] F[oreign] A[ffairs].

[FO 12737/135/13/44]

Sir Edward Grey to Sir F. Bertie
Foreign Office, March 15, 1913

Sir,
  I asked M. Cambon to come to see me this afternoon. I informed him that the Austrian reply to the last Russian proposal was very unfavourable. It was, in effect, that Austria could not consider the proposal of a Commission with regard to the question of Djakova except on the basis that the Commission was to be free to decide the ownership of Djakova. Count Berchtold added that he thought a continuance of the reunions of Ambassadors would be useless unless an agreement could be come to about the Albanian frontier which would not be dependent upon the attitude of a Balkan State.
  I told M. Cambon what I had said to Count Mensdorff. I observed that the situation was very serious, and I asked M. Cambon to inform the French Government, that they might take it into consideration.
  He agreed that the situation was very serious, and he promised to inform his Government. He said that, if the reunion was broken up, the responsibility would rest on Austria.
  I replied that it would no doubt be the case that the reunions would be discontinued because Austria was not willing to go on with them, but there would follow a bitter dispute between Austria and Russia as to which was responsible for the break-up of the reunions. Russia would say that they were broken up because Austria had imposed conditions on their continuance. Austria would say that she had been obliged to bring matters to a head because of the delays, for which Russia was responsible, of some weeks after Christmas and some days recently; delays which were dragging things on to

the prejudice of Austria; the suspicion in the Austrian mind being that things were being deliberately delayed in order to confront Austria with the "fait accompli" of the fall of Scutari.

I am, &c.,
E. Grey

[FO 8627/135/13/44]

Sir Edward Grey to Sir G. Buchanan
Foreign Office, February 20, 1913, 10.45 p.m.

Austrian Ambassador informs me that Austrian M[inister for] F[oreign] A[ffairs] would agree to exclude the town of Dibra and the valley of the Reka from Albania, but could only propose this if it would result in a settlement by the rest of the last Austrian line being accepted. He urges also importance of not letting question of Albanian frontier drag on longer. He urged me to recommend this proposal.

I said that if Austria would give up both Djakova and Dibra I would press for a settlement, but that if she would give up only one, I would do no more than transmit the proposal.

Austrian Ambassador was very emphatic that Austria could not give way on both towns. The Austrian Gov[ernmen]t could not give way on more than three of the five places in dispute: Prizrend, Ipek and Dibra as against Scutari and Djakova. This was a last attempt to come to an accord on the delimitation of Albania. He was instructed not to conceal from me the gravity of the situation or the dangers involved in a further postponement of the solution of delimitation of Albania which was a danger to the peaceful solution of the Balkan crisis.

Austrian M[inister for] F[oreign] A[ffairs] asked me therefore to take this communication as a proof of his honest endeavour to avoid at the last hour the breakdown of the Ambassadors' Conference and all the consequences this would have.

Subsequently I saw German Ambassador. He was positive that Austria could not be induced to give way about both Djakova and Dibra. He informs me that German Gov[ernmen]t have used their utmost endeavours at Vienna in last few days: and Italian Ambassador tells me the same of his Gov[ernmen]t. I believe that both Gov[ernmen]ts have spoken strongly at Vienna and that it has taken much pressure to secure concession of Dibra.

I am sure that German Ambassador here has done his utmost and if Russian M[inister for] F[oreign] A[ffairs] doubts whether more might not be obtained through Berlin he might speak to German Ambassador at St. Petersburgh or direct at Berlin.

I have used every argument, such as pointing out how much Austria had gained by solution of port question, but my impression is that no more than this last offer can be obtained and that if Russian M[inister for] F[oreign] A[ffairs] holds out for both Djakova and Dibra he must be prepared to face break up of Conference of Ambassadors here unless he subsequently gives way on one of the towns. I think Austria might be induced to give way on Djakova instead of Dibra, if that was preferred but not upon both.

Djakova is I am told a town of only 6,000 inhabitants: Russia can fairly say that but for her influence Prizrend and Ipek as well as Dibra would have been included in Albania and that Servia and Montenegro would never have been allowed to join hands across the Sandjak. From this point of view settlement of Balkan crisis, even if Djakova goes to Albania does not look favourable for Austria, especially if judged from standpoint of four years ago.

You should inform M[inister for] F[oreign] A[ffairs].

[FO 8853/185/18/44]

Sir Edward Grey to Sir F. Cartwright
Foreign Office, February 20, 1913

The Austrian Ambassador made to me this morning the communication described in my telegram, number 168, of to-day to Sir G. Buchanan.

I told him that, if Djakova as well as Dibra was conceded, I thought that Russia would accept the last Austrian line for the frontier of Albania. At any rate, I should be prepared to urge its acceptance. But I saw great difficulty in getting Russia to agree if only one of the points was conceded. I urged upon the Ambassador that the Austrian solution about the Adriatic port had been accepted; that Scutari was now to be given up as Austria wished; and that unless both Djakova and Dibra could be conceded to Servia there would be very great difficulty in reaching an agreement.

The Ambassador contended, on the other hand, that the settlement of the Adriatic port question was an essential part of the autonomy of Albania, and that, as regards the frontier of Albania, there had been five places in dispute: Scutari, Prisrend, Ipek, Djakova, and Dibra; and Austria could not give way on more than three of these. Except for Scutari, Albania would really have no towns if Djakova and Dibra were both excluded from her. Each town was the economic centre of a large district, and if Albania did not have the town in each case the Albanians who came for their supplies to the district would be obliged to pay an extra duty on every thing they bought.

The Ambassador left with me the following "aide-mémoire," which he had prepared very roughly and could only leave with me purely as an "aide-mémoire" of the situation.

I am, &c.,
E. Grey

Enclosure
Aide-mémoire

The arguments laid down in my "note explicative" and those brought forward in repeated discussions have no doubt made it clear that further concessions on our side would be contrary to the indispensable necessities upon which, in our opinion, the creation of an "Albanie viable" would depend and render the creation of an "Albanie viable" impossible for ethnographic, economical and international reasons.

I am desired to point out, that by the last Russian counter proposal it is just the towns which are left out, and of which Albania would have already so few, and that certain districts which undoubtedly are considered purely Albanian are deprived of their economical centres.

Under these circumstances the difference between the last two proposals of delimitation,—although it certainly has become smaller—still appears to be so great, that a dead-lock could hardly be overcome.

On the other side, every postponement in the solution of the question of Albanian delimitation is a danger to the peaceful solution of the Balkan crisis.

We are aware that Sir E. Grey is making every effort to bring about the maintenance of the peace, and we therefore should deeply regret if the conference should break down. In deference to Sir E. Grey we are prepared to make another attempt to get over the dead-lock. We are quite ready that the last Russian proposal should be discussed point by point and we hope to give herewith a new proof of our good-will.

Should—as it unfortunately seems to be very likely—this discussion prove to be without result, we could not look without concern at the idea suggested by Sir E. Grey of settling the question of delimitation by a commission. I have had opportunities to bring forward our arguments in the conference as well as in different conversations. Our principal arguments are that such an international commission would lead to protracted deliberations and long delay; the danger of massacres between the different nationalities is very real: we have had a precedent on a very similar occasion when statistical examinations were to be made in Macedonia.

Any loss of time could only aggravate the situation. We could sooner make up our minds to make another and very last sacrifice. We should be prepared to cede the Reka valley and the town of Dibra, but of course on the explicit condition that the rest of the frontiers would be accepted integrally. (The remainder of the Sandjak of Dibra would be left with Albania.)

This concession, which we are only prepared to make if Sir E. Grey could recommend it as a safe basis for acceptance by a unanimous decision of the Ambassadors' conference, would also make allowance for the—although perhaps not quite justified—principle put forward at different occasions by the Russians of establishing a balance in the number of the concessions to be made from both sides. We should give up Prisren, Ipek and Dibra; Russia only Scutari and Djakova.

Should Sir E. Grey find himself in a position to try this last attempt to come to an accord at the Ambassadors' conference on the question of the delimitation, it must of course be left to him to decide, whether he would try to get the consent of Russia to a proposal made by him on the said base, by direct enquiry in St. Petersburgh or through Count Benckendorff.

In any case, I have not to concede to Sir E. Grey the gravity of the situation or the dangers involved in a further postponement of the solution of the pending question.

Count Berchtold hopes Sir E. Grey will take this communication as a proof of his honest endeavour to avoid, at the last hour, the breakdown of the Ambassadors' conference and all the consequences it would have.

[FO 8229/135/13/44]

Sir G. Buchanan to Sir Edward Grey
St. Petersburgh, February 20, 1913

    Assistant Minister for Foreign Affairs sent for me this afternoon and asked me in the name of the Minister, who was engaged at a Cabinet Council, to inform you that Russian Ambassador had been instructed to state at to-morrow's meeting of the Ambassadors that, while yielding on questions of Tarabosch, Luma, and Radomir, Russia, for ecclesiastical and other reasons which Ambassador (group omitted?) will no doubt explain, could not consent to exclusion of Djakova and Dibra from Servian territory. His Excellency added that, after having protested against use of expression "last word" by Austria, Russian Government were loath to use it themselves, but Russian Ambassador would state that he saw no possibility of his Government making any further concessions.
    Minister for Foreign Affairs hopes he may count upon support of French Ambassador and yourself. He would be very glad if you could see Russian Ambassador before the Ambassadors meet.
    Servian Minister told me this morning that he had informed Russian Government that under no circumstances would his Government withdraw their troops from Dibra and Djakova.
    Assistant Minister for Foreign Affairs is much preoccupied at hearing that Roumania contemplates recalling her Minister from Sophia and calling out her reserves.

Minute:
    The Austrians are ready to give way about Dibra (or perhaps Djakova instead). Dibra is the larger town and there is

a Slav (Bulgar) and orthodox element—a fairly strong one—
there and in the surrounding district. There is nothing of the kind
at Djakova. The Austrians are in the right in this case and really
fairly reasonable. It will be absurd if we break down about a
town of 6,000 inhabitants to which the Slav claimants have only
one claim—that of possession. But of course that is a strong
one.

[FO 8905/185/13/44]

Sir Edward Grey to Sir E. Goschen.
Foreign Office, February 23, 1913, 7.30 a.m.

In transmitting last Austrian proposal about Dibra to Russian M[inister for] F[oreign] A[ffairs] I not only put it in the most favourable aspect that I could, but took care to embody in my communication the grave statements on which the Austrian Ambassador laid stress in his communication to me.

I have now received a reply from Russian M[inister for] F[oreign] A[ffairs], in which he says that Russia cannot consent to hand over to a Mussulman Albania, towns of Dibra and Djakova where there are Slav religious institutions. Servia would not withdraw her troops from these towns and Russia could not be indifferent to an attempt to expel Servia by force from either of them.

Djakova is I understand a town of only 6,000 inhabitants; it is the town not a large territory that is in dispute and this is the one outstanding point on which the whole diplomatic settlement will be made or wrecked. It seems unreasonable and intolerable that this should be allowed to cause serious trouble between Great Powers, but a question of prestige has become involved in it.

Austria has secured her settlement as regards an Adriatic port; Scutari will also be conceded, a town of vastly more size and importance than Djakova and Dibra or both put together. I cannot believe that to allow Djakova and Dibra to Servia would be regarded as any loss of prestige to Austria, when the Albanian settlement came to be reviewed as a whole.

On the other hand Russia is already criticized for having abandoned Servian claim to a territorial port: the Russian Gov[ernmen]t and even the Emperor will be attacked for refusing to support Montenegro about Scutari or agreeing that she should be prevented from obtaining or retaining it. If in addition to this Russia yields about Djakova and becomes a consenting party to the eviction of Servia from it by force, the position of the Russian Gov[ernmen]t may become impossible.

For these reasons I cannot after the Adrianople port and Scutari have been conceded press Russian Gov[ernmen]t further about Djakova. The only suggestion I could make would be the reference of outstanding points of dispute to an international commission to report on the local conditions; but this I understand is not agreeable to Austria.

Austrian M[inister for] Foreign] A[ffairs] while being very firm in his communications about Djakova has made them so friendly in tone as regards myself that I am very reluctant to make any appeal to him on this point, which he might resent.

But my own efforts to secure a settlement are very nearly exhausted, and it is necessary to put the position before German, Austrian, Italian Ministers for] F[oreign] A[ffairs] as it is. We have so nearly reached a settlement; and yet without Djakova being conceded to Servia a settlement becomes impossible.

There is no risk that I can see of the question becoming acute until an attempt is made to expel Servia by force, but I cannot well avoid a statement in debate on King's speech when new Session of Parliament opens on March 10 and if we have to confess then that there is a diplomatic deadlock it will make a very bad impression; if on the other hand in next fortnight we register an agreement about Albanian frontier at meetings of Ambassadors there will be enormous relief. But to bring the question before meeting of Ambassadors while Austria and Russia are irreconcilable about Djakova would precipitate deadlock, emphasize disagreement and make it appear that Powers were divided into two opposite camps according to diplomatic support given to Austria and Russia respectively at Ambassadors' meeting. The meetings of Ambassadors have hitherto been most favourably free from such a division.

You should inform M[inister for] F[oreign] A[ffairs] of the whole substance of this telegram.

[FO 8654/135/13/44]

Sir E. Goschen to Sir Edward Grey
Berlin, February 23, 1913

    Secretary of State for Foreign Affairs much depressed by your communication. He says that all he can do is to repeat it to Vienna, but he does not think that it will have much effect. He had already gone as far as he could in extracting concessions from the Austrian Government, and even that respecting Dibra had been made in deference to Germany's wishes. He greatly feared that deadlock of which you spoke was imminent unless Russia gave way. He again maintained that balance of concession was in favour of Austria, and spoke strongly as to the peace of Europe being endangered by Balkan States acting through Russia. He realised your position as regards Russia, and hoped that you would understand his as regards Austria. He was as anxious as you to obtain a settlement, but was at the end of his tether as regards advice and suggestions.

    Scutari would probably fall soon, and the situation would then become even graver. He also had been given to understand that Austria was against international commission to report on local conditions, which had surprised him, as he thought they would be gainers by it.

    As he had no suggestions to make, I begged him to consider your communication carefully, and to let me know tomorrow if he could do anything, but he said that he was sure he could do no more than repeat what you said to Vienna.

[FO 9542/135/13/44]

Sir Edward Grey to Sir G. Buchanan
Foreign Office, February 28, 1913, 4:15 p.m.

I recently addressed C[oun]t Berchtold through Sir F. Cartwright with the view of endeavouring to persuade him to give way about Djakova and I advanced all the arguments which it seemed to me would be most likely to influence him favourably.

I have received a reply through C[oun]t Mensdorff, which I am afraid does not hold out any hope of his yielding over Djakova. He maintains that Austria has already consented to all the localities in N[orth]-E[ast] Albania where a Servian minority exists side by side with an Albanian majority being detached from Albania, but that it would really be asking too much if Austria were to agree to the incorporation into Servia of districts purely Albanian. H[is] E[xcellency] advances various arguments against the cession of the town of Djakova, and points out that Austria is ready to cede Ipek, Prisrend, with the fertile plain of Metoja, and Dibra and Russia has ceded only Scutari and Tarabosh while "making difficulties in regard to the environs of that town."

In regard to the alternative of an international commission to be sent to Djakova, C[oun]t Berchtold says that to this proposal "it might be objected that before the arrival of the commission, efforts might be made to transform by force Djakova into a Servian town."

You should inform M[inister for] F[oreign] A[ffairs] of above, and say that I would be prepared to urge the intern[ational] commission proposal once more on C[oun]t Berchtold if M[inister for] F[oreign] A[ffairs] would consent to this alternative.

[FO 8654/135/13/44]

Sir Edward Grey to Sir E. Goschen
Foreign Office, February 28, 1913, 12.30 P.M.

    I certainly understand Herr von Jagow's position as regards Austria and the corresponding difficulty of our own position with regard to Russia makes me not only understand but sympathize. It must be borne in mind that if Austria gives way about Djakova as well as Dibra and Russia thereupon accepts the rest of the last Austrian line, Russia becomes a party to agreeing that Montenegro is to be prevented from obtaining or retaining Scutari and that Scutari ceases to become a danger to European peace. Russia must also become a party to seeing that Servia withdraws from all places inside the agreed Albanian frontier. I think Herr von Jagow hardly realizes how difficult it would be for Russia to become a party to an agreement that would entail compelling both Servia to withdraw from Djakova and Montenegro from Scutari. Russia might agree to one or the other but not to both and, as Scutari is far more important than Djakova to Albania, it is presumably Djakova that should be conceded to Servia rather than Scutari to Montenegro. There is some hope that commercial arrangements might be devised as regards Djakova that would make the possession of the town a matter of less intrinsic importance to Albania.

    You should speak in this sense to M[inister for] F[oreign] A[ffairs].

[FO 9787/135/13/44]

Sir Edward Grey to Sir E. Goschen
Foreign Office, March 4, 1913, 8 p.m.

It seems to me that if Austria gets her way about the Adriatic port and Scutari, which are the two big questions, she will have a balance of diplomatic prestige to her credit on which she could well afford to draw the small amount that would be required to concede a little place like Djakova, which is hardly known to the public by name.

And German M[inister for] F[oreign] A[ffairs] seems not to realize that if Djakova as well as Dibra were conceded and Russia, (as I believe would then be the case), accepted the rest of the last Austrian line, the Scutari difficulty would be disposed of. For Russia would be bound to take part or to acquiesce in whatever measures were necessary to exclude Montenegro or Servia from taking or retaining places on the Albanian side of the agreed line.

It is precisely because acceptance of the last Austrian proposal would entail upon Russia consent to excluding both Montenegro from Scutari and Servia from Djakova by force that Russia cannot accept it. She must sacrifice some prestige in becoming a party to use of compulsion against either Montenegro or Servia. It is too much to expect her to be put in this position against both simultaneously. All it seems to me that Russia asks is an agreement that will relieve her from the necessity of consenting to compulsion of Servia as well as of Montenegro. This should hardly be construed as acting in such a way as to diminish Austrian influence and prestige.

I realize the good-will of the German Minister for F[oreign] A[ffairs] and the difficulty of his position and I can't press him to do what he thinks is unfair, but you should give him substance of this telegram if only to explain the difficulty of my position in pressing Russian M[inister for] F[oreign] A[ffairs] to give way further.

If Servia were allowed to retain Djakova I think any reasonable compromise about commercial conditions or anything else favourable to neighbouring Albanian territory, that Austria put forward should be considered, but German Ambassador here fears that neither this nor certainty that concession of Djakova would settle all difficulties about Scutari will be sufficient to induce Austria to give way.

[FO 10592/185/13/44]

Sir Edward Grey to Sir R. Paget
Foreign Office, March 4, 1913

The Servian Chargé d'Affaires repeated to me to-day, by instructions from his Government, all the arguments in favour of the retention by Servia of Ipek, Djakova, and Dibra.

I said that for some weeks I had used every diplomatic effort to secure that the four places, Prizrend, Ipek, Djakova, and Dibra, should by agreement be excluded from Albania. I quite understood the Servian point of view, but the Chargé d'Affaires must know our point of view, which was that, while as much as possible should be obtained by diplomatic methods, and if, say, two or three out of these four places could be obtained by diplomacy, it would be quite intolerable that a European war should take place about the one or two places that diplomacy could not obtain.

The Chargé d'Affaires expressed his Government's gratitude for what we had done and said that he was instructed to make it clear that Servia did not contemplate the threat of a European war. But Djakova, of which I had spoken as a town of only 6,000 inhabitants, was essential to Servia as a strategic frontier. If Servia did not get Djakova, the Albanian frontier would be a constant source of trouble and danger to Servia. She would not force a war about Djakova, but as she was in possession of the town she could not possibly consent to withdraw, and could be compelled to do so only by force. It would therefore not be her fault if there was war. Austria would certainly acquire influence in Albania, and there would still be a Macedonian question after the war with Turkey was over. It was therefore essential that Servia should have a good strategic frontier.

I said that, if there were to be a Macedonian question and future developments after the war with Turkey was over, these would not really be affected by the question whether Djakova was given to Albania or not at present. I did not know what the Servian arrangements with Bulgaria were, but I assumed that Servia was certain to get the Sandjak and Uskub, including a large part of Macedonia. In addition, she could probably secure that Prizrend and Ipek should go either to her or to Montenegro. Was she really prepared to put all this to the risk of war with Austria because she could not get both Djakova and Dibra? If she was, she would seem to me to be like a man who, having come sooner than he expected into a large estate, committed suicide because there were one or two fields on the boundary which he could not obtain.

The conversation continued for some time, and I urged that Servia should be content with the very large gains that certainly could be secured by diplomatic methods, even if it were eventually found that these methods were not sufficient to secure everything that she desired.

I am, &c.,
E. Grey

[FO 10595/135/13/44]

Sir F. Cartwright to Sir Edward Grey
Vienna, March 6, 1913

      I enquired of the Austrian Minister for Foreign Affairs to-day whether he saw any prospect of a solution being reached on the question of Djakova. He said that he had just received a telegram from Count Mensdorff stating that he had discussed the question with you and that you had referred matter back to St. Petersburgh. Impression I received from his rather vague language was that it was not quite hopeless to expect to see him give way with regard to Djakova in return for suitable compensations. His Excellency laid much stress on necessity for Powers to come to a rapid settlement of Albanian frontier question. He also said that it was essential that the future of Scutari should be definitely settled and not left in uncertainty. He meant by this that the European Powers should definitely inform Balkan States that they had drawn frontier line of Northern Albania and would permit no further discussion of it. He thought that if the six Powers did so there was a probability that Montenegro and Servia would resign themselves to their decision.

[FO 11179/135/13/44]

Sir Edward Grey to Sir F. Cartwright
Foreign Office, March 6, 1913

Sir,
  At the meeting of Ambassadors this afternoon, the following resolution was come to:—

  "En ce qui concerne la délimitation du nord et du nord-est de l'Albanie, la Réunion pense qu'un accord général est possible sur les différents points qui ont été abordés dans des conversations particulières.

  "La solution de la question de Djakova, qui reste en suspens, étendrait cet accord à toute la frontière.

  "Cette question étant réservée, la Réunion pense qu'on pourrait discuter la délimitation de la frontière au sud-est et au sud de l'Albanie."

  There was a general feeling that this resolution, though it did not settle the question of Djakova, would make the settlement of this question more easy, and that real progress had been made by putting on record the fact that this was in effect the only outstanding question of importance. The tone in which the matter was discussed was most friendly on all sides, and there was a general feeling that settlement was in the air.

  The following resolution, bearing on the question of the Albanian frontier, was then agreed to:—

  "La Réunion se demande si, après les récentes communications des Représentants Serbe et Monténégrin, il ne serait pas opportun de renouveler à Belgrade et de faire à Cettigné la communication faite au Chargé d'Affaires de Serbie par Sir E. Grey de la part de la Réunion, le 23 janvier dernier, au sujet de l'évacuation, après la délimitation de l'Albanie, des points occupés par les troupes Serbes."

The Ambassadors as well as myself had all received the same communication from the Albanian Delegates on the subject of the distress in Albania, particularly at Vallona.

I said that I was prepared to send instructions to the British Minister in Athens to make to the Greek Government the desired representation, and the following resolution was agreed to:—

"Les Délégués Albanais à Londres ont remis à Sir E. Grey et aux Ambassadeurs un mémorandum signalant la triste situation des habitants de Vallona et de ses environs qui, bloqués de tous côtés par les belligérants, ne peuvent se procurer des vivres et sont exposés à mourir de faim.

"La Réunion pense qu'il y aurait urgence à demander au Gouvernement Hellénique de permettre le ravitaillement de ces populations, en prenant toutes les mesures qu'il jugera utiles pour la surveillance des bâtiments chargés de ce service.

"Sir E. Grey envoie des instructions dans ce sens au Représentant Britannique à Athènes."

Finally, the following resolution was agreed to on the subject of the Ottoman Debt:—

"Les Ambassades à Paris ayant été invitées par le Gouvernement Français à se faire représenter dans la commission technique chargée d'étudier les questions financières qui feront l'objet de dispositions spéciales dans le futur Traité de Paix, la Réunion pense qu'il convient d'adresser à Paris toutes les communications relatives à ces questions."

I said that we were satisfied with the "project which had now been drawn up, as far as it went. If no further alterations were to be made in it, it was unnecessary to discuss the matter here. If there were to be further alterations, they had better be discussed in Paris. So far as we were concerned, we had no more to suggest.

I am, &c.,
E. Grey

[FO 10595/135/13/44]

Sir Edward Grey to Sir F. Cartwright
Foreign Office, March 7, 1913, 10.45 p.m.

At the meeting with Ambassadors yesterday the Albanian question was discussed and the following resolution was agreed to:—

"En ce qui concerne la délimitation du nord et du nord-est de l'Albanie, la Réunion pense qu'un accord général est possible sur les différents points qui ont été abordés dans des conversations particulières.

La solution de la question de Djakova qui reste en suspens, étendrait cet accord à toute la frontière.

Cette question étant réservée, la Réunion pense qu'on pourrait discuter la délimitation de la frontière au sud-est et au sud de l'Albanie."

I think this marks an advance towards an agreement.

It was followed by a further resolution.

"La Réunion se demande si, après les récentes communications des Représentants Serbe et Monténégrin, il ne serait pas opportun de renouveler à Belgrade et de faire à Cettigné la communication, faite au Ch[argé] d'Aff[aires] de Serbie par Sir E. Grey de la part de la Réunion le 23 janvier dernier, au sujet de l'évacuation, après la délimitation de l'Albanie, des points occupés par les troupes serbes."

These two resolutions imply that if there was agreement about Djakova, Count Berchtold's desire that the future of Scutari should be definitely settled and not left in uncertainty and that the European Powers should definitely inform Balkan States that they had drawn the frontier line of Northern Albania and would permit no further discussion of it, could be realized.

It would entail an intimation from all the Powers to Montenegro that she must renounce Scutari.

The difficulty is to find some compromise which would avoid a similar intimation to Servia that she must evacuate Djakova. It seems impossible to expect Russia to become a party to anything that would entail both intimations. The language of Russian M[inister for] F[oreign] A[ffairs] to me has never varied on this point.

On the other hand I believe Russia would not exclude consideration of any compromise, which secured material advantages, especially commercial for Albanians in district of Djakova, but obviated necessity of ordering Servians to evacuate the town.

I am ready to discuss the possibility of this with Russian Ambassador and Austrian Ambassador here separately whenever they desire it and to bring the question before the meeting with Ambassadors directly there [if] is a prospect of agreement. You should inform Minister for F[oreign] A[ffairs].

[FO 11222/11222/13/44]

Memorandum communicated by M. de Etter
March 8, 1913
Confidentiel

    Après la délimitation de l'Albanie, la réunion des Ambassadeurs devra s'occuper du statut organique et administratif de la nouvelle Albanie.

    L'Autriche-Hongrie, on le sait, désire une Albanie indépendante; de son côté, le Gouvernement Russe s'est prononcé en faveur du maintien en Albanie de la souveraineté du Sultan. Il paraîtrait que l'Autriche-Hongrie pense pour le trône d'Albanie à un Prince Catholique; l'Italie préférerait un Prince Protestant.

    Ces points de vue différents des Gouvernements Austro-Hongrois et Italien ont été signalés à S[ain]t-Pétersbourg confidentiellement par le Chargé d'affaires d'Italie, qui a offert au Gouvernement Impérial l'appui du Gouvernement Italien pour l'opposition qu'il compte faire au projet Austro-Hongrois.

    Il paraîtrait qu'en ces circonstances, le mieux serait que les Puissances abandonnent à l'Autriche-Hongrie et à l'Italie le soin d'élaborer le statut futur de l'Albanie, quitte à y introduire les amendements qu'elles jugeraient nécessaires.

    Le Gouvernement Impérial pense toutefois qu'il importerait de maintenir le principe que l'Albanie constitue une province autonome sous la souveraineté de la Turquie. Le point essentiel serait d'éviter l'établissement d'une prépondérance politique exclusivement autrichienne. Le futur Prince, pour affermir sa position, devra nécessairement s'assurer d'un appui ailleurs qu'en Albanie, un appui que le Cabinet de Vienne sera tout disposé à lui accorder.

Introduire un élément dynastique ne ferait dans l'opinion du Gouvernement Impérial que compliquer la tâche que devra assumer le futur Prince d'Albanie au moment de son avènement.

D'autres considérations militent en faveur du maintien en Albanie de la souveraineté du Sultan.

La cession éventuelle de Scutari à l'Albanie, sera de fait due moins aux efforts de la diplomatie Autrichienne qu'à la résistance tenace de la garnison Turque; le droit moral de la Turquie de conserver la souveraineté en Albanie, acquis par la force des armes, ne pourrait donc guère être mis en question.

Il est douteux que les mesures élaborées à Londres par les Puissances réussissent et suffisent à garantir pleinement l'ordre et la sécurité, et à prévenir des collisions entre les populations Albanaises—de race et religion différentes—si l'autorité administrative locale ne dispose pas d'une force réelle suffisante. On ne voit pas sur quelle force pourrait s'appuyer un Prince étranger au début de son administration. La nécessité d'un détachement international, pour protéger son entrée en pouvoir, ainsi que son installation, s'imposera vraisemblablement; mais l'exemple de la Crète semble démontrer l'insuffisance d'un pareil ordre de choses et ses conséquences souvent fâcheuses.

Les Puissances auront de même à pourvoir à l'impérieux devoir de veiller à la protection des populations chrétiennes, qui, après l'évacuation des troupes Serbes, resteraient livrées à leurs propres ressources et exposées aux actes de vengeance et de fanatisme des tribus turbulentes de l'Albanie.

C'est en s'inspirant de toutes ces considérations que le Gouvernement Impérial croit devoir se prononcer en faveur d'une Albanie neutre, franchement autonome, confiée à l'administration d'un Vali Turc et placée sous le contrôle international Européen, conformément à celui qui a déjà été accepté et dont les détails devront être empreints du même esprit.

[FO 11424/135/13/44]

Sir Edward Grey to Sir G. Buchanan
Foreign Office, March 10, 1913, 10 p.m.

At Berlin and Vienna I am constantly met by the argument that even if Austria had given way about Djakova there would still be trouble about Scutari. I have always replied that if once a line was agreed upon, Russia would necessarily be a party to whatever pressure was necessary to make the line respected and that even if Scutari was taken after a line had been agreed to, it would make no difference.

But I have not been able to convince German or Austrian M[inister for] F[oreign] A[ffairs] that this is the view taken in St. Petersburgh.

It would be of the greatest value if Russian M[inister for] F[oreign] A[ffairs] would make it quite clear that if the question of Djakova is settled, he would join in preventing Montenegro from going to Scutari and in securing the recall of Servian troops from territories agreed to be Albanian.

If this was assured and it was made clear that in the event of Djakova not being given to Albania, the Albanians of the district would be given commercial advantages there. I understand that Austria would agree to refer the question of Djakova to an international commission.

Contention of Austrian M[inister for] F[oreign] A[ffairs] is that he continually receives trustworthy news that Servians act in such a way in territories occupied by them not only against Mahommedans, but also against Slav Catholics, that he could not defend cession of a town like Djakova, inhabited exclusively by Albanian Catholics and Mahommedans without being able to count upon sense of justice of an international commission.

Austrian M[inister for] F[oreign] A[ffairs] was originally opposed altogether to any such commission and Russian M[inister for] F[oreign] A[ffairs] was disposed to favour it, he was indeed at one time prepared if need be to propose something of the kind through Russian Ambassador here.

I understand that Russian M[inister for] F[oreign] A[ffairs] is now opposed to an international commission for Djakova but it seems to me very difficult to refuse one, if only to say what guarantees are necessary for the Albanian population at Djakova, if the town is given to Servia. I am sorry to say that British Consular reports go some way to confirm allegations of outrages in territories occupied by Servians.

You should inform M[inister for] F[oreign] A[ffairs] of whole substance of this telegram and ask his view, which I should like to have as soon as possible; I feel that things are moving towards a settlement and that no time should be lost in attaining one before some unfavourable turn or incident takes place. Austrian M[inister for] F[oreign] A[ffairs] is becoming very anxious about increased Servian military activity in Northern Albania.

[FO 11607/11607/13/44]

Memorandum communicated by Count Mensdorff
March 10, 1913

Count Berchtold expresses his best thanks to Sir E. Grey for all his endeavours in the interest of peace which he hopes will be successful.

We assume that the communication intended to be made to the Servian and Montenegrin Governments would be accompanied by an intimation that they should evacuate at once the territory which is no more in dispute.

Count Berchtold wishes me not to conceal from Sir E. Grey that the news received in the last days and also frankly admitted by the Belgrade Government, according to which considerable Servian forces sent to Albania via Salonika are already at sea, have very considerably increased his anxiety, whether these troops are meant to force the capture of Scutari, or—which would be even worse—whether they are intended to effect a definite settlement of Servia on the Adriatic coast, ignoring the decision of the Powers. Anyhow the landing of these troops, which must be expected in the very next days, [sic] would very materially modify the situation. It would make it clear to the whole world that Servia does not intend to take any notice of the decision of the Powers or of the interests of the neighbouring monarchy, which could not fail to be looked upon by our public opinion as a provocation.

We had and we have still the earnest desire to assert these interests through the concert of the Powers, interests which we are obliged to defend under all circumstances.

The imminent arrival of the Servian expeditions on Albanian soil threatens to make the situation a very critical one indeed, unless the praiseworthy efforts of Sir E. Grey succeed and the action of the Powers at Belgrade and Cettinjé can be made immediately.

[FO 11609/135/13/44]

Sir Edward Grey to Sir F. Cartwright
Foreign Office, March 10, 1913

Sir,
 Count Mensdorff, referring to-day to what had passed between Sir Edward Goschen and the German Minister for Foreign Affairs, said that, if an assurance could be given by Russia that she would formally bind herself to prevent Montenegro from retaining Scutari and to secure the recall of Servian troops from territory agreed to be Albanian, and if Russia would agree that, should Djakova not be given to Albania, commercial advantages would be allowed in the neighbouring territory, it would be of the greatest value if Count Berchtold could know that this was so. Would Russia give this assurance if Austria, without giving up Djakova, agreed that the question of Djakova should be referred to an International Commission? Count Berchtold could not give up Djakova, because he continually received from trustworthy sources news that the Servians acted in such a barbarous way in the territory occupied by them, not only against Mahommedans but also against Slav Catholics, that he could not defend before his conscience and public opinion the cession of a town inhabited exclusively by Albanian Catholics and Mahommedans until he was able to count upon the sense of justice of an International Commission.
 I replied that Sir Edward Goschen had, on my instructions, told the German Minister for Foreign Affairs that I presumed that Russia would agree to whatever was necessary to prevent Montenegro from holding Scutari once Russia had agreed to a delimitation of the Albanian frontier so that it included Scutari in Albania. All the Powers, when they had

agreed to a line, were bound to see that Servia and Montenegro respected the line: to do otherwise would be to tear up the agreement. If Austria gave up Djakova, and Russia then agreed to a line that gave Scutari to Albania, and subsequently made difficulties about the exclusion of Montenegro from Scutari, I could not countenance such a proceeding. But, after what Count Mensdorff had said, I should have no difficulty in asking M. Sazonoff to make the position clear.

I am, &c.,
E. Grey

[FO 11259/135/18/44]

Sir F. Cartwright to Sir Edward Grey
Vienna, March 10, 1918
Confidential

    I communicated to the M[inister for] F[oreign] A[ffairs] this morning the substance of your tel[egram] no. 93 of Mar[ch] 7. H[is] E[xcellency] is of the opinion that unnecessary importance is attached to Djakova question and he has made to me the following suggestion with regard to it. He thinks that the ambassadors in London might now declare as definitely traced the Northern and the North-eastern frontiers of Albania, including Scutari in that state. The district of Djakova would be left undecided and would eventually be settled by a local commission. Meanwhile Servia would be left in possession of the town.
    The essential point for the Austrian M[inister for] F[oreign] A[ffairs] is that the siege of Scutari should cease and that Montenegro should be warned off that town. It is also essential in his opinion that Servia should withdraw her troops from the Adriatic as soon as the Powers accept the northern frontier of Albania as traced by the ambassadors with the undecided gap of Djakova.
    The M[inister for] F[oreign] A[ffairs] seemed to me very anxious about the attitude of Servia as she was showing a desire to force on the new military operations in northern Albania, which looked like an intention to defy the will of the Powers. He said that Austria-Hungary had behaved loyally to Europe in not interfering during the course of the war, although its results touched her more closely than any other Power. He therefore hoped you would use your influence to bring about a

prompt settlement with regard to the Scutari question and the withdrawal of the Servians from the Adriatic.

Count Mensdorff has been instructed to speak to you in the above sense.

Minute:
The Russians don't like the idea of the Commission. But they are willing apparently to warn Montenegro off Scutari without saying anything about Djakova. But they will hardly agree to the definite declaration desired by C[oun]t Berchtold – at least I sh[oul]d think not.

Sir Edward Grey to Sir G. Buchanan
London, March 11, 1913
Private

My dear Buchanan,

It is difficult to find time for writing private letters, but I am continually writing telegrams to you about the Albanian question.

In both Berlin and Vienna I have rubbed in the impossibility of Russia's becoming a party to some thing which would entail using compulsion against both Montenegro and Servia. In other words: Russia is prepared to see Montenegro made to renounce Scutari, provided that she is not also put in the position of forcing Servia to evacuate Djakova. It has been weary work, but I hope that you impress upon Sazonoff how very strongly I have put the Russian view in both Berlin and Vienna.

I am having Cartwright's telegram, number 35, repeated to you for your information. It has come since I received a communication from Mensdorff which was evidently intended to be the same, and on which I founded a telegram to you. If Sazonoff is still opposed to leaving the question to be settled by a Commission while Servia retains possession of the town, he might at least make a counter-proposal that, while Servia was left in possession of the town, a Commission should be employed, not to decide the ultimate possession of Djakova, but to say what guarantees would be required for the Albanian population and what commercial advantages, such as a free zone for the district, should be given. We have really got to a point when a breakdown of the diplomatic work would be ridiculous as well as deplorable. You may make any use that you think discreet and desirable of Cartwright's telegram, number 35, in talking to Sazonoff.

My view about the terms of peace is that the Powers should state that Turkey must concede and the Allies accept that the Turkish frontier should be the Enos-Media line; that the question of the Islands should be left to the decision of the Powers; that Turkish territory west of the new frontier should be ceded, except Albania, of which the status and limits should be left to the Powers; that the Allies should renounce any claim to an indemnity; but that, having renounced this, they should be admitted to the discussions in Paris which are to decide the allocation of the Debt.

Since I dictated this, I have had to deal with two of its subjects by telegram but I send it nevertheless.

Yours sincerely,
E. Grey

[FO 11632/135/13/44]

Sir F. Cartwright to Sir Edward Grey
Vienna, March 12, 1913

      Austrian Minister for Foreign Affairs begged me to-day to convey to you his thanks for all the efforts you are making in the cause of peace and for your support of his last proposal with regard to Djakova. He said, however, that it was to be regretted that Russia was delaying her reply, as it was a matter of vital importance that the frontier of Northern Albania should be settled by the Powers without loss of time, and especially before the fall of Scutari. His Excellency complained very much of the military measures taken by Servia to hurry its fall. Should Scutari fall, he said, the situation would become very grave.

[FO 12370/135/13/44]

Sir Edward Grey to Sir F. Cartwright
Foreign Office, March 13, 1913

Sir,
I gave Count Mensdorff to-day a copy of the written reply of M. Sazonoff, as given in Sir George Buchanan's telegram number 89. I added verbally that M. Sazonoff explained that he did not ask that the assurance which he suggested should be given by Austria direct to the Russian Government, and that it would be quite sufficient if an assurance such as he desired were given verbally by the Austrian Ambassador to me.

On this, I pointed out that, though M. Sazonoff had not raised the point, it was quite clear to me that, if Russia were to make public that she had come to an agreement about the line of the Albanian frontier, she would also have to make public that there was an assurance that Servia would not have to evacuate Djakova. Djakova was a town of only 6,000 inhabitants, but the whole difficulty of the Russian position was this: Russia was a great Slav State, and she could not allow herself to be put in the position of siding against both the Slav countries of Montenegro and Servia at the same time on the points of Scutari and Djakova; in other words, in the Slav question of the moment Russia could not agree to be placed in the position of having to take the entire anti-Slav side. If Russia could have an assurance that Servia was not to be turned out of Djakova and Dibra, she could give this assurance to Servia, and tell her that she had no reason for discontent; and Russia could then concentrate upon bringing pressure to bear on Montenegro to renounce Scutari. Russia could do this, but she could not take the anti-Slav line against both Servia and Montenegro. If

Austria agreed to the principle that Servia should not be turned out of Djakova, I should express, indeed I had already expressed, the opinion to the Russian Ambassador that Russia should not make difficulties about the smaller points, such as the questions of the Boyana and the Lake, which still remained open.

Count Mensdorff expressed some disappointment that the Russian reply had not gone further, and said that he could not tell what view his Government would take of it. He would transmit it to his Government, but meanwhile it was difficult for him to discuss it.

I said that I did not wish to ask him to discuss it this afternoon. It was a great relief to me to have been able to give a Russian reply, and I regretted very much the delay which there had been in obtaining a reply to the last Austrian suggestion about an International Commission. Indeed it had been my intention this afternoon, if the reply had not arrived, to deprecate very strongly any further delay. I was able to deprecate delay, and had done so already; but as the Ambassador knew, I was in a difficult position with regard to pressing Russia to yield further. Before last Christmas, the prominence given in the Press to the question of Servian access to the Adriatic had led Europe to suppose that on the settlement of this question depended the peace of Europe. This question, with the limelight upon it, had been settled in the Austrian sense. As soon as this was done, I had told the German and Italian Ambassadors as Count Mensdorff knew, that I must support Russia, if she desired support, with regard to the question of Scutari. Russia had now practically given way about Scutari, on the condition that Djakova and Dibra went to Servia. I could not press Russia to yield about Djakova without appearing to press her to go on yielding all along the line. I had explained to Count Mensdorff how difficult it would be for her to yield further. He might be sure, that whatever the difficulties were, I had not done anything to make them worse, and in transmitting the Austrian proposals

I had been careful not to say anything that might put them in an unfavourable light.

Count Mensdorff said very cordially that he was quite sure of this, and that the part which I had played was very much appreciated.

Finally, I left with him the Russian reply, saying that it was the best that could be obtained.

I am, &c.,
E. Grey

[FO 12440/185/13/44]

Sir Edward Grey to Sir F. Cartwright
Foreign Office, March 14, 1913

Sir,

Count Mensdorff informed me to-day that the Austrian Government had received through the Servian Minister in Vienna, and I think through their Minister in Belgrade also, the same sort of information that we had received about the Servian attitude respecting Scutari, as explained in Sir Ralph Paget's telegram, number 53, of the 13th instant. The Servians had, in effect, given the Austrians to understand that, if the Powers would only intimate that Scutari was to go to Albania, the decision would be accepted as far as the Servians were concerned. This made it all the more urgent that the Powers should make a statement as to Scutari.

I said that everything depended upon Djakova. I again went over the ground as to the impossibility of Russia putting herself in a position of hostility to both Montenegro and Servia at the same time. But, if the Austrian Government could accept the last Russian proposal about Djakova, I thought that a collective intimation ought to be made, in both Belgrade and Cettinjé, to the effect that the Powers had advanced so far in their agreement about the Albanian frontier that they were in a position to say that Scutari was to go to Albania. In fact, I said that, if Count Mensdorff could inform me that the Austrian Government accepted the last Russian proposal about Djakova, I would take upon myself to say in both Belgrade and Cettinjé that the Powers had virtually agreed that Scutari was to go to Albania; and I would ask the meeting of Ambassadors to have this confirmed immediately, and turned into a collective "démarche."

I am, &c.,
E. Grey

[FO 12445/135/13/44]

Sir Edward Grey to Sir F. Bertie
Foreign Office, March 14, 1913

Sir,
  The French Ambassador spoke to me to-day about the Albanian frontier question, Scutari, and the Near Eastern situation generally.
  I told him what had passed with the Italian Ambassador this afternoon. I said that, if the Austrian reply was unfavourable, I should then say to Austria that, after the settlement of the question of the Adriatic littoral and the conditional settlement of the question of Scutari, I could not do any more with Russia; and I should say to Russia that it had been a very difficult matter to get Austria to give way about Dibra, that the concession of referring Djakova to a Commission had been obtained, but that this had exhausted everything that I could do in Vienna, and I must leave the question as it stood as a result of these arrangements.
  M. Cambon agreed that this would be the situation, and he did not suggest that I could do anything more.

I am, &c.,
E. Grey

[FO 12425/135/18/44]

Sir Edward Grey to Buchanan
Foreign Office, March 15, 1913, 11 p.m.

  Austrian Ambassador has given me reply to last communication about Djakova and Albanian frontier. Reply was verbal but is quite definite that Austria cannot go further in way of conciliation than to accept an international commission to decide to whom Djakova should belong. Only if this commission had decided against Djakova being Albanian would the commission have to secure economic and other guarantees for protection of non-Servian population. I fear that on this point, reply of Austrian M[inister for] F[oreign] A[ffairs] is final and that concession of Dibra and assent to an international commission for Djakova are the last concessions that can be obtained from Vienna.

  Austrian Ambassador also gave me to understand that Austrian M[inister for] F[oreign] A[ffairs] considered that further meetings of Reunion would be of no use unless the North and North-East frontiers of Albania could be settled at them without the carrying out of a decision arrived at being made dependent upon the attitude of Balkan States. This no doubt means that refusal of any Balkan State to evacuate or renounce a place assigned to Albania must be no reason for not giving effect to any decision come to at the Reunion.

  A decision after last reply of Austrian Gov[ernmen]t can of course only be arrived at exclusively of the question of Djakova, the settlement of which would be reserved for a Commission.

  I told Austrian Ambassador that the reply of Austrian Gov[ernmen]t brought me very near to the point of saying that there was no more I could do in the matter, but that this was a decision too serious for me to take without consideration and that meanwhile I should inform Russian M[inister for] F[oreign] A[ffairs] of purport of Austrian reply.

You should inform M[inister for] F[oreign] A[ffairs], and ask him to give very serious consideration to the situation and to let me know as soon as possible whether he would be prepared to come to a decision about the North and North-East frontiers of Albania, exclusive of Djakova and leaving the whole decision as regards Djakova to a Commission.

What I fear is that the fall of Scutari will precipitate separate action on the part of Austria and create a serious if not critical situation unless an agreement about the frontier is speedily come to.

[FO 12736/135/13/44]

Sir Edward Grey to Sir F. Cartwright
Foreign Office, March 15, 1913

Sir,
 Count Mensdorff asked to see me, at short notice, before the meeting of Ambassadors to-day, and gave me verbally the Austrian reply to the last Russian proposal about Albania.
 The Austrian reply was that the last Russian proposal appeared "indiscutable" to Count Berchtold. The intention of M. Sazonoff to give "en principe" Djakova to Servia and to reduce the activity of the International Commission to the economic question could not be considered, all the more so as the news received during the last few days about Servian-Montenegrin atrocities against Mahommedan and Catholic Albanians had strengthened Count Berchtold's conviction that Austria could not go further in the way of conciliation than to accept the International Commission, suggested by me, to be sent to Djakova. The mission of this Commission would be to decide to whom Djakova should belong; only in case this Commission had decided against Djakova being Albanian, the Commission would have to secure not only economic guarantees, but also guarantees for an effective and lasting protection of the religious rights and liberties of the urban and rural non-Servian population. Concerning the argument of M. Sazonoff making his participation in a "démarche" at Cettinjé and Belgrade dependent on Austria's assent to the abandonment of Djakova to Servia, because Servia could never recall her troops from that town, Count Berchtold could only look upon this argument as a recognition of the right of a Balkan State to resist a decision taken by the Ambassadors' reunion in London, a principle

which Austria could not admit. In Vienna the impression seemed to gain ground that, up to now, the deliberations of the reunion had had only a theoretical result. At the first occasion when one ought to pass from theory to practice, obstacles were met with. The argument of M. Sazonoff about Servian resistance raised serious doubts about how the decisions of the reunion could be carried into effect at all. It would appear aimless to continue theoretical deliberations as long as these doubts were not dispelled by a unanimous decision of the reunion of Ambassadors, imposing upon Montenegro and Servia the obligation to evacuate the territories already allotted to Albania and to stop the war operations in the said territories. At present, Austria would therefore consider further meetings of the reunion useless, as long as I was not in a position to invite the Austrian Ambassador to attend a reunion in which the north and north-east frontiers of Albania—exclusively of the question of Djakova, the settlement of which would be reserved—could be settled, without the carrying into effect of this decision being made dependent upon the attitude of Balkan States interested in the matter. Should this be impossible, and, much against the Austrian wish, I decided to make a pause in the deliberations of the Ambassadors. Austria would have to reserve the liberty of her decision concerning events which might occur during that time.

    I said that this brought me very near to the point of saying that I could not do any more, that no settlement could be come to, and that the meetings of Ambassadors must be discontinued. In that case, I should have to make a statement in Parliament of what my part had been, and of why I could do no more. But the situation was too serious for me to come to any decision without reflection. I proposed, therefore, to take Sunday (to-morrow) to consider the matter. This afternoon I would merely inform the Russian and French Ambassadors of the purport of what Count Mensdorff had told me, and telegraph it to St. Petersburg.

Count Mensdorff begged me not to come to any decision such as I had indicated without first telling him. He was most anxious to do anything in his power to soften matters. He impressed upon me that the instructions which he had received, and which were brusque in tone, were not intended to represent the form of a communication to be made to me.

I observed that Count Berchtold's impression that Russia was establishing the principle that giving effect to a decision of the Powers should be made dependent upon the attitude of one of the Balkan States interested appeared to me to be due to a misunderstanding. The principle that Balkan States must defer to the wishes of the Powers was not disputed by Russia. She had agreed to its application in the case of the Adriatic littoral, and it would be applied in the case of Scutari if Servia was left in possession of Djakova. I therefore did not construe the Russian proposal as meaning more than that Russia was unable to concur in pressing Servia to evacuate Djakova as well as in pressing Servia to evacuate the littoral, and Montenegro to renounce Scutari. For these reasons, it was not a principle that was in dispute, but the application of a principle to the particular case of Djakova. I asked Count Mensdorff to point out this to Count Berchtold, as the inherent difficulties of the subject ought not to be made worse by a misunderstanding on a point of form.

Count Mensdorff said that he would do this.

With regard to the statement that I had suggested an International Commission with regard to the question of Djakova, I said that my recollection was that I was the first to suggest an International Commission if need be to consider the question of the whole Albanian frontier. Austria had been decidedly opposed to this suggestion. Russia had been favourable to it, if it became necessary. Subsequently, when only the question of Djakova remained to be settled and every thing depended upon it, Count Mensdorff had told me that he thought it possible that, if a Commission were limited to just this small district, Austria might accept the Commission. But

M. Sazonoff had never committed himself as favourable to anything except the original idea of a Commission for the whole frontier.

Count Mensdorff agreed in my recollection of the history of the proposal.

I am, &c.,
E. Grey

[FO 13002/135/13/44]

Sir Edward Grey to Sir F. Cartwright
Foreign Office, March 18, 1913

Sir,
    I spoke to the Austrian Ambassador to-day as reported in my telegram number 239 to Sir George Buchanan. I said that I hoped progress would now be made towards a settlement by direct communication between St. Petersburg and Vienna: the more there was of this, the better. The Ambassador would, I assumed, receive his next information about the Russian views from Vienna. While this communication was taking place we could, of course, not make any progress in the reunions towards a settlement; but I thought that we might improve matters by coming to some such resolution as the following, which I wrote down for him as a sketch:—

    "A collective démarche should be made at Belgrade and Cettinjé, repeating that Albania has been reserved for delimitation by the Powers; that until that delimitation has taken place no action by Servia or Montenegro in Albania can be regarded as having acquired rights; and that, for instance, if Scutari falls, the destiny of Scutari will be decided by the Powers, and not by the Montenegrin occupation."

    Count Mensdorff: seemed pleased with this idea.

I am, &c.,
E. Grey

[FO 12894/135/13/44]

Memorandum by Sir A. Nicolson
Foreign Office, March 18, 1913

The following is a translation from the Russian of a telegram sent yesterday by M. Sazonow to the Russian Ambass[ado]r at Vienna:—

Russia has no objection to a Commission in regard to Djakova, but wishes to know the basis on which the Commission will work. Ethnographical considerations must be avoided, and the Russian Gov[ernmen]t think it indispensable that the Commission should be required to establish the undeniable fact of the geographical and economic connection between Djakova and Servia, and that this should be the guiding principle of the Commission.

"If the Austro-Hungarian Gov[ernmen]t consent to express confidentially to Sir E. Grey their concurrence with the above, C[oun]t Benckendorff will receive instructions to agree to submit the question of Djakova to an international Commission."

A. N[icolson]

[FO 13283/135/18/44]

Sir Edward Grey to Sir F. Cartwright
Foreign Office, March 19, 1913

Sir,
    The Austrian Ambassador informed me to-day of the communications that had taken place between St. Petersburg and Vienna through the Austrian Ambassador in St. Petersburg. According to these, M. Sazonoff had said that everything was conditional upon the settlement of the question of Djakova. M. Sazonoff wanted a Commission that would deal with geographical and economic conditions, and not make the settlement of the question depend upon ethnographical considerations. M. Sazonoff had stated that every thing that had been agreed to in the reunions of Ambassadors was conditional upon the settlement of Djakova. Count Berchtold also considered that everything hitherto conceded by Austria would be "non avenu" if no agreement was arrived at; that Ipek and Prizrend, for instance, would be claimed for Albania.
    Count Mensdorff then told me that Count Berchtold must insist that the object of the Commission should be to decide to whom Djakova should belong. Should the Commission decide against Djakova being Albanian, the Commission would have to secure not only economic guarantees but also guarantees for an effective and lasting protection of the religious and national rights and liberties of the urban and rural non-Servian population. If these conditions were made the basis of the instructions given to the Commission, Count Berchtold would be willing to meet M. Sazonoff in so far that he would leave the composition of the Commission to me. Count Mensdorff was to ask me whether,

"provided M. Sazonoff consented," I would undertake to name the members of the Commission.

I replied that I could not be responsible for anything but the appointment of an impartial Commission. If Austria and Russia liked to arrange between them that a Commission should be composed so as to give a particular decision about Djakova, I should, of course, have no objection. But, if the appointment of the Commission was referred to me, with the object stated by Count Berchtold, I could not lay myself open to the reproach of having appointed a biassed Commission in order to secure that it should decide in favour of giving Djakova to Servia. I would, therefore, tell M. Sazonoff that, if I appointed a Commission, it must be an impartial one. I was quite prepared to discuss its composition and terms of reference with Count Berchtold and M. Sazonoff, and accept any terms of reference to which they agreed, but any Commission for which I was responsible must be impartial in giving a decision according to the terms of reference. I would communicate with M. Sazonoff to see whether, as the composition and terms of reference of the Commission required careful consideration, some explicit statement could not be made at once to the effect that the Powers had decided that Scutari was to go to Albania, and that the question of Djakova, the only point left undecided, was under discussion. It should also be announced that meanwhile Servia would not be disturbed in her occupation of the town.

Count Mensdorff said that, if this were done, the siege of Scutari ought to be raised.

I agreed that this was so.

I am, &c.,
E. Grey

[FO 12846/135/13/44]

Sir G. Buchanan to Sir Edward Grey
St. Petersburgh, March 19, 1913, 8.32 p.m.

On my informing Minister for F[oreign] A[ffairs] today of what you had told Austrian Ambass[ado]r, H[is] E[xcellency] said that he had not telegraphed to Vienna but had had conversation with Austrian Ambass[ado]r on the subject. He maintains that the whole object of the Commission is to save Austria's amour propre and that all it has to do is to find a pretext for giving Djakova to Servia. The fact that the town gravitates to the east and not to the west would furnish pretext desired and delegates might be instructed to leave ethnographical considerations out of account. He does not care on what they base their decision but insists that Djakova must be given to Servia in exchange for Scutari.

As regards the latter town I said that I personally thought it was essential that some settlement about Albanian frontier should be come to at once that would make it clear that Russia had no intention of supporting Montenegrin claim to it. Otherwise when the crisis came she might have to choose between making it a casus belli which she did not want or exposing herself to humiliation. I then read to him proposal which you were to submit to Ambassadors to-day. He said that he had no objection to make to it. Russia was ready to go to almost any length with a view to imposing the will of the Powers on Montenegro as long as she was not asked to fire a shot or to consent to Austria being given European mandate. If diplomatic pressure did not succeed, he thought that course he had suggested to me last night would be the best (see my tel[egram] No. 100 of Mar[ch] 19).

Sir G. Buchanan to Sir E. Grey
St. Petersburgh, March 19, 1913
Private

My dear Sir Edward,
    I have not failed to impress on Sazonow how strenuously you have been urging the Russian view at Vienna and Berlin, and he is very grateful for all that you have done. I have not, however, succeeded in inducing him to consent to leaving the question of Diakovo to be decided by an International Commission. He would have no objection to such a Commission if it is only to be used as a golden bridge over which Austria may beat a graceful retreat and allow Diakovo to be declared Servian. Austria, he assured me, only wanted to save her face and the Commission must therefore be so composed and its members furnished with such instructions as will ensure the attainment of the object for which, he maintains, it was originally intended, namely, the settlement of the Diakovo question in a sense favourable to Russia. From the language held to me by the Austrian Ambassador—which I reported in one of my telegrams—Sazonow would appear to have some grounds for holding this view; but I cannot guarantee that Count Thurn has correctly interpreted the views of his Government. One thing seems clear, namely that Sazonow will not say his last word about Scutari until he has some assurance that Diakovo will in the end be given to Servia.
    As you will have already learnt from my telegrams I impressed on him your views with regard to the former place both in a conversation which I had with him last night at the German Embassy, and in one which I had with him at the Ministry to-day. Provided that he gets Diakovo he is ready to go almost any lengths in bringing pressure to bear on Montenegro to abandon Scutari. The only reserves which he

makes are that Russia must not be expected to "tirer du canon" and that Austria must not be entrusted with the mandate of imposing the will of the Powers on Montenegro. He will join in any diplomatic action which the Powers may decide to take at Cettigné, and—though he has not said so officially—he will acquiesce in a collective naval blockade of Antivari, in which the fleets of Russia's ally and of Russia's friend participate. If diplomatic pressure fails and if we must have recourse to force, such collective naval action is, as he repeated to me to-day, the best way of applying it.

[FO 13284/9085/13/44]

Sir Edward Grey to Sir F. Cartwright
Foreign Office, March 19, 1913

Sir,
  At the meeting with the Ambassadors to-day, in the course of the discussion that resulted from the resolutions, recorded in telegrams of to-day, about the conditions of peace between Turkey and the Allies, and about the destiny of Scutari being left to the Powers, the Austrian Ambassador proposed the following resolution respecting an indemnity:—
  "La question d'une indemnité de guerre sera traitée par la commission internationale de Paris en connexité [sic] avec la question d'un règlement équitable de la participation des alliés à la dette ottomane et aux charges financières des territoires qui leur seront attribués. Les alliés ainsi que la Turquie seront invités de prendre part aux délibérations de cette commission."
  This resolution might take the place of point 4 in the conditions of peace which we had drawn up.
  The German Ambassador at once took objection to anything that would admit the principle of an indemnity. I agreed in this objection; and it was ascertained that all the others felt that the Austrian proposal was open to the objection that it admitted the principle of an indemnity, and would give rise to discussion that would cause a most unfortunate delay in formulating any conditions of peace.
  Count Mensdorff therefore did not press the proposal, and said that he would report to Count Berchtold that the other members of the reunion were all opposed to it.
  We then received from the Italian Ambassador the following proposal for the southern frontier of Albania:—

"La frontière partirait de la rive méridionale du lac d'Okhrida entre le couvent de S[ain]t-Naoum qui resterait hors de l'Albanie et le bourg de Starova et suivrait d'abord les hauteurs entre le lac de Malik (ou lac de Soviani) d'un côté et le lac de Presba de l'autre côté, puis la crête des collines formant le partage d'eau entre les bassins du Dévol et de la Bistritza (Haliacmon) en laissant le district de Kortcha (Koritza) à l'Albanie. Elle se dirigerait ensuite passant à l'ouest de Kastoria, Lapsista et Grévéna lesquelles villes resteraient hors de l'Albanie vers le sud sur le village de Kipourio au sud-ouest de Grévéna et suivrait puis les crêtes qui forment la ligne de séparation entre les bassins: au nord, de la Voïoussa et de ses tributaires; au sud, du Salamvrias, de l'Arta et de leurs tributaires jusqu'à la source du Kalamas dans le voisinage du Han Kalabaki, laissant au sud la ville de Janina ainsi que Metzovo qui resteront acquis à la Grèce. La frontière suivrait puis le thalweg du Kalamas jusqu'au point le plus rapproché à Aidonat (Paramythia) d'où laissant ce district et celui de Murghelitche (Margariti) à l'Albanie elle passerait par la crête des montagnes au sud au village de Glykys et suivrait le thalweg de la rivière Glykys jusqu'à son embouchure dans la mer Jonienne sur la rade de Phanari (ou Porto di Spîanza)."

We said that this must be taken into consideration, but we could not express any opinion upon it this afternoon.

It was agreed that the next meeting should be on Tuesday, 25th instant, at 4 o'clock, and that the Roumanian Minister should be invited to attend it, in order to inform us of the views of his Government respecting the Koutzo-Vlachs inhabiting that part of territory that would now come under discussion as being on the Albanian frontier or part of the south of Albania

I am, &c.,
E. Grey

[FO 12847/185/13/44]

Sir Edward Grey to Sir G. Buchanan
Foreign Office, March 20, 1913, 11.30 p.m.

It is a delicate matter for me to undertake this duty but I am willing to do so, if it will enable Russian M[inister for] F[oreign] A[ffairs] to join in a public communiqué that the Powers are all agreed that Scutari is to go to Albania and that the siege should therefore be raised.

It must however be understood that though if desired by both Austrian and Russian Gov[ernmen]ts I accept in principle the task of composing the commission I can only proceed with it on terms of reference defining its object and scope that are agreed to by both Gov[ernmen]ts.

For me to appoint a commission regarded by Austrian M[inister for] F[oreign] A[ffairs] as having the duty of deciding whether Djakova should be Albanian or Servian and by Russian M[inister for] F[oreign] A[ffairs] as having for its whole object (see your tel[egram] No. 101) to save Austria's amour propre by finding a pretext for giving Djakova to Servia would expose me to certain reproach of bad faith from one side or the other.

Information from British Minister at Cettinjé is that representations on behalf of civil population of Scutari have produced no effect, that the greatest bitterness is being shown against Albanians and that shells are being thrown indiscriminately into the town.

Austrians say their consulate has been damaged and Austro-Hungarian orphanage and a monastery destroyed and foreign flags not respected and they are sending ships of war to waters of Southern Dalmatia.

All this makes it urgent to announce some agreement so that any demonstration against Montenegro may be one in which other Powers such as France and England could take part and may not take the form of separate action taken by Austria for her own objects. It will be more difficult to arrive at any agreement after such separate action than before it.

[FO 13787/135/13/44]

Sir Edward Grey to Sir G. Buchanan
Foreign Office, March 21, 1913, 5 p.m.

    Austrian Ambassador has informed me that Austrian Gov[ernmen]t will give up Djakova on the understanding that there will be a promise to secure effective protection of Albanian and Catholic minorities in those territories which are going to Servia and Montenegro, and also a further understanding that the rest of the line of North and North-East Albania should be settled according to the last Austrian proposal; also that the immediate cessation of hostilities in and the evacuation of those territories allotted to Albania should be demanded and secured by the six Powers in Belgrade and Cettinjé. I earnestly hope that Russian M[inister for] F[oreign] A[ffairs] will agree to this and consent to a communiqué on these lines. Servia assured of Dibra and Djakova will then presumably accept the intimation of the Powers and withdraw from Scutari, and Montenegro can hardly persist alone. It seems to be of greatest importance to avoid delay; if Montenegro proceeds with present indiscriminate attacks upon Scutari and a massacre occurs it will alienate all sympathy here.

    I hope to get Ambassadors to take note of this Austrian Communication to-morrow and to recommend some communiqué to their Gov[ernmen]ts. It seems to me that, now Austrians have given way about Djakova, the whole question should be settled.

[FO 14813/18799/18/44]

Sir Edward Grey to Sir F. Cartwright
Foreign Office, March 28, 1913

Sir,

At the meeting of Ambassadors this afternoon, I reported the request of M. Skouloudis, the Greek Delegate, to be admitted to the reunion as M. Misu, the Roumanian Minister, had.

The Italian Ambassador pointed out that, if the Greek Representative was admitted to discuss the whole of the southern frontier of Albania, the Servians and others might complain that they had not been admitted to discuss the parts of the frontier which interested them, and Albanians also might ask to be heard.

The French Ambassador observed that the others had not yet requested to be heard, and the questions other than those connected with the south of Albania were already settled. A sense of grievance might be caused if, after the Roumanian Minister had been admitted, the Greek Delegate was not heard.

I said that I thought it would be inconvenient if M. Skouloudis discussed the whole Southern Albanian question with us after we had settled the other parts of Albania without hearing the Servians and others; but, on the other hand, now that M. Misu had been allowed to put before us personally the views of his Government concerning the Koutzo-Vlachs, it would be rather hard if M. Skouloudis was not given an opportunity of replying to M. Misu with the views of the Greek Government.

Eventually, it was agreed that I should give M. Skouloudis a copy of the "résumé" which M. Misu had sent and which I had communicated to the reunion; and that M. Skouloudis should be asked to reply in writing to the points raised by M. Misu. I would then communicate this reply to the reunion.

The Austrian Ambassador informed us that his Government had instructed their Representatives in Cettinjé and Belgrade not to oppose any proposal made by the Russian Representatives in the sense of the resolution come to by the reunion on the 25th instant, respecting the evacuation by Servia and Montenegro of territories occupied by them inside Albania.

We then discussed the Italian Ambassador's proposition about the southern frontier of Albania.

The French Ambassador and I pointed out the hardship to Greece of not getting possession of the coast exactly opposite to Corfu. I said that it was not necessary that the frontier of Albania should go in a direct line inland from the point chosen on the coast, but it would be hard for Greece not to have the coast.

The Italian Ambassador contended most emphatically against this, saying that it would mean the cession to Greece of the port just south of Cape Kephali, which was the outlet for all that "hinterland" of Albania, and could be made into a naval station. He said that the Italian Government would agree that Greece should have up to the line of the Kalamas, but they could not possibly go beyond this.

It was agreed to regard this discussion as a preliminary one, on which each Ambassador would make his own report to his Government.

Finally, the following resolution was adopted:—

"Le Prince Lichnowsky fait observer qu'on pourrait envisager dès maintenant l'emploi de mesures coercitives pour le cas où le Roi Nicolas refuserait de se rendre à la communication collective des Puissances, ou ferait attendre trop longtemps sa réponse.

"Sir E. Grey dit que, dans le cas où l'emploi de pareilles mesures deviendrait nécessaire, il conviendrait de recourir à une démonstration navale internationale et de s'y apprêter en envoyant des bâtiments de guerre à portée des eaux monténégrines. L'Amirauté anglaise a déjà été invitée à prendre des dispositions à cet effet.

"La réunion partage l'opinion de Sir E. Grey."

I am, &c.,
E. Grey

[FO 15163/15676/13/44]

Sir Edward Grey to Sir G. Buchanan
Foreign Office, March 31, 1913, 10.45 p.m.

At meeting of Ambassadors to-day it was agreed that in view of latest news from Cettinjé a naval demonstration at Antivari would be necessary.

When it takes place I would suggest that naval commanders should be instructed to advise the Governments what steps could be taken to bring any pressure to bear. A landing of international force is the most obvious step, but we ought first to know from naval commanders what this would involve.

[FO 15167/135/13/44]

Sir Edward Grey to Count de Salis
Foreign Office, April 1, 1913

Sir,
  M. Popovitch, Montenegrin delegate, called this afternoon to enquire whether it was true that a naval demonstration was about to be made against Montenegro. Sir A. Nicolson told him that unless Montenegro accepted the decision of the Powers and raised the siege of Scutari, it was extremely probable that a naval demonstration would be made; and that it was to the interest of Montenegro to accept without delay the decisions of the Powers. He said that a naval demonstration would have no effect. Sir A. Nicolson replied that in such a case it might be necessary to employ other measures. Sir A. Nicolson said that it would be unfair if he did not state very clearly to M. Popovitch that the Powers had unanimously come to the decision—and Montenegro must not count upon any divisions among the Powers—that Scutari was to be included in the future Albania. On that point the Powers were immovably firm, and it would be but common prudence for Montenegro to bow to that decision. Even if Scutari were to fall, the situation would not be changed and Montenegro would have to evacuate it. Why then continue a siege which was quite without any object, and which only led to a useless waste of men? Sir A. N[icolson] did not wish to employ harsh terms, but it was really an act of folly for Montenegro to set herself up in opposition to the will of Europe. By accepting the decisions of the Powers, Montenegro would secure their good-will, and her future would be assured. M. Popovitch said that the Montenegrin people could not possibly abandon what had been the chief object of their going to war; they could not live without

some means of securing a simple livelihood which their barren mountains and the desolate tracts which the Powers proposed to give them could not afford. He proceeded in this strain at some length, appealing to the equity and benevolence of H[is] M[ajesty's] Gov[ernmen]t not to be hard on a small people who had lost much, had always struggled to gain a bare existence, and who were now condemned to perpetual poverty. Sir A. N[icolson] said he could only repeat his former statements, and that he could hold out no hope to M. Popovitch whatever that the Powers would modify their decisions. M. Popovitch was much distressed and said that Montenegro would then have to perish, or be absorbed by Austria-Hungary, as she could not possibly yield.

I am, &c.,
E. Grey

[FO 17253/18799/13/44]

Sir Edward Grey to Sir F. Bertie
Foreign Office, April 10, 1913

Sir,
 M. Cambon spoke to me to-day about the southern frontier of Albania. He pointed out the exceeding difficulty of enforcing an agreement unacceptable to Greece.

I said that this had been preoccupying me also. I was reluctant to become a party to an agreement unless it could be enforced. There could be no question of our joining in a naval demonstration against Greece.

M. Cambon confirmed my impression that France also would not join in a demonstration.

I said that Germany, whose Court was now much interested in the Greek Court, would presumably not like to take any forcible steps; and I did not suppose that Italy alone would undertake the task of turning the Greeks out.

M. Cambon asked me if I had discussed this difficulty with the German Government.

I replied that I had not yet done so. I was afraid of impeding the chance of securing a cessation of hostilities on the terms of our last reply to the Allies. If we could settle the southern frontier of Albania in a week, it would be a help to securing a cessation of hostilities. But to discuss the frontier without settling it would probably be an inducement to Greece to work for a negative or evasive reply about the cessation of hostilities. I had impressed upon the Greek Minister this afternoon that I thought that, until the critical question of the terms of peace had advanced sufficiently to secure a cessation of hostilities, and till the critical question of Scutari, which was so closely bound up with the first question, was settled, the

Powers could not proceed to an agreement about the southern frontier of Albania. I wished Greece to feel that she had nothing to gain in this respect by prolonging the war. I would propose, therefore, that we should present our reply to the Allies, as I hoped that we should do this week. We should then wait to know whether it resulted in a cessation of hostilities, and only after that should we proceed to discuss the south of Albania. When the time came, it should be pointed out how essential it was to have some idea of how the agreement was to be enforced, before we arranged it.

  M. Cambon entirely concurred in this, and said that it would be necessary for Austria and Italy to make some proposal that Greece could reasonably accept.

I am, &c.
E. Grey

[FO 17814/185/18/44]

Sir Edward Grey to Sir F. Elliot
Foreign Office, April 14, 1913, 3.30 p.m.

Foll[owin]g is revised identic text comm[unicate]d by Russian and Austrian Amba[ssado]rs here as to N[orth] and N[orth]-E[ast] frontier of Albania:—

La frontière de l'Albanie partira de la côte Adriatique à l'embouchure de la Boïana, et suivra le thalweg de ce fleuve jusqu'au village de Goritza, situé sur la rive droite. De là elle atteint le sommet des montagnes séparant la Boïana du lac de Scutari, en laissant le Tarabosch à l'Albanie. Elle traverse le lac près du village Zogay qui reste à l'Albanie, jusqu'à la baie de Licheny-Hoti, d'où elle suit la frontière entre les tribus de Grouda et Hoti, cédées au Monténégro d'une part et les tribus de Castrati et Clémenti d'autre part, laissant ces deux tribus à l'Albanie.

Elle se confond ensuite avec les limites actuelles entre les tribus monténégrines de Koutchi d'un côté, et la tribu de Clémenti de l'autre côté jusqu'au territoire de Goussigné et Plawa, elle laisse ces villes avec leurs dépendances au Monténégro en suivant la chaîne principale et la ligne du partage des eaux entre le Lim d'un côté et le Drin de l'autre. Elle quitte cette chaîne pour gagner la crête des collines au sud de la ville de Diakowa qui est laissée hors de l'Albanie, et continue sur cette crête jusqu'au Drin Blanc. Elle suit le cours de ce fleuve jusqu'à l'ouest de Prisren et ensuite la ligne frontière entre le district de Prisren et le district de Liouma laissant ce dernier à l'Albanie.

De là elle suit la crête de la montagne Korab en laissant à l'Albanie le district de la Basse Dibra et hors de l'Albanie le district de Reka. Quittant cette crête un peu au nord de la ville de Dibra qui reste hors de l'Albanie, la frontière gagne le Drin Noir qu'elle remonte jusqu'au village de Loukowo, d'où, en se dirigeant par les crêtes principales, séparant le bassin du Drin de celui du Shkoumbi et en laissant Strouga hors de l'Albanie, elle gagne la rive du lac d'Ochrida dans les environs du village Lin.

You may comm[unica]te it to Gov[ernmen]t to which you are accredited as soon as your colleagues are similarly instructed.

[FO 18031/14538/18/44]

Sir Edward Grey to Sir F. Bertie
Foreign Office, April 21, 1913

Sir,
    At the meeting of Ambassadors held to-day, it was ascertained that all the Powers had in principle agreed to the offer of financial assistance to be made to the Montenegrin Government, though the Austro-Hungarian Ambassador had not himself received any specific instructions on the point. It was considered desirable that the offer should be made to the Montenegrin Government, but as it appeared likely that King Nicolas would have some difficulty in justifying the acceptance of financial aid if it implied the raising of the siege of Scutari, a proposal was accepted by the Ambassadors that he should be sounded confidentially as to whether he would fall in with the suggestion that Turkey should be asked if she would consent to surrender Scutari to the Powers. Before approaching the Ottoman Government confidentially on the subject, it was considered desirable to obtain a formal engagement from King Nicolas and his Government that the flags of the Powers if hoisted over the town would be respected, and that he would be able to justify to his people the raising of the siege if the Ottoman Government placed the town in the hands of the Powers. A resolution was accordingly passed by the meeting of the Ambassadors in the above sense, and you will have received its text by telegraphy.
    An enquiry was made at the meeting as to whether some further measures than a blockade might not be necessary; but the proposal to land detachments from the international fleet did not meet with unanimous acceptance, and it was consequently withdrawn. A suggestion was made that the retirement of the

Servian troops might have so eased the close investment of the town as to permit the international fleet taking some measures to revictual the besieged place. This suggestion was withdrawn when it was pointed out that the international fleet could not, without committing a belligerent act, assist in provisioning a beleagured town.

I am, &c.,
E. Grey

[FO 20463/185/13/44]

Sir Edward Grey to Sir F. Cartwright
Foreign Office, May 1, 1913.

Sir,
    At the reunion this afternoon, I stated that the British Government had approved the statement that I had made at the last reunion respecting their attitude, but that the words "as far as Scutari is concerned" ("en ce qui concerne la question de Scutari") should be added after the words "disinterest herself in his fate" ("se désintéressera de son sort").
    Count Mensdorff then made the following verbal communication—
    "La dernière réunion n'est pas tombée d'accord sur les mesures de coercition à employer contre le Monténégro pour le cas où la démarche collective faite à Cettigné ne donnerait pas de résultat prompt et satisfaisant. Nous nous trouvons par conséquent vis-à-vis de la situation que j'avais annoncée dans mes communications antérieures, c'est-à-dire que le Gouvernement Austro-Hongrois se réserve de prendre les mesures nécessaires pour mettre à exécution les résolutions des Puissances.
    "Les vues exprimées au cours de la dernière réunion par les Représentants de plusieurs Puissances sur les mesures de coercition à prendre nous font espérer que d'autres Puissances ne refuseront pas de coopérer avec nous dans les opérations sur terre ou dans une action navale, bien qu'une résolution n'avait pas été prise à ce sujet dans la dernière réunion.
    "L'objection formulée par M. l'Ambassadeur de France contre le débarquement de troupes ne parait pas fondée au Comte Berchtold. Mon Gouvernement est au contraire d'avis qu'il ne serait pas impossible qu'un débarquement— même

sans combat—servirait au Roi Nicolas de motif suffisant pour justifier vis-à-vis de son peuple sa soumission à la volonté des Puissances. Il est toutefois évident qu'une pareille action ne saurait avoir l'effet voulu si l'on déclarait dès à présent—ainsi que M. Sazonow l'avait suggéré dans une conversation avec le Comte Thurn—de se borner à l'occupation des ports sans pousser plus loin les opérations militaires.

"Quant à l'avis de Sir Edward Grey de déclarer dès à présent au Roi Nicolas que, s'il se soumet à la volonté des Puissances, elles discuteront avec lui après l'évacuation de Scutari des compensations raisonnables, le Gouvernement Austro-Hongrois fait observer ce qui suit:—

"Le Monténégro doit avant tout respecter la volonté des Puissances et évacuer Scutari sans que les Puissances lui fassent envisager des compensations. Ainsi que nous l'avons déclaré maintes fois, nous ne pourrions prendre en considération des compensations territoriales aux dépens de la frontière Nord et Nord-Est de l'Albanie, fixée d'une manière définitive par les Puissances. Si après l'évacuation de Scutari les Puissances venaient à envisager les mesures économiques à prendre pour assurer à ce pays épuisé les moyens d'existence, nous nous réservons de prendre part à une conversation à ce sujet."

I then informed the Ambassadors that, after I had seen them separately yesterday, I had received the following communication, which M. Popovich had made to Sir Arthur Nicolson:—

"J'ai l'ordre de mon Gouvernement de demander au G[ouvernemen]t R[oya]l d'Angleterre, si dans le cas où le Monténégro cédant à la volonté des Gr[andes] Puissances et faisant le sacrifice de ses ambitions les plus naturelles—en acceptant la solution Scutari à L'Albanie—les G[ran]d[e]s Puissances lui accorderaient une compensation territoriale digne de ses sacrifices et dont la ligne frontière passerait... a
vec une aide efficace pour rétablir sa situation économique et rendre la vie plus possible à ses habitants."

I explained that this communication had been made quite spontaneously and unexpectedly. It was not the result of any suggestion by us or discussion with us. I made the following observations to the reunion upon it. The communication volunteered spontaneously by M. Popovitch was a "fait nouveau," and seemed to indicate that King Nicolas was beginning to realise how serious the situation was. In view of this, the British Government could not say that the last resort had yet been reached, and under the circumstances an effort, even if it were the last, was worth making to avoid a resort to force. This effort might take the form of a strong representation stating that, if the Montenegrin Government evacuated Scutari peaceably as demanded by the Powers, the Montenegrin Government would receive financial help, which had already been under the consideration of the Powers, to improve the economic situation of Montenegro; but that, if they did not evacuate Scutari, they would certainly be expelled by one method or another, they would have to abandon the hope of help from the Powers, and the consequences would be disastrous.

The German Ambassador at once expressed an opinion favourable to my observations.

The Italian Ambassador did the same.

Finally all the Ambassadors agreed to my observations, and said that they would refer them to their Governments.

I gave all the Ambassadors copies of the communication that M. Popovitch had made. After what the Austrian Ambassador had been instructed to say about territorial compensation, it was clearly impossible for him to enter upon any discussion of this communication; but all the Ambassadors said that they would send it to their Governments.

I gave to the Ambassadors copies of the draft of a Treaty embodying the points in dispute between Turkey and the Allies, as approved by the Powers.

The Ambassadors all expressed approval of it, except the French Ambassador: who, while not differing from anything in the substance of it, said that his Government did not think that there was any advantage in this method of procedure, but would defer to the general opinion.

It was urged, in the interests of peace, that I should give the draft to the belligerents as quickly as possible.

I said that, as both the Turkish Ambassador and Bulgarian Minister had asked for a draft, I would give them this draft, pointing out that it contained only what the Powers had already approved, and that I assumed there was nothing in it to which any of the Governments of the Powers would object; and telling them that they might take it and make what use they pleased of it. I would point out also that it did not deal with questions between the belligerents and the Powers, which would have to be discussed with them afterwards, but only with questions between Turkey and the Allies.

Lastly, the German Ambassador brought forward the wish of the Turkish Government to get leave to send to Asia Minor their troops in Albania, whom they could not feed there.

All the Ambassadors were in a position to agree to this, except the Russian Ambassador, who had no instructions.

I am, &c.,
E. Grey

[FO 20486/20477/13/41]

Sir E. Goschen to Sir Edward Grey
Berlin, May 4, 1913

    The negotiations said to be in progress between Vienna and Rome on the subject of Albania are being followed with close interest in Berlin diplomatic circles, and especially by Balkan representatives, and latest report that Italy contemplates the occupation not only of Vallona but also of Santi Quaranta is causing them considerable uneasiness. The occupation of these two places, and especially the latter, would, of course, affect Greece most, and Greek Chargé d'Affaires in conversation with me and my French colleague has not concealed his great uneasiness as to the excitement it would cause in Greece. We have both warned Greek Chargé d'Affaires of the danger of a conflict with a naval Power like Italy, and have impressed on him the necessity for Greece to avoid any act which might provoke such a conflict. He pointed out, however, with regard to designs attributed to Austria and Italy, that there never has been any question of a mandate for those two Powers as regards Albania; that idea of an independent Albania was sanctioned by Europe on their demand, and that therefore they should be the last to nip their own idea in the bud by dividing up Albania between them. It seemed to him that the very first condition of Albanian independence was its neutrality, and he had every reason to believe that was the (group omitted: ?) view held by Russia.

    It seems to my French colleague and myself that, as difficulties which may arise out of the Albanian question may possibly become even graver than those connected with Scutari, points raised by Greek Chargé d'Affaires are worthy of consideration, and that it might be prudent, should the current rumours prove correct, that a hint should be given in proper quarters that Albanian question is one which concerns the whole of Europe.

      I have ventured to put these considerations before you as there can be no doubt that occupation of Santi Quaranta especially would be very serious blow to Greek interests, and might if resented by Greece lead to complications which, as possibly affecting future of islands, might be matter of concern to His Majesty's Government.

[FO 20974/135/18/44]

Sir Edward Grey to Sir E. Goschen
Foreign Office, May 5, 1913

Sir,
    I told the German Ambassador this morning the news that King Nicholas had given way about Scutari.
    He joined with me in expressing the greatest satisfaction.
    I took the opportunity to say that it was all the more satisfactory because there were rumours that, had Austria been obliged to take action separately, it might have led to a division of Albania between Austria and Italy, and have affected even the question of the Ægean Islands. The moment that any Power occupied territory separately, or claimed territory for itself, the whole foundation on which we had been proceeding would be cut away; for all our proceedings had been on the assumption that no Power was going to ask for any territory for itself as a result of the Balkan troubles.

I am, &c.,
E. Grey

[FO 21208/20810/13/44]

Sir Edward Grey to Sir F. Cartwright
Foreign Office, May 5, 1913

Sir,
At the meeting with the Ambassadors this afternoon, I informed them of the communication from the King of Montenegro, saying that he placed the fate of the town of Scutari in the hands of the Powers.

Count Mensdorff informed the reunion of the information that he had given me this morning.

The following resolution was then adopted:—

"Sir Edward Grey, ayant reçu un message du Roi de Monténégro déclarant qu'il remet le sort de la ville de Scutari entre les mains des Puissances, la Réunion est d'avis qu'il y a lieu de prendre acte avec satisfaction de cette déclaration. Les Représentants des Puissances à Cettigné feront savoir en même temps au Gouvernement Monténégrin que des dispositions sont prises pour assurer la remise de la ville aux Commandants de l'escadre internationale. Ils réclameront l'envoi aux autorités monténégrines de Scutari d'instructions leur prescrivant de procéder d'accord avec les Commandants à l'évacuation de la ville."

It was decided that I should send instructions in this sense to His Majesty's Minister in Cettinjé, on which he should act as soon as all his Colleagues were similarly instructed.

The meeting also arrived at the following resolution:—

"La Réunion pense également qu'il y a lieu de prescrire à l'Amiral commandant l'escadre internationale de se mettre en rapport avec les autorités monténégrines de Scutari pour fixer le jour où une Commission composée d'officiers désignés par les Commandants et accompagnée de détachements internationaux procédera à la prise de possession de la ville au nom des Puissances. Cette Commission réglera les détails de l'évacuation et de l'enlèvement du matériel de guerre. Les Puissances resteront en possession de la ville jusqu'à l'organisation d'un Gouvernement autonome. Le blocus sera levé aussitôt après la prise de possession."

Count Mensdorff pointed out that Count Berchtold had made no reply to the Montenegrin request for the postponement of Austrian action, and contemplated that the Montenegrins should apply to the naval Commanders of the International Fleet to take over Scutari.

I urged that it would be a great pity to dwell upon a point of form, and to wait for the Montenegrins to communicate with the naval Commanders. The latter had better be instructed to communicate at once with the Montenegrins in Scutari.

The meeting then proceeded to the consideration of the repatriation of the Turkish troops in Albania, and the following resolution was arrived at:—

"La Sublime Porte ayant réclamé le concours des Puissances pour qu'aucun obstacle ne soit apporté au repatriement des troupes ottomanes d'Albanie, la Réunion pense qu'il y a lieu de prescrire aux Représentants des Puissances à Athènes de prier le Gouvernement Hellénique de ne pas s'opposer au transport des troupes repatriées par le Gouvernement Ottoman."

It was agreed that the next meeting should take place on Thursday, the 8th instant.

The Italian Ambassador stated that the project for the organisation of Albania, which the Austrian and Italian Governments had been requested, in accordance with the decision of the meeting of the Ambassadors some months ago, to draw up, was now ready.

It was decided that this should be communicated to us at the next meeting.

I took the opportunity of observing that we were now back on the "terrain" of international action as regards Scutari, and that it would be very desirable that we should keep on this "terrain." If it became necessary to take measures in Albania for the preservation of order, they should be international.

I am, &c.,
E. Grey

[FO 21566/20477/13/44]

Sir Edward Grey to Sir R. Rodd
Foreign Office, May 7, 1913

Sir,
            The Italian Ambassador informed me to-day that the Italian Minister for Foreign Affairs, in talking to the German Ambassador in Rome, had given the following review of the situation. He thought that feeling in Vienna would now subside, and that then the remaining questions should be surveyed in a calm spirit. Every action in Albania by Austria and Italy should be avoided. It was true that there might be a certain amount of disorder in Albania, but there had been disorder there for centuries, and it need not be taken too seriously. The Italian proposals for the reorganisation of Albania had been accepted by Austria, they were based on European control, which was what Italy had always advocated. There must be no talk of compensation for Montenegro, especially not of territorial compensation. If territorial concessions to Montenegro were mentioned while Austria was in her present spirit, she would refuse categorically, and the door would be shut on them for ever. The object should be to assure to Montenegro a certain degree of welfare, to make her an element of order rather than a source of agitation. She should be given financial help, and the delimitation of the boundaries agreed upon by the Powers should be traced eventually with a benevolent disposition. It should be recognised, after what had happened, that the Great Powers must not play with fire; they must respect the limit beyond which no Great Power could give way, and be careful of entering upon a slippery path that might be dangerous.
            I said that these were most excellent sentiments, with which I entirely agreed; and, with regard to the application of

what the Ambassador had last said, I hoped that the Ægean Islands would be borne in mind, because, if any Great Power claimed or retained one of the Ægean Islands, we should feel that the whole strategic position in the Mediterranean was being altered, and our interests in that way affected.

The Ambassador proceeded to speak of the south of Albania, and told me the utmost limits that Italy could concede to Greece.

I observed that we must not drift into the position, from which we had just emerged about Scutari, of coming to an agreement, and then being confronted with the defiance of Greece and the problem of how to turn her out by force, for she already occupied a great part of the territory that Italy wished to reserve for Albania. It would, therefore, be desirable that Italy should find some means of getting Greece to accept a boundary of southern Albania on which the Powers could agree; and I suggested that concessions about the Ægean Islands might be used by Italy for this purpose.

The Italian Ambassador abounded [sic] in this sense. He said that it was his own idea, and that he had been pressing it strongly on his Government.

But, when I came to instance Rhodes as one of the Islands that I had in mind, he said that it was quite impossible for the Italian Government to give up Rhodes to Greece. They were bound to restore it to Turkey.

I said that, if Italy could not give Rhodes to Greece because it belonged to Turkey, and if Turkey signed a Treaty by which she left the decision as regards the Islands to the Powers, the Powers were then free to decide what should be the fate of Rhodes.

The Ambassador urged that Turkey could not leave Rhodes to the decision of the Powers, because it was in the occupation of Italy, and Turkey had to fulfil some obligations to Italy before the Island could be restored to her.

I observed that when it was suggested that Rhodes might be ceded by Italy to Greece, the reply was that this could not be done because it belonged to Turkey; when it was suggested that Rhodes could be ceded to Greece because it was Turkish, the reply was that this could not be done because Italy was in occupation on certain conditions. It was clear that Turkey and Italy between them had the fate of Rhodes in their hands, and the occupation by Italy was already beginning to excite some suspicion and apprehension.

The Ambassador assured me that we need be under no apprehension whatever as to Rhodes being retained permanently by Italy. She was not going to claim it.

He informed me that, as regards other Islands, by which I understood him to mean Mytilene and Chios in particular, Austria was quite willing that they should go to Greece, but the difficulty was in Berlin.

I am. &c.,
E. Grey

[FO 22131/9564/13/44]

Sir Edward Grey to Sir F. Cartwright
Foreign Office, May 8, 1913

Sir,
    The Austro-Hungarian and Italian Ambassadors communicated to the reunion to-day a project of organisation for Albania, and the following record was made:—
    "Les Ambassadeurs de l'Autriche-Hongrie et de l'Italie ont communiqué à la Réunion un projet d'organisation de l'Albanie en faisant observer qu'il a été préparé conformément à la résolution prise par la Réunion en décembre dernier. Les deux Ambassadeurs ont déclaré que l'Article VII de ce projet n'était pas encore définitif.
    "L'Ambassadeur de l'Autriche-Hongrie a dit, en motivant son opinion, que son Gouvernement préférerait supprimer les Articles I et II relatifs à la suzeraineté du Sultan et écarter cette suzeraineté.
    "L'Ambassadeur de l'Italie s'est exprimé dans le même sens.
    "On a décidé de soumettre ce projet d'organisation à l'examen des différents Gouvernements."
    The Austro-Hungarian Ambassador made verbally the following observations in support of his view:—
    "L'Ambassadeur d'Autriche-Hongrie d'ordre de son Gouvernement propose d'éliminer dans le projet d'organisation de l'Albanie la stipulation établissant une suzeraineté du Sultan.

Motifs

    1° Quand la réunion a admis le 17 décembre la suzeraineté du Sultan la situation ne se présentait pas comme aujourd'hui. Alors il semblait possible que la Turquie conserverait une plus grande partie de ses possessions en Europe; on pouvait même s'attendre à voir une Macédoine autonome. Aujourd'hui que les événements de la guerre ont refoulé la Turquie derrière la ligne Midia-Énos, la distance immense qui sépare la Turquie et l'Albanie rend tout lien de suzeraineté à peu près impossible.

2° Une suzeraineté turque en Albanie devrait avoir pour conséquence logique le maintien de la suzeraineté turque sur le territoire également autonome du Mont-Athos, qui est beaucoup plus rapproché de Constantinople que l'Albanie, ce qui serait aussi contraire aux désirs des couvents du Mont-Athos que le serait la suzeraineté du Sultan à l'intérêt des Albanais.

3° L'opinion publique en Turquie est opposée au maintien de la suzeraineté turque sur l'Albanie qui ne pouvant être que purement nominale ne serait d'aucun avantage pour la Turquie et lui créerait seulement des difficultés comme l'ont fait jusqu'à présent toutes les suzerainetés plus ou moins fictives créées par le Congrès de Berlin.

4° Les Albanais et surtout les Chrétiens sont opposés à la suzeraineté turque qui pourrait inspirer aux Albanais musulmans des velléités de domination sur leurs compatriotes chrétiens comme c'était le cas au temps du régime turc.

5° Comme l'Albanie doit être neutralisée, le maintien de la suzeraineté turque créerait des complications pour le cas que la Turquie serait impliquée dans une guerre; ce qui pourrait alors faire naître parmi la population musulmane des aspirations et des tentatives de venir se ranger dans la guerre à côté de leur suzerain, la Turquie.

I read to the Ambassadors the information received in the telegram of May 7th from the Vice-Admiral, respecting the taking over of Scutari. A paraphrase of the telegram was given to the Ambassadors.

I said that I presumed that all the Governments would have received the same information from their respective Naval Officers. The procedure proposed seemed quite straightforward, and instructions would be sent to the Vice-Admiral to proceed as he proposed when his Colleagues were ready to co-operate.

I informed the reunion of what the Bulgarian Minister had said to me about defining the line from Énos to Media. I also communicated to the meeting the "aide-memoire" from the Turkish Ambassador about the Treaty of Peace. The following was then recorded:—

"Sir E. Grey a fait connaitre une communication du Ministre de Bulgarie relative à la délimitation de la frontière Turco-Bulgare entre Midia et Énos. Cette ligne serait établie à travers les points suivants à partir de Midia: Sarai, Muratli, au sud d'Airabol, entre Keshan et Malgara, pour aboutir sur le versant de la Mer Egée a l'est d'Énos.

"Le 5 avril M. Gueshoff avait exprimé aux Représentants des Puissances à Sofia le désir de voir adopter cette ligne, mais en se réservant de consulter à ce sujet les Alliés de la Bulgarie. Aucune communication officielle dans ce sens n'a été adressée depuis aux Puissances.

"L'Ambassadeur de l'Autriche-Hongrie dit avoir reçu de son Gouvernement l'instruction d'appuyer une demande bulgare qui aurait fait au commencement d'avril l'objet d'une note du Gouvernement de Sofia, mais la Réunion n'a pas connaissance de cette note.

"Elle a admis, sur la demande du Gouvernement Bulgare, que la ligne Énos-Midia serait considérée comme base de négociations et non comme frontière définitive. Mais, ainsi qu'elle l'a indiqué dans l'Article II du projet du Traité de Paix approuvé par toutes les Puissances et communiqué en ce moment à tous les belligérants, les détails de la délimitation doivent être régies par une Commission Internationale qui, de l'avis de la Réunion, comprendrait des délégués de toutes les Puissances.

"La Réunion estime donc qu'il n'y a pas lieu de revenir sur cette façon de procéder, et qu'il ne convient pas d'examiner un voeu ayant pour objet la fixation détaillée de tous les points de la ligne.

"Sir E. Grey a communiqué à la Réunion une note de Tewfik Pasha aux termes de laquelle la Sublime Porte accepte les principes posés par la Réunion au sujet de cette délimitation."

The German Ambassador brought forward a request from the Roumanian Minister in London that the amnesty for the Koutzo-Vlachs should be dealt with in the Treaty of Peace.

After some discussion, I pointed out that the object of the draft Treaty was to enable the Allies and Turkey to sign something and demobilise as quickly as possible. If we tried to make use of this draft to secure special advantages for the Koutzo-Vlachs or others, we should delay or defeat altogether the primary object of the draft, which was to induce the Turks and Allies to make peace quickly.

Finally, it was decided to deal with the request of the Roumanian Minister by a resolution in general terms applying to all minorities, and the following was adopted:—

"La Réunion pense qu'il convient de recommander aux Alliés de proclamer aussitôt après la conclusion de la paix une amnistie générale pour tous les faits de guerre et la participation des minorités de race ou de religion aux opérations militaires."

I am, &c.,
E. Grey

This attitude of H[is] E[xcellency]'s on Scutari question is however conditional on Servia obtaining Djakova.

[FO 23425/13799/13/44]

Sir Edward Grey to Sir R. Rodd
Foreign Office, May 19, 1913

Sir,
  The Italian Ambassador informed me to-day that the point about the Ægean Islands had been settled favourably. Italy would give up to Greece the islands that she occupied, to facilitate a settlement of the southern Albanian frontier. But Italy must remain firm about three conditions: (1) that the Greek frontier must not be north of the point that he had last indicated to me; (2) that the whole of the Corfu Canal must be neutralised; and (3) that the small island of Saseno, near the Bay of Vallona, must go to Albania. Italy could not, owing to her obligations to Turkey, make this proposal about the islands herself, but it might be made by a third party. It was a great sacrifice on the part of Italy, for, as I might have seen by the morning's papers, there was still fighting in Cyrenaica, and a considerable number of Turkish troops were still there. To agree to give up the islands while this was the case was a sacrifice.
  I asked whether any progress had been made in Berlin respecting other islands.
  The Ambassador replied that he could not speak definitely, but he believed that things were going well as regards Mytilene and Chios. He pressed me for my views.
  I said that I had not seen the Russian Ambassador or the French Ambassador at all last week. I would make the best use I could of what he had told me to ease the situation, but I could not say anything more definite at present.

I am, &c.,
E. Grey

[FO 23424/9564/13/44]

Sir Edward Grey to Sir R. Paget
Foreign Office, May 19, 1913

Sir,
    The Servian Delegates came to see me to-day. They wished to raise some points about the northern Albanian frontier, which they said would be an impracticable one as it stood at present according to the decision of the Powers.
    I said that, for several months, we had been told that the frontier would be impracticable unless Djakova went to Albania; and I explained that, if any points were to be raised at all, this point of Djakova and others would be reopened.
    One of the delegates said that apparently, then, "noli me tangere" was the motto with regard to the Albanian frontier.
    To this I assented.
    They then urged that the guarantees given by the Powers about Servian access to the Adriatic should be inserted after the third Article of the Treaty, and said that they were instructed not to sign the Treaty unless these guarantees were put into it.
    I replied that these guarantees could not be put into a Treaty between Turkey and the Allies. If they were put into a formal instrument, it must be one signed by the Powers who gave the guarantees, and the Powers would not sign the Treaty between the Allies and Turkey. I had no doubt that the Powers would confirm these guarantees either by inserting them in the Statute for the organisation of Albania or in some other instrument that they would sign.
    The Delegates gave me to understand that, if they were assured that the guarantees would be inserted in the Statute for

Albania, they might be able to get instructions to sign the Treaty of Peace.

I said that it appeared from this that their only difficulty about signing the Treaty was their wish to have the guarantees confirmed.

They assented to this.

I told them that I would bring the matter before the meeting with the Ambassadors to-morrow.

The delegates expressed a wish that I should again open the Peace Conference. I said that I had never closed the Conference, which had only been suspended; a formal reopening did not therefore appear to be necessary, but when they were all ready to sign the Treaty and conclude peace I would do whatever they all desired.

I am, &c.,
E. Grey

[FO 25582/9564/13/44]

Sir Edward Grey to Sir F. Cartwright
Foreign Office, May 30, 1913

At the reunion to-day the following resolution was adopted:—

"Sir E. Grey informe la réunion de la signature de la paix par les délégués du Gouvernement Ottoman et des États Alliés.

"Il ajoute que la réunion reste maintenant en présence des questions précises à la solution desquelles il est d'autant plus nécessaire de limiter ses travaux que des questions nouvelles qui ne sont pas de sa compétence pourraient se poser et qu'elle serait ainsi amener à sortir du programme tracé par les différents Gouvernements.

"Ces questions sont: (1) L'organisation de l'Albanie. Il ne peut s'agir d'une organisation de détail, mais il importe que l'accord se fasse entre les Puissances sur les lignes générales de l'institution de l'état autonome. (2) La délimitation de la frontière Albanaise au sud-est et au sud. (3) La question des Îles de la Mer Egée.

"Une fois ces questions épuisées, il conviendrait d'ajourner la réunion."

I then observed that the questions of the Ægean Islands and of the south of Albania were so closely connected that the two must practically be settled together.

The Italian Ambassador agreed, but said that, as Italy was under an obligation to restore the Ægean Islands that she occupied to Turkey, she could not do anything inconsistent with that obligation. It was apparent, however, from what he said that if, as part of the settlement, the Powers decided that the Islands occupied by Italy were to go to Greece, Italy would be prepared to agree. Indeed the Ambassador said that, should the Islands go to Greece, conditions of neutralisation and the arrangement of details to soothe the "amour-propre" of Turkey should be taken into consideration.

The German Ambassador said that, in view of all the difficulties, he thought that all the Islands might go to Greece, except Tenedos and Imbros. It was understood, of course, that Thasos was to go to Bulgaria, as had been agreed some time ago.

With regard to the south of Albania, the Italian Ambassador said that the two cardinal points were that Thalia and Stilos on the coast and Koritza in the hinterland should be included in Albania.

I summed up the discussion by saying that a sketch of settlement had emerged under which, if Thalia and Stilos and Koritza were kept for Albania, all the Ægean Islands except Tenedos and Imbros, which would be left to Turkey, and Thasos, which was to go to Bulgaria, should go to Greece under conditions of neutralisation and with what might be arranged to satisfy the "amour-propre" of Turkey. I doubted whether the reunion would wish to go so far to-day as to treat this as a definite proposition, and I suggested that each Ambassador should make his own report to his Government with a view to considering whether a discussion of southern Albania and the Ægean Islands should be entered upon with the object of attaining some such settlement.

The French Ambassador agreed, and said that it was necessary to "tater le terrain."

The following resolution, unanimously passed by the Naval Commission in Scutari, was communicated to the reunion:—

"The commission are unanimously of opinion [that] the Montenegrin troops have worked and are still working very well indeed in the removal of war material from the town and forts. The work has been so expeditiously carried out that it will be complete in nearly a week less than the minimum time that was originally anticipated."

The Austrian Ambassador observed that there were places, beyond the immediate one supervised by the Naval Commission, which Montenegro must evacuate.

M. Cambon reported that the Comte Voinovitch, one of the Montenegrin Delegates to the Peace Conference, had stated that Montenegro had security that she could offer eventually in the form of tobacco or other monopolies, but that it was an immediate necessity for her to get some money at once, and that he hoped that the financiers to whom the Montenegrin Government applied would be encouraged by the Powers to give them a small loan for immediate necessities.

No one raised any objection to this, it being understood that the further question of a loan guaranteed by the Powers could not arise until after complete evacuation of Albanian territory.

Early in the discussion, the Italian Ambassador said that his Government wished to reply to the proposal that M. Cambon had made about the organisation of a provisional administration for Albania. He was not yet ready to give their answer, but he wished to give it later. We did not, therefore, proceed further to-day with the discussion of the French Ambassador's proposal.

The Austrian Ambassador, while making no objection to this procedure, observed that it would not be very courteous to "passer outre" altogether with regard to the proposal for the reorganisation of Albania which had been drawn up by the Italian and Austrian Governments at the request of the reunion, and which had been submitted to it.

I am, &c.,
E. Grey

[FO 34451/14809/13/44]

Sir Edward Grey to Mr. Carnegie
Foreign Office, July 25, 1913, 4.30 p.m.

The Reunions have now worked practically without intermission for many months: it is essential that the personnel including myself should get as much rest as circumstances will admit and I propose to adjourn the meetings after next week. Whether they are resumed after an interval can be decided by circumstances and the wishes of the Gov[ernmen]ts later on.

Apart from this, the latest startling developments in the Balkans, while not ripe for final decisions, prevent the various Governments from giving more than a secondary attention to remaining questions affecting Albania and the Islands respecting which decisions are necessary to complete the work originally taken up by the Reunions.

There has also of late been a tendency to multiply conditions of detail and points of form rather than of substance and the very facility with which points can be raised and discussed at the Reunions seems to encourage this tendency. Progress as regards the organization of Albania and settlement of its Southern frontier has been greatly impeded in this way.

I still hope it may be possible next week to agree about the commission of control for Albania and to ask Swedish Gov[ernmen]t to select officers for Gendarmerie and to settle some points about protection of Albanian Minorities, &e.

Italians now show a disposition to reserve question of Islands, at any rate those in their occupation, till claims of Greece are dealt with as a whole; this will delay a decision about Koritza and Stylos.

I would suggest therefore that after next week all questions that remain should for the present be dealt with

through the ordinary channels between the Powers or in whatever manner the Powers consider most convenient.
You should inform M[inister for] F[oreign] A[ffairs].

Sir Edward Grey to Sir F. Cartwright
Foreign Office, October 4 1913

ADMIRAL BURNEY telegraphs as follows, 28th September:-
"On 24th September, on receipt of assurance from Montenegrin Government, I sent a letter to the Malissori informing them that Montenegro would not advance or attack them unless provoked to do so, and requested the tribe to return to their territory. This morning I learn privately from reliable sources that Austrian representative here sent a provocative letter to the tribe yesterday cancelling my letter."

The above is typical instance of the attitude of the Austrians at Scutari, and throws unpleasant light on the causes which are at the bottom of the campaign of intrigues conducted against the British admiral. It is difficult to understand what motive the Austrian authorities can have in thus deliberately endeavouring to promote unrest among the Albanian frontier tribes. The impression produced on His Majesty's Government is deplorable. Fortunately most of the tribesmen have, according to further telegram just received from the admiral, decided to act on his advice and have returned to their territory. You may make use of the above in speaking confidentially to the Minister for Foreign Affairs, making it quite plain that I have entire confidence in his own loyalty and good intentions.

Sir Edward Grey to Sir F. Cartwright
Foreign Office, October 4, 1913.

ALBANIA

At the moment of considering Count Berchtold's note of 24th September enclosed in your Excellency's despatch No. 154 of 24th September, I received your telegram No. 148 of 1st October, and also a verbal communication from the Austro-Hungarian Chargé d'Affaires here, complaining that Sir C. Burney was continuing to hold meetings of the Commission of Admirals notwithstanding notification from Austrian admiral that he would not attend until recent decision respecting Drin bridge was rescinded.

Austro-Hungarian Government refuse to recognise validity of any decisions of Commission not agreed to by Austrian admiral, and propose on this ground withdrawal of Commission without waiting until Committee of Control is constituted and assembles. They suggest immediate transfer of Commission's administrative functions to Provisional Government at Vallona, whilst military duties would continue to be exercised by international contingents under supreme command of senior officer.

I am asking Admiralty to call upon Sir C. Burney for report on circumstances in which he decided to hold further meetings without Austrian admiral—a course in which all his other colleagues appear to have concurred. On receipt of report I shall be able to form opinion whether Sir C. Burney had any other choice of action in view of the deliberate and apparently indefinite withdrawal of Austrian admiral, and whether it can be admitted that any one Power can claim the right to paralyse work of the Commission by merely ordering its admiral not to attend the meetings.

His Majesty's Government are not at present prepared to agree that Commission can relinquish its functions before the Committee of Control have advised the six Governments as to the existence of a competent authority at Scutari to whom administrative duties can properly be transferred, and the proposal to leave international contingents in absolute inactivity and without any specific duties at Scutari until Albanian Government have organised a force sufficient to cope with external enemies is not one that His Majesty's Government can support. They do not, moreover, share the belief that there is any serious danger of a fresh Montenegrin attack on Scutari. Nor do the circumstances in which withdrawal of Commission of Admirals is now proposed encourage the expectation that military contingents will not find themselves exposed to similar difficulties to those encountered by the Commission in the discharge of its duties.

If His Majesty's Government consent to allow the British contingent to remain for the moment, they do so on the understanding that the Committee of Control sets to work without further delay and recommends a satisfactory arrangement for the relief of the admirals.

The most convenient course appears to His Majesty's Government to be that the admirals should remain at Scutari till the Commission of Control is in Albania. The admirals could then relinquish their duties, and the international contingents would remain for a time if desired. Should this be also the view of the other Powers, His Majesty's Government will act accordingly, but should it be decided to withdraw the admirals before the Commission of Control is in existence His Majesty's Government could not leave the British contingent to be at the disposal of the Provisional Albanian Government, uncontrolled by any international authority, and would withdraw the British contingent at once with Admiral Burney.

Sir Edward Grey to Sir F. Cartwright
Foreign Office, October 8, 1913

Following from Sir C. Burney, No. 71 of 4th October:-

"With reference to Admiralty telegram No. 34 of 2nd October, minutes of Commission have not been kept as complete record of meetings of Commission, but only as a guide for a future administration taking over the town.

"It is not understood how first Austro-Hungarian admiral can deny that bridge over Drinasa (referred to in Admiralty telegram as Drin River) was ever discussed, as he himself proposed to have military bridge sent here for it, and also where bridge question is mentioned in minutes it appears over his signature. The bridge was frequently discussed with first Austro-Hungarian admiral, and on 21st July it was decided to employ the Italian company to repair it. I am informed now by Italian admiral that he telegraphed to his Government to that effect directly after meeting of Commission on that day.

"With regard to majority vote, one was taken on 5th September by Austro-Hungarian admiral to decide the incompatibility of the assistant harbour-master being also an agent for an Italian steamship company, and was decided in favour of Austro-Hungarian admiral against Italian admiral.

"One was also taken on a former occasion when Italian admiral, backed by Austro-Hungarian admiral, proposed that consuls should again attend the meetings of the Commission.

"It would be quite impossible to continue work of commission on the lines of all decisions having to be unanimous as one member of the Commission with an obstructive policy could defeat the objects of the Commission.

"Copies of minutes have not previously been forwarded, as they were not considered of interest. A complete copy is now being prepared, and will be forwarded."

Your Excellency should inform the Austrian Minister for Foreign Affairs that, in view of this definite statement of Sir C. Burney, His Majesty's Government trust that the Austro-Hungarian Government will call upon the Austrian admiral to explain his statement that (a) question of bridge was never previously discussed, and (b) it was complete and unjustifiable innovation to take a majority vote in the Commission.

Sir Edward Grey to Mr. Dering
Foreign Office, October 8, 1913

Sir,
    The Italian Chargé d'Affaires read to Sir E. Crowe on the 24th ultimo a number of long telegrams from the Italian consul at Yanina, according to which the Greek Government were taking systematic measures to mislead the frontier-delimitation commission as to the wishes and political aspirations of the inhabitants of those Albanian districts still in Greek occupation. The Greek authorities had, more particularly, recently convoked an assembly of notables at Yanina, and endeavoured to persuade them to pronounce strongly in favour of annexation to Greece. The notables had, however, declined to commit themselves.
    Sir E. Crowe observed that this rather tended to demonstrate how difficult it would be for the Greek authorities, assuming the correctness of the information, to carry opinion in Albania with them. Moreover, he thought that the commissioners of the Powers, being able and honest men, were not at all likely to be deceived by such manoeuvres and intrigues as were being ascribed to the Greek Government and Greek secret agents. The commission had now at last started work, and this would do more than anything else to create a situation in which Greece would find it difficult to defy the decision of the Powers.

I am, &c.,
E. Grey

Sir Edward Grey to Mr. Dering
Foreign Office, October 8, 1913

Sir,

The Italian Chargé d'Affaires enquired on the 24th ultimo whether His Majesty's Government had received from the Greek Government a request for intervention based on a communication from the Oecumenical Patriarch in favour of Greek Orthodox Christians in Albania. The Italian Government, who had received such a request, were disposed to reply that the position of Albanians who were not Greek subjects in no way concerned the Greek Government, more particularly since the latter had categorically declined to interpose with the Patriarch when there had been a question of securing his intervention in Macedonia. On that occasion the Greek Government had declared that the Patriarch was entirely independent of any but the Turkish Government, and would certainly resent any representation being addressed to him by Greece, with whom he was not concerned.

Sir E. Crowe informed Prince Borghese that there was no record of a similar request having been received here from the Greek Government. Should such a request be made, he had little doubt that I should reply that the six Powers had appointed an International Commission of Control to advise and report on the question of governing and administering Albania, and that it would be for that Commission to deal with all matters of this kind.

I am, &c.,
E. Grey

Sir Edward Grey to Vice-Admiral Sir C. Burney
Foreign Officer, October 8, 1913

ITALIAN Government propose that, to meet every eventuality consequent on Montenegrin mobilisation, small international detachment from contingents at Scutari should occupy Mount Tarabosh.

Please telegraph your views.

Sir Edward Grey to Sir F. Cartwright
Foreign Office, October 13, 1913

I TOLD the Austrian Ambassador to-day that your Excellency had received an aide-mémoire from the Austrian Government in the sense of what Count Mensdorff had said to Sir Eyre Crowe last week. I showed him the telegraphic summary of the aide-mémoire, and then read to him the reply that I was sending to Vienna. I also told him of the communication to the other Powers that I was making of the Austrian aide-mémoire, and of my views on it.

Count Mensdorff thought that the matter might now be arranged on these lines. He said that he had pointed out in Vienna that there did not seem to be much difference in substance between my views and those of Count Berchtold. He hoped that things would now be settled.

I said that the telegram giving the summary of the aide-mémoire had been received here only last evening; I had seen it on my arrival in London this morning, and had sent off my reply before luncheon; so that no time had been lost.

I told Count Mensdorff that this was all that I had to communicate to him officially.

I then went on to say that, during the last, few weeks, I had felt more anger about some incidents in Scutari than I had about anything else in the whole of the Balkan crisis.

Admiral Burney had been doing his best to smooth things when some of the tribes threatened to attack Montenegro; he had used his influence, and had succeeded in calming them; and, after he had done so, one of the Austrian officials had told the tribes to pay no attention to Admiral Burney. I also pointed out how unfair it was for the Austrian admiral to object to a decision being taken by a majority vote in the Council of Admirals, when, on the 5th September last, a decision in that very way had been taken by the Austrian admiral, and one on a former occasion by the Italian admiral supported by the Austrian admiral, as pointed out in Admiral Burney's telegram No. 71 of the 4th instant. In fact, the attitude of the Austrian admiral had really been much like the opposition to which a political party resorted when it wished to prevent anything being done, or any progress being made. I had felt so indignant at the unfairness with which Admiral Burney was being treated that I had contemplated asking the Prime Minister to agree to the withdrawal of Admiral Burney and the whole of the British contingent to agree, in effect, to our washing our hands of matters at Scutari altogether, in which case we should have published papers giving an account of the incidents to which I had referred, and showing how things had been made impossible for us.

The incidents to which I had referred had already been brought to the notice of the Foreign Office in Vienna, and, therefore, I was not asking Count Mensdorff to make a new representation about them; but I should like Count Berchtold to know how indignant I had felt, and that I had even contemplated a complete withdrawal of the British admiral and force, and a publication of papers. Now, however, I hoped that things might be settled in the way I had proposed in reply to the last Austrian proposal.

Count Mensdorff said that it seemed incredible that an Austrian official could have acted with regard to the tribes in the way I had stated, and be had no knowledge of all these incidents. He would, however, let Count Berchtold know how strongly I had felt about them. He said that he thought there must have been a good deal of muddle, and perhaps if he had been in London and able to discuss matters with me we might have prevented some of this. That there should be any misunderstanding with me was, he felt sure, quite contrary to Count Berchtold's wishes.

I said that the same thing had occurred to me, and I had thought that, had Count Mensdorff and I been in touch, we might have avoided some of the trouble. I also observed that Count Berchtold had been away on a holiday, and the sort of obstruction that had occurred had been just what Austrian subordinate officials might have instigated when matters were left uncontrolled. To illustrate the inconvenience of what had occurred, I gave the hypothetical case of the Commission of Control coming to some decision which the British representative regarded as unsatisfactory, and the British representative being instructed to withdraw from the Commission without there being any discussion or attempt to come to an agreement with the other Powers.

Count Mensdorff urged that the Austrian admiral had not withdrawn till something had been decided in his absence.

I observed that the length of time that he had been kept without instructions had made it impossible for the Commission to suspend matters any longer.

We then had some friendly and sympathetic conversation with regard to the troubles of the last twelve months. We agreed that if, when the Balkan war began in October 1912, we could have been assured that there would be no war between the Great Powers and that in October 1913 no one of the Great Powers would be mobilised, we should have been well content in spite of whatever else of trouble there had been.

Count Mensdorff recalled a critical moment, when the Montenegrins were in Scutari, and it was difficult to see how they could be induced to leave.

I remarked that that was one of the things that had made me feel so much what had occurred with regard to Admiral Burney. I had taken a very strenuous part in securing an international naval demonstration to get the Montenegrins out of Scutari, as Austria wished, and I had made great efforts, which were eventually successful, to secure the participation of the French, without which there could not have been a naval demonstration. I could not have expected that, after that, Admiral Burney would have been so unfairly treated in Scutari.

I am, &c.,
E. Grey

Mr. Dering to Sir Edward Grey
Rome, October 13, 1913

Sir,

ON receipt of your instructions I duly communicated to the Italian Government, on the 6th instant, the views of His Majesty's Government on the proposal by the Austro-Hungarian Government for the withdrawal of the Commission of Admirals and as to the retention of the international military contingents at Scutari. I stated that you were calling upon Admiral Burney for a report as to the difficulty which had arisen in connection with his Austro-Hungarian colleague and, at a later date, on receipt of information from you that Admiral Burney's attitude appeared to be entirely justified, thought it advisable to let Marquis di San Giuliano know this also.

A memorandum of the views of the Italian Government which his Excellency had promised me has just been received, and I hasten to transmit a copy herewith. Although the last sentence of the second paragraph may appear somewhat obscure, it becomes evident later in the memorandum that the Italian Government do not consider that a unanimous vote is required for the decisions of the Commission of Admirals, and it is definitely stated that they are not prepared to disavow any decision taken by Rear-Admiral Patris.

It appears probable now that the meeting of the Commission of Control may not take place so soon as the 15th instant if some of the members are unable to be present until the 23rd instant, so that the suggestion of the Italian Government for adjusting the difference of opinion which has unfortunately arisen may not prove so valuable as they would hope. In order, however, that you may be in possession of the Italian views without delay, I have felt it necessary to telegraph the main points of the enclosed memorandum in advance to-day.

I have, &c.,
Herbert G. Dering

Sir Edward Grey to Mr. Dering
Foreign Office, October 13, 1913

Sir,

THE Italian Chargé d'Affaires read to Sir E. Crowe on the 7th instant a telegram from the Italian consul at Vallona. Ismael Khemal had informed the latter, in discussing his difficulties with Essad Pasha, that he would as soon as Mr. Lamb arrived ask him for his advice as to what he should do, and act on that advice whatever it was. The Italian consul had urged Ismael Khemal that the proper thing for him to do was to come to a friendly understanding with Essad.

Prince Borghese was instructed to express the hope of the Italian Government that Mr. Lamb would be directed to give similar advice, and in any case to act only after consultation with his Italian colleague.

Sir E. Crowe replied that Mr. Lamb would without doubt, in accordance with his general instructions, consult not merely his Italian but all his colleagues, and take no isolated action whatever. It seemed to Sir E. Crowe quite unnecessary to give fresh directions on this point. Nor had he any doubt that the Committee of Control would be unanimous in favouring any reasonable local arrangements designed to keep the peace and promote harmony between the various elements in Albania.

I am, &c.,
E. Grey

Sir Edward Grey to Sir F. Cartwright
Foreign Office, October 13, 1913

Sir,

COUNT MENSDORFF to-day left with me the enclosed statement, which had been made to him, and which he had reported to his Government.

He also observed that the question of markets at Dibra and Djakova had proved very important, as be had foreseen. The refusal of the use of these markets to the Albanians had been the cause of the trouble with the Servians on the Albanian frontier. The Albanians who tried to use these markets had been shot by the Servians.

I said that these accounts of outrages were deplorable. It had become so much the fashion to give accounts of outrages that one could not always be sure of the truth, but I was afraid that in the Balkan peninsula generally many very horrible things had occurred. Busy with other things, as we had all been, and preoccupied with the great object of preserving peace between the Great Powers, we had no doubt overlooked some points that might have been helpful. In the case of Djakova and Dibra, it might perhaps have saved some trouble if some of the Powers had sent vice-consuls to those places to report what happened. Their presence would have been a wholesome check.

I am, &c.,
E. Grey

Enclosure in No. 63
Telegram communicated by Count Mensdorff

PLUS de 2,000 habitants de Struga, Ochidra et alentours se trouvent réfugiés Elbassan et dans campagne. Nous avons fui atrocités serbes, qui ont incendiés village et massacré paysans innocents. Le 23 septembre trente-cinq Albanais out été emprisonnés, Ochrida, plus cinq Dibriotes de passage. Les Dibriotes, savoir, les nommés Hamid Behajet et Murad, ont été lendemain étranglés avec fil de fer. Quatre notables dibriotes ont été assassinés coups de baïonnette. Craignant exaspérations et explosions, population souffrant innombrables crimes et vexations, les Serbes se retirèrent jusque Petrina à la suite évènements Dibra. A leur retour, Serbes massacrèrent villageois innocents. Reste population, terrifié, prirent fuite territoire albanais dans misère affreuse. Tous réfugiés, la plupart femmes et enfants, souffrent misère famine et ne peuvent rentrer foyer, car Serbes ont fait massacre, malgré parole donnée. Prions votre Excellence prendre mesures pour garantir vie et biens de milliers de femmes et enfants par commission européenne à fin rentrer foyer avant hiver.—Au nom réfugiés, Ochrida et Struga: AHMED HUSEIN, HASOU TAHHIN, AGUEL PAPAOVASILOF, DR. MURTEZA.

Consul-General Lamb to Sir Edward Grey
Valona, October 16, 1913

Sir,

I HAVE the honour to report that the International Commission of Control held its first preliminary meeting here this afternoon at the municipality, the council room of which had appeared to myself and most of my colleagues to be the most appropriate locality available. Commendatore Leoni, as "doyen d'âge," assumed the presidency for this occasion, but it was agreed without opposition that in future the presidency should be filled by each delegate à tour de rôle, for one month at a time, and in alphabetical order of the countries represented. For the first month, therefore, the meetings will be presided over by the German delegate.

On the opening of the deliberations the Italian delegate raised the question of the formal recognition of the Provisional Government. Apparently Ismail Kemal Bey had hinted to him that he had no official knowledge of the constitution of the Commission, nor of the identity of its members. I pointed out that our situation towards him was the same, since we had no official notification of the constitution of the Provisional Government, nor of the identity of the Ministers composing it. The Austrian delegate, however, proposed that the Commission should write to Ismail Kemal Bey informing him of its entry upon its duties, and at the same time inviting him to designate a fit and proper person to fill the post of "delegate of Albania," who, according to the decision of the Conference of Ambassadors, is to form part of the Commission, but as to the manner of whose selection nothing was decided.

I felt bound to object to this that, although Ismail Kemal Bey's Government is incontestably the "autorité existante" at Valona, we have nothing to show how far its authority is recognised outside this town, whilst we do know that it is not recognised anywhere north of the Schkomnbi. I maintained, therefore, that we should avoid any action that might have the appearance of recognising it as the Government of Albania. The question of officially notifying our constitution to Ismail Kemal Bey was thereupon dropped, and the discussion continued upon that of the method of selection of the Albanian delegate, upon which, as might have been anticipated, there manifested itself a considerable divergency of opinion amongst the members of the Commission. The Austrian delegate maintained that the only possible course was to apply to Ismail Kemal Bey to appoint a representative, practically admitting in the course of his argument that the only object in compelling us to assemble in so undesirable a locality as Valona was to secure the recognition of Ismail Kemal Bey's Cabinet as the Government of Albania. I, on the contrary, argued that the decision of the Ambassadorial Conference spoke clearly of a "délégué de l'Albanie," and that the Government of Valona, openly repudiated by two-thirds of the country, could not be treated as representing Albania. The country looks to the Commission to save it from the anarchy which must necessarily follow on a perpetuation of its present internal dissensions, and it behoves the Commission consequently to maintain an attitude of the strictest impartiality. To put itself in the pocket of the Provisional Government of Valona would entail the complete loss, in the eyes of those portions of the population which do not recognise the latter, of all prestige and consideration—the moral influence which constitutes its only force.

  I was very strongly in favour of some form of election or popular selection, such, for instance, as might have been obtained by a reference to the municipalities of the four or live principal centres. If that were considered too difficult, I should then be in favour of selection by the Commission pure and simple. All Albania would, I am convinced, accept our choice so long as it fell on someone not specially committed to any one faction. The Austrian, however, remained firm in maintaining his proposal, which represented the deliberate policy of his Government, and in this he was somewhat half-heartedly supported by his Italian colleague, who appeared to me to be acting against his own personal convictions.

Finally a compromise was arrived at, by which it was agreed that each delegate should submit to his Government the two alternatives set forth in my telegram No. 6 of to-day's date, i.e., either to invite the existing authorities at Valona, Durazzo, and Scutari to submit to us telegraphically the names of two competent, persons, from amongst whom we should proceed to select one by lot, or else to invite the Provisional Government to designate our collaborator. I should have preferred selection by the Commission to "tirage au sort," amongst the names submitted to us, but the majority were of opinion that it would be impossible for us to arrive at an agreement within any reasonable time.

The sitting was brought to an end after some discussion upon the internal organisation of the Commission and its common expenditure, which will form the subject of a separate despatch.

I have, &c.,
Harry H. Lamb

Sir Edward Grey to Sir E. Goschen
Foreign Office, October 18, 1913

Separate action by Austria, before even consulting other Powers, makes things very difficult; the usual course would be not to take separate action till after some attempt and failure to obtain co-operation of other Powers. For Austria to present an ultimatum to Servia and then to demand the support of other Powers is in a sense to confront the Powers with an ultimatum.

Apart from this, I think Servia has some ground of complaint owing to delay of the Powers in establishing any settled government in Albania.

I am, however, prepared to support at Belgrade the decisions of the Ambassadors Conference in London respecting frontier between Albania and Servia and to advise Servian Government to give an assurance that Servia will respect that frontier, and that her troops have only crossed it as an emergency measure and will be withdrawn at the earliest practicable moment.

Consul-General Lamb to Sir Edward Grey
Vallona, October 19, 1913

  AUSTRIAN colleague evidently has positive instructions not only to recognise Provisional Government here, but also to impose its acceptance on the whole of Albania. Such a line on the part of the Commission could only lead to anarchy and to internecine strife, degenerating into civil war. Majority of my colleagues are of opinion that our policy should be to recognise that there are separate local authorities in Northern, Southern, and Central Albania, and to endeavour to establish control over the three.
  French and Russian colleagues received instructions to proceed to appoint Governor of Scutari as soon as others receive similar instructions. This is step in the right direction. Am I authorised to concur?

Sir E. Grey to Sir F. Cartwright
Foreign Office, October 22, 1913

Sir,

COUNT MENSDORFF read to me to-day a long telegram that he had received from Vienna informing him of the explanation of the views of His Majesty's Government that had been given to Count Berchtold by your Excellency. The statement seemed to correspond with views that I had expressed at Berlin about the Austrian action, and it had elicited from Count Berchtold the reply that Austria did not intend to separate from the Powers, but that in this instance her action had been the only means of avoiding delay in giving effect to the decision of the Powers about the Serbo-Albanian frontier.

I then observed to Count Mensdorff that there was always a risk in separate ultimatums, or action by one Power, of disturbing agreement between the Powers; but that as in this case the risk had not materialised, and as the Servians had accepted the ultimatum, and as we had not ourselves contemplated disturbing the agreement of the Powers, it was unnecessary for me to emphasise this point now.

Argumentatively, on the merits of the question, the Servians could urge that it was the Albanians who had first violated what for the sake of convenience I would call the London frontier, and the Servians might ask for assurances that when their troops were withdrawn, the Albanians would not violate the frontier again. We ought all—and the Austrian Government especially—to consider what answer we should give to this request if it was made.

I told Count Mensdorff what I had said to Herr von Kühlmann on Monday about discouraging any demands on the part of Servia for a rectification of the frontier, and said that, on the merits of the case, the reports which had reached me of what, to put it mildly, I would call provocative treatment by the Servians of Albanians in territory occupied by Servia had made me personally feel rather lukewarm about Servian complaints.

Assuming the crisis of the Servian frontier difficulty to be over, there were two points which I thought especially important.

The first was that the Commission of Control should work smoothly; there was apparently some difference of opinion about recognition of the Provisional Government. Count Mensdorff said that his Government felt that, considering all the circumstances, it was surprising how little internal trouble there had been in Albania and how well things have been worked; we ought to recognise this and be careful not to upset it.

I quite agreed and said this was exactly the point—let us recognise the Provisional Government wherever its authority was already accepted in Albania, but where other local authorities were working well do not let us upset what was well by forcing the authority of the Provisional Government upon districts that would resent it. I observed that the Provisional Government was apparently Ismail Kemal, and all I had heard of this gentleman in recent years made me rather a lukewarm admirer of him. Nevertheless, by all means let us recognise the Provisional Government where it was willingly accepted in Albania. But the resolution of the reunion of Ambassadors agreeing to the Commission of Control had spoken of "autorités indigènes existantes," or some phrase in the plural, and the Commission had better recognise any local authorities that were in existence and had proved acceptable in their districts.

The other point to which I wished to draw attention was the importance of appointing a Prince quickly. Mr. Lamb, our representative on the Commission of Control, had pressed the importance of this point very strongly. I said to Count Mensdorff on this point what I had said to Herr von Kühlmann on Monday.

I am, &c.,
E. Grey

Consul-General Lamb to Sir Edward Grey
Vallona, October 22, 1913

Sir,

IN continuation of my immediately preceding despatch of yesterday's date, I have the honour to transmit herewith copies of the procès-verbaux of the second and third meetings of the International Commission of Control, which took place on the 18th and 20th instant respectively.

There is nothing which calls for any further remarks in the record of these meetings, the greater part of which was taken up with the settlement of preliminary questions concerning the internal organisation of the Commission itself and discussions on the general situation, which must necessarily remain without definite result until our respective Governments shall have instructed us to what extent we are to recognise respectively the Provisional Government of Vallona and the other regional authorities now existing de facto in Albania.

I take the opportunity of annexing to this despatch copy of a numerously signed petition which was presented to the Commission on the 20th instant, begging it to hasten as much as possible the constitution of a definitive Administration and the nomination of the Prince, which the signatories declare to be the only means of putting an end to existing dissensions and preventing still greater calamities. This is in complete agreement with the desire expressed by Essad Pasha and the "Senate of Central Albania" in the telegram of which I had the honour to transmit you a copy in my despatch No. 1 of the 15th and with the opinion which I myself formed and ventured to lay privately before you immediately on my arrival in this country. I have not the slightest doubt that it represents the general feeling throughout Albania.

I have, &c.,
Harry H. Lamb

Enclosure 1 in No. 158.
Procès-verbal of Second Meeting of International Commission of Control.

AUJOURD'HUI, 18 octobre, 1913, la Commission internationale de Contrôle s'est réunie à la Municipalité, sous la présidence de M. le Dr. Winckel, délégué de l'Allemagne, lequel, conformément à la décision prise au cours de la séance précédente, assume la présidence pour la durée d'un mois.

M. Leoni fait observer que d'après les renseignements qui lui out été fournis, la somme de 250 fr. fixée au cours de la première séance comme appointements pour le secrétaire de la Commission sont très insuffisants ct il ajoute qu'il faudrait les porter à 500 fr. La justesse de cette observation a été admise, mais la Commission croit préférable de remettre à une date ultérieure sa décision finale et un nouvel appel à la contribution des Puissances.

Sur la proposition de M. Petriaef, la Commission décide que toutes les questions administratives seront adoptées à la majorité des voix, et que toutes celles de caractère politique devront retenir l'unanimité, mais ne prendront pas de caractère définitif si un des délégués croit nécessaire de déférer la question aux Puissances.

M. Leoni ayant attiré l'attention de la Commission sur l'opportunité d'une tentative de réconciliation entre Ismail Kemal Bey et Essad Pacha, la discussion s'engage sur ce point. Après un échange de vues, auquel participent tous les délégués, aucune décision n'est intervenue. Cependant, sur la proposition de M. Petrovitch, il a été admis que la liberté entière serait laissée à ceux des délégués qui, à titre strictement privé, voudraient causer avec Ismail Bey sur cette question.

A 1 heure la séance est levée et renvoyée à lundi matin, à 10 heures.

Valona, le 18 octobre, 1913.

Enclosure 2 in No. 158.
Procès-verbal of Third Meeting of International Commission of Control.

CE JOURD'HUI, 20 octobre, 1913, à 10 heures du matin, troisième réunion de la Commission internationale de Contrôle, à la Municipalité, sous la présidence de M. le Dr. Winckel, délégué de l'Allemagne.

Dès le début de la séance, M. Krajewski lit la déclaration suivante, dont il demande l'inscription au procès-verbal:—

"Je prie la Commission imternationale de Contrôle de vouloir bien prendre note et consigner dans le procès-verbal de la réunion d'aujourd'hui, 20 octobre, 1913:

1. Que MM. G. Freyssenge et Daudet, le premier représentant et le second ingénieur de MM. Jean et Georges Hersent et J. Mesnier, domiciliés à Paris, 60, Rue de Londres, ont déposé, le 5 juin, 1913, entre les mains de Malid [sic] Bey, Ministre de l'Intérieur et par interim des Travaux publics du Gouvernement provisoire de l'Albanie, une demande de concession des ports de Valona et Santi Quaranta et des voies ferrées, dont le tracé, restant à déterminer après entente et études sur le terrain, relierait aux deux ports précités les localités dont ces ports doivent former le débouché naturel, soit le tracé Valona, Bérat, Tépéléni, Argyrocastro et Santi Quaranta, ainsi que tous embranchements partant de ces ports;

2. Que cette demande a été enregistrée, le 5 juin, 1913, par le Gouvernement provisoire, ainsi qu'il résulte d'une lettre qui a été écrité par Mufid Bey en sa qualité officielle et qui se trouve entre les mains du groupe en question;

3. Que cette demande a été confirmée par lettre adressée, le 24 juillet, 1913, par MM. Jean et Georges Hersent et J. Mesnier à Ismaïl Kemal Bey, Président du Gouvernement provisoire. En prenant en considération ce qui precède, je me réserve, le moment venu, de faire établir devant qui de droit le

droit de priorité pour le groupe français en question pour la concession dont le détail a été donné ci-dessus."

La Commission, prenant en considération la déclaration du délégué français, en autorise l'inscription au procès-verbal de ce jour.

MM. Petrovitch et Leoni rendent compte de l'entrevue que chacun d'eux a eu séparément avec Ismaïl Kemal Bey sur la question de la réconciliation entre les deux Gouvernements provisoires. La discussion s'engage de nouveau sur cette question, qui est enfin renvoyée à une date ultérieure.

Deux des délégués n'ayant pas encore reçu l'instructions de leur Gouvernement, la Commission ne peut pas discuter la question de la nomination du Gouverneur de Scutari.

Sur la proposition de Mr. Lamb, la Commission est d'avis qu'il est de l'intérêt de l'Albanie de hâter autant que possible l'arrivée de l'officier chargé de l'organisation de la gendarmerie, et à cet effet elle décide que chacun des délégués enverra à son Gouvernement le télégramme identique suivant:—

"La Commission Internationale de Contrôle, dans sa séance de ce jour, émet à l'unanimité le voeu que les Puissances prennent leurs dispositions pour hâter l'arrivée de l'officier chargé de l'organisation de la gendarmerie albanaise."

A midi un quart la séance est levée et renvoyée à demain, mardi, à 10 heures du matin.

Enclosure 3 in No. 158
Joint Letter addressed to the President of International Commission of Control.

NOUS soussignés avons l'honneur d'attirer la bienveillante et sérieuse attention de la Commission international de Contrôle sur l'état anormal de l'Albanie et de la prier de vouloir bien remédier à cet état de choses, dont la prolongation pourrait compliquer davantage la situation et causer par conséquent à la nation des maux irrémédiables.

Le caractère provisoire des institutions gouvernementaux, la mauvaise administration, la discorde, les rivalités personnelles ne pourraient prendre fin, à notre humble avis, qu'avec un seul Gouvernement définitif et légitime dans le pays.
Les six Grandes Puissances gagneraient certes le plus grand titre à la reconnaissance du peuple albanais en accélérant le choix du futur Souverain et en nous évitant par leurs bons offices un conflit intérieur, funeste à l'Albanie.

EKREM BEY VLORA,
Vice-Président du Conseil national,
H. AVNI BEY DELVINO,
HAIDAR KOLONIA,
VELI KLISSOURA,
TAHSIN ABDUL,
MUSTAPHA,
BABA-SALIH,
HAKKI,
REMZI T. BORSHI,
KOL TROMARA,
THEODOR KOTTI,
VASILI S. MATTO,
ZIHNI ABBAS KANINA,
AZIZ MUTCHO of VALONA,
MESHTAN (?), of ARGYROCASTRO,
KHALIL BABA (?), of SCUTARI,
ALOUSH TAIIA,
MEHMET MUFTI,
HUSNI,
ARIF KOLOYA,
IDEM. J. KOSTOURI,
STAVRI M. KARODI,
SOLO,
VLASI ZIMRO,
KADRI LIBOHOVO,

SHKRI TCHOTCHO of ARGYROCASTRO,
&c., &c.

Mr. Dering to Sir Edward Grey
Rome, October 24, 1913

Italian Government have now replied respecting Albanian delegate on Commission of Control.

They consider Mufid Bey, Libohova, would be suitable candidate owing to his personal and family position, his experience in Ottoman administration, and ability to exercise influence on Albanian Government. Notwithstanding the personal hostility to his nomination on the part of Ismail Kemal, which is unjustified, Italian Government have undertaken to support his candidature, and hope His Majesty's Government will do likewise.

Sir Edward Grey to Sir F. Cartwright
Foreign Office, October 24, 1913

I HAVE told Count Mensdorff, with reference to the withdrawal of Servian troops from Albania, that the Servian Government could urge that the Albanians had been the first to violate the frontier laid down at the London Conference, and that we all, and the Austrian Government especially, ought to consider what answer we should give to their request for assurances that, when their troops were withdrawn, the Albanians would not repeat the violation.

There were two further points in regard to Albania which I thought especially important.

The first was that the Commission of Control should work smoothly. There was apparently some difference of opinion about the recognition of the Provisional Government. I thought we might recognise the Provisional Government wherever its authority was already accepted in Albania, but where other local authorities were working well we should not upset matters by forcing the authority of the Provisional Government upon districts that would resent it, especially as the Provisional Government was apparently only Ismail Kemal, whose personality did not inspire His Majesty's Government, with much confidence. The resolution of the Ambassadors in defining the mandate of the Commission of Control had spoken of "autorités indigènes existantes," and the Commission had better recognise any local authorities that were in existence and had proved acceptable in their districts.

The other point to which I wished to draw attention was the importance of appointing a Prince without further delay. Our commissioner had pressed this point very strongly.

Consul-General Lamb to Sir Edward Grey
Vallona, October 25, 1913

Sir,

EVER since my arrival in this place, innumerable complaints have continued to reach me concerning the acts of injustice, violence, and pillage, committed by the Greeks, to the detriment of the Mussulman population, in the districts occupied by them in Southern Albania.

Though not attaining to the degree of savagery of which the Serbs are accused on the Eastern border, for which, indeed, they have not had even the Servian's pretext of "attempted insurrection," the Greeks seem to have resorted to every means, short of wholesale murder, in order to terrorise and reduce to silence all that part of the population which they have found themselves unable by other methods to convince of its purely "Hellenic" origin and sympathies. Their action is all the more cynical and inexcusable in that it is being carried on in districts lying beyond the frontier definitely allotted to Greece by the decisions of London, and its patent object is to blot out all signs of a non-Hellenic population (in a region which, ethnologically at least, is almost purely Albanian) before the arrival of the Frontier Commission.

The enclosed memorandum contains a certain number of specific instances, for which one of my most reliable informants is prepared to vouch, and refers principally to the neighbourhood of Argyrocastro. Whilst necessarily unable to verify the statements contained therein, I have practically no doubt of their veracity. Similar conduct has been systematically resorted to by the Greek authorities at Koritza ever since their first occupation of that place.

I am sending a copy of this despatch and its enclosure to His Britannic Majesty's Legation in Athens.

I have, &c.,
Harry H. Lamb

Sir Edward Grey to Sir F. Bertie
Foreign Office, October 27, 1913

Sir,

M. de FLEURIAU informed Sir E. Crowe on the 18th October that the German Government had made to the French Government the same communication as that which we have received from Berlin respecting the Austrian ultimatum to Servia. He was unable to tell Sir E. Crowe anything precise as to what the French Government proposed to do, but he said the Austrian proceeding, and the manner in which it was made the subject of communications from the German Government, were considered at Paris exceedingly strange.

Sir E. Crowe thought it right to tell M. de Fleuriau of the reply which I had sent to Berlin, and the instructions to Mr Crankanthorpe at Belgrade. Sir E. Crowe also read to him the relevant parts of Mr. Crankanthorpe's telegram No. 256, and called his attention to the fact that, although the Austrian communication to Servia was made on the 15th October, we had heard nothing from Austria direct up to now. He said the French Government were in the same anomalous position.

M. de Fleuriau then added, speaking, as he said, without any instructions or official authority, that the French Government were beginning to feel very anxious about the whole question of Albania. The reports they were receiving from the several international commissions indicated growing and perpetual friction and foreshadowed the complete breakdown of the international machinery in Albania. There was, consequently, a strong disposition in Paris to withdraw from Albania altogether and adopt, with regard to it, the attitude which Austria and Germany had formerly taken up in the Cretan question; the French Government would, in that case, withdraw all their commissioners and also the French military contingent at Scutari.

I am, &c.,
E. Grey

Sir Edward Greg to Sir F. Cartwright
Foreign Office, October 27, 1913

Sir,
    BARON GAUTSCH informed Sir E. Crowe officially on the 21st October that his Government had received a reply from the Servian Government agreeing to the Austrian demand for immediate evacuation, and saying that the necessary orders to that effect had been given. It was accordingly to be expected that all Servian troops would be withdrawn from Albanian territory by the 26th October.

I am, &c.,
E. Grey

Sir Edward Grey to Sir F. Bertie
Foreign Office, October 29, 1913

  I OBSERVED to M. Cambon to-day that the Austrian policy obviously was to turn the international control of Albania into an Austrian control. This policy might result in an absolute deadlock on the Commission of Control and the Commission for Delimitating the Southern Frontier. We ought to consider what we should do in such an event. Had we any real interest in making an effort to prevent Austria from pushing her interests in Albania, or should we throw the whole thing up and leave it to Austria and Italy to settle the Albanian question? An absolute deadlock might occur at any moment, and we ought to be prepared.
  M. Cambon said that he would put the question to M. Pichon.

I am, &c.,
E. Grey

Sir Edward Grey to Mr. Dering
Foreign Office, October 29, 1913

Sir,

THE Italian Chargé d'Affaires made to Sir E. Crowe this afternoon the same communication that Count Mensdorff had just made to Sir A. Nicolson, respecting the obstruction alleged to be offered by the Greeks to the work of the Commission of Delimitation in Southern Albania.

Sir E. Crowe pointed out to Prince Borghese that the interpretation put by his Government on the attitude of the inhabitants who refused entry into their houses to the Delimitation Commission, was not the only possible one. It might be, as they thought, that this was evidence that the people were Albanians who had been threatened by the Greeks if they were to reveal their true nationality and language, although it seemed to Sir E. Crowe curious, knowing the character of Albanians to be what it is, that an overwhelming majority of them, such as they are represented to form, should be terrorised in this way by a small minority of despised Greeks. But there was another possible explanation: the Greek portion of the inhabitants might have resolved to offer at least passive resistance to the Commission, who, in their eyes, are charged with the mission to transfer certain Greek-speaking, or largely Greek-speaking, districts to Albania.

Sir E. Crowe said we were ourselves puzzled as to the interpretation to be placed on the situation, and were awaiting further reports on this point from our commissioner.

As regards the requirement that the delimitation was to be finished, whatever happened, by the 30th November, Sir E. Crowe said it would hardly do to base this requirement, as the Italian Government proposed to do, on the resolution of the Ambassadors' Conference. That resolution also declared that the delimitation should begin on the 1st September. When the time came, neither the Italian nor the Austrian delegates were ready. They did not, so far as Sir E. Crowe remembered, appear at Corfu (after Brindisi had been abandoned as the meeting place) till the middle of September, and the work on the spot did not begin until about the 23rd September, when at least our commissioner expressed the opinion that it would be quite impossible to finish by the 30th November.

I am, &c.,
E. Grey

Sir Edward Grey to Sir F. Bertie
Foreign Office, October 29, 1913

Sir,

M. CAMBON spoke to me to-day about Albania.

I explained our view that the Provisional Government of Ismail Kemal should be recognised in the district where its authority was accepted, but that in other districts, where the authority of the Provisional Government was not accepted, the native district governments should be recognised.

M. Cambon also spoke to me of the difference of opinion with regard to the Dutch officers. The Austrian and Italian view was that they should be dependent upon the Provisional Government, and one suggestion apparently had been made that they should carry out their task of enquiry in consultation with the Minister of War for Albania. This was absurd; there was no such person. The view of the French Government was that the Dutch officers should study the question in the closest relations with the Commission of Control.

I said that I agreed that they should carry out their work in consultation with the Commission, and communicate, as far as they found it necessary, not only with the Provisional Government of Ismail Kemal, but also with other native authorities.

I am, &c.,
E. Grey

Sir Edward Grey to Mr. O'Beirne
Foreign Office, October 29, 1913

Sir,

THE Russian Chargé d'Affaires read to Sir E. Crowe on the 21st October a telegram from his Foreign Office, according to which the Commission of Control was in great difficulties over the question of recognition of Albanian authorities. The Austrians and Italians had suggested that the Commission should direct their efforts to bringing about a reconciliation between Ismail Kemal and Essad Pasha. But the majority of the Commission considered this to be quite hopeless.

The Russian Commissioner therefore recommended that the Commission should refuse to recognise either Ismail Kemal or Essad, and nominate separate Governors for Durazzo, Elbassan, and Scutari. The Russian Government enquired whether I would support this solution.

Sir E. Crowe said he did not think I would be willing to express any opinion on this question now. I had not the materials for forming an independent judgment. The whole object of a commission on the spot was to try and settle matters of this kind themselves. The proper course would therefore seem to let the Commission discuss the various proposals for a solution, and only if they found it impossible to arrive at any arrangement to refer to their Governments. In the present instance we had received no report from our commissioner.

M. de Etter quite agreed with what Sir E. Crowe said, and expressed himself as glad to recommend the view Sir E. Crowe had expressed to M. Neratof.

I am, &c.,
E. Grey

Sir Edward Grey to Sir F. Cartwright
Foreign Office, October 30, 1913

Sir,

I TOLD Count Mensdorff to-day, with reference to his communication of yesterday to Sir Arthur Nicolson about the Southern Frontier Commission in Albania, that I was puzzled as to why the inhabitants were closing their doors against the Commission. Colonel Doughty-Wylie had reported the great obstruction that was caused thereby to the work of the Commission, and I had telegraphed to him to ascertain to what motive this obstruction was attributed. It might be, as the Austrian Government supposed, that the doors were closed by Albanians who had been terrorised by Greeks; or, on the other hand, it might be that the people in question were Greeks who wished to boycott the Commission and its work. When I received some information, I should know what inferences to draw.

As to the prospect of the work of the Commission not being concluded by the 30th November, I said that it must be borne in mind that the Italian and Austrian representatives had not arrived till the 14th September, and it had therefore not been possible to begin the work as soon as was expected.

Count Mensdorff assured me that the delay had been due in this case to the French, who had not sent their representative.

I said that, in any case, I would wait till nearer the end of November before coming to any decision as to what should be done after that.

I am, &c.,
E. Grey

I promised that H[is] M[ajesty's] Gov[ernmen]t would instruct the British Admiral accordingly, to take the necessary action as soon as all his Colleagues were similarly instructed.

Sir Edward Grey to Sir F. Bertie
Foreign Office, October 30, 1913

SERVIAN Government state they have information that Albanians within Albanian territory are preparing fresh attack against Djakova and Prisrend to be delivered before arrival on the spot of the International Delimitation Commission.

I presume this communication has been made to all the Powers.

I pointed out to Austro-Hungarian Ambassador here a week ago that the Powers ought to be prepared to consider what reply could be given if Servia asked them to ensure that withdrawal of Servian troops should not be followed by a renewed violation of frontier fixed by the Powers through Conference of Ambassadors.

I should be glad to know what answer should, in the opinion of the Government to which you are accredited, be given to Servia.

Sir Edward Grey to Sir F. Cartwright
Foreign Office, October 30, 1913

Sir,

I TOLD Count Mensdorff to-day that the Servians had now asked for assurances against the violation of the London frontier by the Albanians, and had yesterday informed us that, according to their information, the Albanians were preparing to attack Djakova and Prisrend. I reminded Count Mensdorff that last week I had spoken to him of this difficulty.

He told me that he had reported what I had said to Count Berchtold, and that the latter, in commenting on it, had observed that there ought to be mutual guarantees on both sides. The Servians could establish on their side blockhouses, as was commonly done on mountainous frontiers, as the Austrians themselves had on part of their frontier with Montenegro. The Servians should also protect the rights of minorities on their own territory, and allow free access to the markets of Djakova and Dibra, for which Austria had stipulated at the reunion of Ambassadors in London. On the Albanian side, the appointment of a Prince, which Count Berchtold was very glad to hear I thought to be urgent, and the establishment of a gendarmerie would be guarantees.

I said that, pending these steps, it might be possible in some way to exercise influence in Albania to prevent the violation of the frontier.

Count Mensdorff expressed the general hope that things would go smoothly.

I said that it was important that there should not be difficulties on the Commission of Control, and I again reminded him that it would be desirable not to force Ismail Kemal down people's throats in Albania, but only to recognise his authority in districts where it was accepted.

He told me that he had reported what I had said to him on this point last week.

I am, &c.,
E. Grey

Consul-General Lamb to Sir Edward Grey
Vallona, October 31, 1913

Sir,

WITH reference to my despatch No. 8 of the 28th instant, I have the honour to transmit herewith copies of the procès-verbaux of the sixth and seventh meetings of the International Commission of Control. In the above-cited and immediately following despatches I have already expressed myself sufficiently in regard to the appointment of Mufid Bey as Albanian delegate on the Commission. I would now merely add that the news of his nomination has been received with evident disappointment by the "Nationalists," representing the great majority of the people who are neither actually nor prospectively Government officials nor agents of a foreign propaganda, and whose confidence the new delegate certainly does not enjoy. As for Ismail Kemal Bey, when the notification was made to him by the president of the Commission, he simply asked by whom the question had been decided, and on being told that it was in accordance with a decision of the Powers, he replied: "In that case, 'je n'ai qu'à m'incliner.'"

Petitions in favour of the immediate designation of the Prince continue to be received by the Commission, which to-day decided in principle that the attention of the Great Powers should be drawn to the prevailing desire. The Russian delegate, indeed, proposed that it should at once take some definite and collective action to this end, but the Austrian and Italian delegates appeared uncertain as to how this proposal would be regarded by their Governments, and so succeeded in postponing any final decision on the subject.

I have, etc.,
Harry H. Lamb

Consul-General Lamb to Sir Edward Grey
Vallona, November 5, 1913

Sir,

IT is generally understood that, before the constitution of the International Commission of Control, pourparlers had been entered into for the appointment of "conseillers techniques," of Austrian and Italian nationality, to the various Ministries composing the Provisional Government. So long as no international agreement existed for the creation of an independent State under the collective guarantee of the six Powers, possibly no exception could justly be taken to this, but the situation seems to me to have undergone a fundamental change on the arrival of the Commission of Control, and I was consequently no little surprised when I was confidentially informed that the Italian vice consul, who has recently returned from a short visit to Rome, had called upon Ismail Kemal Bey and somewhat vehemently insisted on the fulfilment of certain promises which would appear to have been previously made in this respect.

Mr. O'Beirne to Sir Edward Grey
St. Petersburgh, November 5, 1913

Minister for Foreign Affairs has left for the Crimea. Assistant Minister for Foreign Affairs informs me that M. Sazonof, previous to his departure, had a conversation with him concerning Albanian question, of which following is the upshot:—

Only questions connected with Albania which seriously interest Russia are delimitation of frontier with Servia and Montenegro and establishment of some Government capable of maintaining order. It is a matter of indifference to Russian Government whether Vallona Government is recognised or another and whether concessions which this Government have given are ratified; and Russia would be prepared, if Great Britain and France concurred, to cease all opposition to Austro-Italian Commission of Control in such matters.

Russian Government, however, wish to know if His Majesty's Government and French Government would not have objections to Austria and Italy thus gaining entire control of Albania and establishing themselves as masters on Albanian coast.

If it is decided not to allow Austria and Italy a free hand in Commission of Control, the three Powers must decide clearly what steps they will take to carry out their wishes on certain points.

M. Sazonof enquired of me on 31st October whether Great Britain, as a Mediterranean naval Power, would object to Italy establishing a naval base at Vallona, a contingency which he thought extremely probable. I had reported this by despatch.

Mr. Dering to Sir Edward Grey
Rome, November 6, 1913

    Minister for Foreign Affairs now informs me that news received from Vallona and Scutari from Italian consuls respecting threatened Albanian attacks is reassuring.

    As regards reply to be given to a Servian request for assurance that withdrawal of their troops would not be followed by renewed violation of frontier, Italian Government suggest that opinion might be expressed to Servian Government that guarantees to this effect should be given not only by Albania but also by Servia. Servia's guarantees could consist of military measures usually adopted on frontier in mountain districts, such as construction of blockhouses and forts and the establishment of a chain of military posts. All provocation directed against Albanians should also be avoided by adopting measures to ensure, in accordance with the wishes of London Conference, protection of minority and free access to markets at Dibra and Djakova; these measures should be put into rigorous effect.

    As regards Albania, Italian Government consider best methods of guarantee, in addition to advice which they personally are constantly giving to respect frontier fixed by London Conference, would be to hasten organisation of that State and of Albanian gendarmerie, and more especially the enthronement of the Prince.

Sir Edward Grey to Mr. T. Russell
Foreign Office, November 7, 1913

Sir,

I ASKED the Austrian Ambassador to-day whether his Government were going to propose the Prince of Wied for the Throne of Albania.

He replied that he had not heard anything on the subject, and he asked me whether we would accept the Prince.

I said that we would accept him, and I did not think that anyone would raise objection to him; but it was necessary that someone should take the step of proposing him.

The Ambassador asked me if I thought that France and Russia would accept the Prince.

I answered that I thought they would not make any objection to him.

The Ambassador said that this was very important, and was something that he would at once telegraph to his Government.

I am, &c.,
E. Grey

Sir Edward Grey to Sir F. Bertie
Foreign Office, November 7, 1913

Sir,

M. CAMBON said to-day that the Prince of Wied had a good personality, but he would probably stipulate that his Throne in Albania should be guaranteed by the Powers; that he should be invited to accept the Throne by the Provisional Government of Albania on behalf of Albania as a whole; and that the Powers should guarantee a loan to Albania. The second condition M. Cambon regarded as out of the question, and he assumed that we could guarantee a loan only if the international control was working well.

I am, &c.,
E. Grey

Sir Edward Grey to Mr. Crackanthorpe
Foreign Office, November 7, 1913

Sir,

THE Servian Chargé d'Affaires stated to Sir E. Crowe on the 31st October that, according to reliable information received by his Government, the proceedings of the Northern Boundary Commission were taking a turn exceedingly unfavourable to Servia. The Commission seemed determined to trace the frontier in such a way as to impose on Servia the maximum difficulty in defending it militarily. This was, in the first instance, due to the spirit in which the delegates of the Triple Alliance Powers carried on their duties; but the really determining factor was the attitude of the British delegate, who seemed to have no will of his own and always gave way to every Austro-Italian demand. If the British delegate would only take an impartial view and stand by it, the Austro-Italian designs would be frustrated.

Sir E. Crowe expressed surprise and resentment at receiving such a communication, and said he refused to lay it before Sir E. Grey. He could not allow vague charges of this kind to be brought against a British officer, who was discharging exceedingly onerous duties to the best of his ability and, Sir E. Crowe had no doubt whatever, with the strictest impartiality; nor did Sir E. Crowe understand how the Servian Government could claim to have reliable information in regard to what passed between the various commissioners.

Sir E. Crowe therefore asked M. Grouitch to inform his Government that this Department declined to discuss the attitude of the British commissioner with him.

I am, &c.,
E. Grey

Sir Edward Grey to Sir F. Bertie
Foreign Office, November 7, 1913

Sir,
         M. de FLEURIAU informed Sir A. Nicolson on the 3rd November that M. Sazonof had instructed the Russian delegate on the South Albanian Delimitation Commission, if he were in a position to confirm the Austro-Italian complaints as to Greek obstruction, to make representations to the Greek local authorities not to place any impediments in the way of the labours of the Commission. M. Pichon said he would be prepared to send similar instructions to the French delegate if His Majesty's Government were to do the same in regard to instructions to the British delegate.

The Greek Minister also, on the 3rd November, said that his Government from the first had given the strictest orders to the local authorities to assist the Commission in every way, and he read to me a long list of grievances in regard to the action both of the Austrian and Italian delegates and complaints as to the people with whom they had surrounded themselves.

M. de Etter also spoke on the same subject, and asked what were my views as to the separate action of Austria and Italy at Athens. Sir A. Nicolson replied that we were awaiting the return of M. Cambon, who would doubtless take the opportunity of his visit to Paris to discuss matters with M. Pichon.

M. Gennadius said he would send Sir A. Nicolson the text of the reply of his Government to the Austro-Italian identic note which had been delivered on the 30th October.

He had been instructed to enquire whether His Majesty's Government admitted that Austria and Italy should act as delegates of the Powers, or whether the latter intended to maintain the decision taken at London that Albania is a matter of international concern.

Sir A. Nicolson told M. Gennadius he would refer this query to me.

My reply to M. Gennadius will be that any action taken separately by one or more of the Great Powers is, in the first instance, a matter to be discussed between the Great Powers themselves.

I have sent the same instructions to the British delegate as the Russians and French have sent, or are ready to send.

I am, &c.,
E. Grey

Sir Edward Grey to Mr. Crackanthorpe
Foreign Office, November 13, 1913

Sir,
 THE Servian Chargé d'Affaires urged to-day that after the Servian withdrawal from Albania the Powers ought to prevent the Albanians from crossing the frontier.
 I said that the way to do this would be for the Powers to expedite the installation of a proper Government in Albania, and the formation of the gendarmerie under Dutch officers; meanwhile they should exercise what influence they could to discourage the Albanians from crossing the frontier. I had expressed this opinion, and had been informed that the Austrian officials were now instructed to use their influence for this purpose.
 The Chargé d'Affaires said that this would be a welcome change, and he began to give an account of how the last Albanian attack upon Djakova and so forth had been organised.
 I said that if we went into these past things there would be no end to our conversation, for there were charges on the other side that the Albanians had been denied access to the markets at Djakova and Dibra, and that Albanian minorities had not been well treated by the Servian authorities.
 The Chargé d'Affaires said that the Albanians would bring arms into the towns if they used the markets.
 We did not, however, continue the conversation further.

I am, &c.,
E. Grey

Sir Edward Grey to Sir F. Elliot
Foreign Office, November 25, 1913

Sir,

THE Greek Minister read to me to-day a telegram protesting against the line that the Greek Government understood was being discussed by the Frontier Commission for the south of Albania. The line proposed would give numbers of Greeks to Albania, thereby putting them under a rule much less civilised than that of Greece, which they would resent and against which they would revolt. There would be all sorts of trouble if such a line was decided upon. He understood that we had proposed this line to the Powers.

I said that a line had been suggested in the Commission, and we had asked the Powers to instruct their delegates to continue the discussion on the basis of this line, in the hope of coming to an agreement. I could not discuss the line outside the Commission. Indeed, it was a matter of detail to be decided according to the merits on the spot by the commissioners. No decision had yet been come to; but I earnestly advised that, when the Commission did come to an agreement, the Greek Government should not dispute the decision of the Powers about Albania.

The Greek Minister continued to deprecate the line.

I continued to repeat the advice, that Greece should accept whatever decisions the Powers came to. I added that if, five years ago, the Greeks had been told that they would get what they had now obtained and occupied, including such important things as Salonica, it would have seemed almost incredible.

The Minister contended that the patriotism that had been displayed and the sacrifices that had been made by Greece were equally unforeseen.

I said that I supposed every one expected his countrymen to be patriotic and to make sacrifices when the occasion demanded.

As the Minister continued to press the question of Albania, saying that it was the interests of Italy and Austria that were being considered, I observed even Great Powers must be allowed sometimes to have interests, as well as the smaller Powers. In this Balkan crisis the Great Powers had claimed exceedingly little for themselves, and their moderation had been remarkable.

The Minister urged that it had suited them to be moderate, because they had thereby kept the peace between themselves.

I observed that I had not said that the moderation of the Powers was a great virtue, but that it had been remarkable.

I am, &c.,
E. Grey

Sir Edward Grey to Mr. Dering
Foreign Office, November 25, 1913

THE Italian and Austrian Governments have suggested that His Majesty's Government should propose the Prince of Wied to the Powers.

I demurred to this procedure, as we have no relations with the Prince of Wied, and I have said that the natural course was for Italy and Austria to propose the Prince to the Powers.

The Italian Ambassador urged that this would cause still further delay, as it would still remain to communicate with the Prince of Wied.

I suggested that the five Ambassadors at Berlin might at once be instructed to approach the German Minister for Foreign Affairs and ask him to inform the Prince of Wied that the Powers wish to designate him as Prince of Albania, and to ask if he will accept the position.

In view of nationality of Prince of Wied, and as he is believed to be at Potsdam now, this seems to be the most appropriate method of communicating with him.

You should inform Minister for Foreign Affairs.

Mr. Akers-Douglas to Sir Edward Grey
Cettinjé, November 26, 1913

Proclamation of annexation made as stated in my telegram No. 137 of 22nd November. Colonel Phillips informed.

I do not think that the Government will yet seriously take steps to occupy all the Hoti-Grouda country, but they maintain that they cannot, in view of public opinion, indefinitely postpone the incorporation of territory which presumably is their own. Realising that those tribes are hostile, they are not best pleased with the acquisition, but, while admitting that there will be opposition, believe that this will soon be overcome. They do not seem to fear general rising.

According to Colonel Phillips, chiefs understood that Montenegro was to wait until the delimitation of boundary was completed. I presume, however, that this cannot be insisted upon, and the Boundary Commission may not arrive there for many months.

I have refrained from advising the Government to take no action, for it is certain that they would in some way throw the responsibility in the event of difficulties [? group omitted] and might perhaps try to make capital out of it (please see Count de Salis's telegram No. 99 of 15th June and despatch No. 56).

Colonel Phillips told me that the telegraph lines had been cut by Essad Pasha.

Sir Edward Grey to Mr. Dering
Foreign Office, November 26, 1913

Sir,
YOU will have observed from the telegram sections that the conduct of the Austro-Hungarian and Italian consuls at Vallona has scarcely seemed to His Majesty's Government compatible with the dignity of the International Mission of Control. As you are aware, it appeared at first as if the Austrian consul was chiefly responsible for this, an impression which the tenour of your telegram No. 201 of the 18th November tended to confirm.

I have, however, now received three despatches from the British representative on the Commission, copies of which I transmit to you herewith.

You will observe from these despatches that the Italian consul seems to have been at least equally active in taking steps independently of the Commission.

You should bring the substance of these despatches in a friendly manner to the knowledge of the Italian Minister for Foreign Affairs, and point out that, while His Majesty's Government have no desire to attach undue importance to the proceedings of Signor de Facendis or to raise unnecessary points of controversy, his action, if persisted in, must, in their opinion, impair the authority, and therewith the utility, of the International Commission that has been set up for the control of Albanian affairs. That Commission is, and should remain, the sole channel through which the Great Powers should exert their influence upon the local authorities.

I am, &c.,
E. Grey

Sir Edward Grey to Sir F. Bertie
Foreign Office, November 26, 1913

Sir,

M. CAMBON told me to-day that the Greek Minister in Paris had urged upon M. Pichon that the decision about the southern frontier of Albania, mentioning Koritza, should be reconsidered by the Ambassadors' reunion. M. Pichon had said that it was impossible to go back upon the question of Koritza, and it could not be reconsidered.

I told M. Cambon of the protest that the Greek Minister had made here yesterday, and of what I had replied, both about the southern frontier of Albania and about the Ægean islands.

M. Cambon said that Greece was to have the islands if Koritza and Stylos went to Albania.

I said that undoubtedly this had been the understanding on which a decision had been arrived at to give Koritza and Stylos to Albania. The Powers had undertaken no obligation towards Greece in the matter, but the understanding between them had been that Greece was to keep all the islands in her occupation except Tenedos and Imbros; and if any other decision was come to about the islands it would be open to any of the Powers to reopen the question of the southern frontier of Albania. I had spoken in this sense to the Italian Ambassador when he had asked me about the matter, and, I thought, also to the German Chargé d'Affaires.

M. Cambon said there had been a report that Sir Rennell Rodd had proposed that the islands should be formed into a separate confederation. M. Cambon asked me whether I had discussed the matter with him.

I said that I had not discussed such a proposal with Sir Rennell Rodd at all. I had given him certain instructions before he returned to Rome, but I had not given him any instructions about the islands in the occupation of Greece. In regard to the islands in the occupation of Italy, I had instructed him to point out to the Italian Minister for Foreign Affairs that the longer this question dragged on, the more awkward it would become, and to urge upon him that the Italian Government should give the islands back to Turkey. The Powers could then decide about their future destiny. All that we could press Italy to do was to give them back to Turkey, in accordance with the Treaty of Lausanne.

M. Cambon showed me some information from Constantinople to the effect that the Turks admitted that they had not yet pressed Italy to restore the Ægean islands that were at present in Italian occupation, but affirmed that they were going to do so.

I am, &c.,
E. Grey

Sir Edward Grey to Count Mensdorff
Foreign Office, November 28, 1913

SIR E. GREY presents his compliments to the Austro-Hungarian Ambassador, and has the honour to acknowledge the receipt of his Excellency's memorandum of the 22nd November.

In deference to the wish of the Austro-Hungarian Government, Sir E. Grey has authorised His Majesty's Chargé d'Affaires at Belgrade to join in making the necessary communication to the Servian Government respecting the Albanian refugees from Servian territory, if all his colleagues are similarly instructed.

As regards access to Dibra and Djakova and the protection of minorities, Sir E. Grey has already made known to the Servian Government his views in a manner which corresponds generally with the desire now expressed by his Excellency, and he does not therefore think it necessary to take further steps now in regard to these specific points.

In regard to the Servian decree respecting public security in the annexed territories, the oppressive nature of these regulations has already, by Sir E. Grey's direction, been forcibly represented to the Servian Chargé d'Affaires in London. Sir E. Grey does not therefore at present propose to take any further action in this connection.

Sir Edward Grey to Sir F. Bertie
Foreign Office, November 28, 1913

Sir,

    I ASKED M. Cambon to-day to make sure that instructions were sent to the French Ambassador in Berlin to join with his colleagues in informing the German Minister for Foreign Affairs that the Powers had agreed to designate the Prince of Wied as Prince of Albania, and to ask Herr von Jagow to communicate with him.

    M. Cambon said that he understood that the French Government had already sent instructions to their Ambassador.

I am, &c.,
E. Grey

Sir Edward Grey to Sir M. de Bunsen
Foreign Office, November 28, 1913

Sir,

THE Austrian Ambassador asked me to-day about the designation of the Prince of Wied.

I said that M. Cambon had expressed himself as favourable to the proposed communication in Berlin, and I hoped, therefore, that the French Government were instructing their Ambassador there to take part in it.

The Austrian Ambassador asked me about a deputation of notables from Albania to the Prince of Wied. The latter was likely to make it a condition that he should be invited in that way by the Albanians.

I said that I did not think that the Powers could organise deputations of notables from Albania. As far as the Powers were concerned, their part was complete when they had designated the Prince; but there was no reason why objection should be taken to deputations of notables from Albania being received by the Prince if they wished to go spontaneously,

The Ambassador said that he assumed that they would go from different parts of Albania.

I am, &c.,
E. Grey

Sir Edward Grey to Sir M. de Bunsen
Foreign Office, December 5, 1913

Sir,

THE Austrian Ambassador read to Sir A. Nicolson to-day a telegram from the Austrian Minister of Foreign Affairs, to the effect that the Moslem Albanians in the south were alarmed lest reprisals might be made upon them when the boundary line was settled and the commission had left.

Count Berchtold was ready to agree to the adoption of any measures which would allay those fears, such as the creation of a native force or some other method, but he laid down two conditions: —

1. That no international force should be employed; and
2. That the date on which the Greek forces were to evacuate Albania should not be deferred.

Sir A. Nicolson said that the question to which he alluded had already been mentioned, and that His Majesty's Government would, he thought, share Count Berchtold's views as to the non-employment of an international force. If, however, the Greeks were to evacuate Albania on the 31st December, it was clear there was not time to organise any native force; and if Greek troops were withdrawn before there was any protective force ready to replace them, there would be great risk of outrages and anarchy. This was the dilemma with which the Powers were confronted, and Sir A. Nicolson felt sure that His Majesty's Government would be glad to consider any way out of the difficulty which was practical.

Count Mensdorff said that he would lay these considerations before Count Berchtold.

I am, &c.,
E. Grey

Sir Edward Grey to Sir F. Bertie
Foreign Office, December 12, 1913

We may now expect any day to hear that South Albanian Boundary Commission has agreed upon a line, and has thus terminated its labours. A serious situation will then arise in view of the evident determination of the Christian population in the border districts to resist incorporation in Albania.

2. In these circumstances it is essential that some force should be available on withdrawal of Greek troops and administration to prevent sanguinary disorder. His Majesty's Government share what they understand to be the general reluctance to employ international contingents for such a purpose.

3. The Austro Hungarian Government have put forward a suggestion that a local militia of sufficient strength might be rapidly formed, and, according to reports received from the British delegate on Commission of Control, the Dutch officers appear to consider it possible to organise 1,000 gendarmerie in three weeks at a cost estimated, roughly, at 6,000 l. a month. It is difficult to form an opinion as to the feasibility and sufficiency of these plans on the scanty information to hand, but everything points to the necessity of allowing sufficient time to make suitable preparations before the date of Greek evacuation.

4. According to the formal resolution of the Ambassadors' Conference, such evacuation could not rightly be demanded until one month after termination of Frontier Commission's labours, that is, in any case not before the middle, or possibly the end, of January, and His Majesty's Government consider the Powers are formally bound to allow not less than this one month's grace.

5. When moment for evacuation does come, the Powers will be faced with the question of the islands, with which that of the South Albanian frontier was deliberately linked during discussions at the Ambassadors' Conference. It will be remembered that the inclusion in Albania of Koritza and Stylos was only agreed to on an understanding between the Powers that the islands except Tenedos and Imbros should go to Greece. Apart from the justice of now giving effect to this honourable understanding, this course will afford the best means of obtaining the co-operation of the Greek Government in a general settlement which will, among other things, go a long way to dispose of the difficulties in Southern Albania.

6. Failing such a settlement, there will clearly be trouble in Greece itself and the danger of further trouble between Greece and Turkey that may reopen larger questions. It is to the interest of all the Powers, including Turkey, that the peace now finally concluded in the Balkans should not now again be broken. A general settlement on the basis outlined by M. Venizelos seems both equitable and practical, and His Majesty's Government hope that the six Powers will agree to co-operate for its immediate realisation.

7. With this view, the Powers should, as soon as possible, after the South Albanian boundary is settled, communicate it to Greece with an intimation that it must be definitely accepted, and with the request for a definite pledge that in due course all the districts incorporated in Albania will be evacuated by the Greek forces at the date named. At the same time, the Greek and Turkish Governments would have to be informed that the Powers have decided not to deprive the Greeks of the islands entirely inhabited by Greeks which they conquered in the late war, except Tenedos and Imbros, which, for strategical reasons, should be handed back to Turkey. Satisfactory guarantees would have to be given by Greece to Turkey that the islands will not be fortified, or used for any naval or military purposes, and that effective measures will be taken for the prevention of smuggling between the islands and

the Turkish mainland, and the Powers should in fairness to Turkey undertake some responsibility to the extent of promising to use their influence with Greece to secure that these conditions are effectively carried out and maintained.

8. In order to make this decision as easy and palatable as possible to Turkey, it is essential that definite arrangements should now be agreed upon by the Powers, and communicated to the Porte, respecting the fate of the islands in Italian occupation. Italy having given the most solemn and unqualified assurances of her determination to withdraw from the islands as soon as the conditions of the Treaty of Lausanne have been fulfilled, the Porte could now be informed, if the Powers were to accept this solution, that they have decided that all these islands should revert to Turkey, subject to the introduction of a suitable form of autonomous administration under the Sultan's sovereignty, and to provisions regarding fortifications, &c., similar to those to be enforced in respect to the Greek islands.

9. His Majesty's Government trust the Powers will appreciate the conciliatory nature of this compromise, to which, contrary to their previously expressed strong preference for the allotting of all the Ægean islands to Greece, they now assent in the interest of an amicable understanding between the Powers, and which M. Venizelos may be urged to accept.

10. I request that you will make a communication in the above sense to the Government to which you are accredited, and urge upon them most earnestly the adoption of the course indicated, as the only one so far as His Majesty's Government can see that is likely to lead to a settlement of a question which, so long as it remains open, will be a standing menace to the peace of Europe and may even precipitate untoward events. It is this apprehension that is the sole motive of His Majesty's Government in making a suggestion to the Powers and urging it upon their consideration at this moment.

Sir Edward Grey to Sir E. Goschen
Foreign Office, December 12, 1913

Sir,

THE German Chargé d'Affaires called on the 5th December and stated to Sir E. Crowe that his Government supported the Austro-Hungarian proposal that if the South Albanian Delimitation Commission had unanimously agreed upon a frontier line, such line should be considered as definitely accepted by the Powers, and not be subject to further modification at the instance of any of the several Governments concerned.

In reply, Sir E. Crowe said that it seemed most unlikely that any Government would, given the actual situation, wish to alter a line on which all their delegates had agreed. On the other hand, he did not see what object could possibly be served by insistence on now laying down categorically in advance that whatever the delegates did must be automatically approved.

Herr von Kühlmann thought that Austria-Hungary's object was to secure that a definite frontier should be fixed at the earliest possible date, in order to hold Greece to the obligation, laid upon her by the Ambassadors' conference, to evacuate Albania by the 31st December. On this point also the German Government supported the Austro-Hungarian demand.

Sir E. Crowe told him of the dilemma in which the Powers were placed by the series of propositions made to-day by the Austro-Hungarian Ambassador to Sir A. Nicolson. Herr von Kühlmann expressed surprise on hearing that Austria-Hungary objected to the employment of an international force to keep order in Southern Albania.

Sir E. Crowe expressed it as his personal opinion that it was not wise to insist on the withdrawal of the only force which could and did keep order in the district, before there was any other force to replace it, and said he could not at all understand this feverish anxiety for the withdrawal of the Greeks by 1st January, whatever happened to the unfortunate natives, if, as both Austria-Hungary and Italy declared, and as Herr von Kühlmann confirmed, those two Powers were quite determined to avoid, if possible, sending in their own troops. There could be no doubt that whenever the six Powers formally demanded the evacuation of Albania, the Greeks would withdraw. But whether this was on the 31st December or some later date seemed to Sir E. Crowe really of minor importance from the Albanian point of view.

Herr von Kühlmann suggested that the Austro-Hungarian Government were adhering to the date of the 31st December because that was the actual date fixed by the Ambassadors' conference. Sir E. Crowe, however, pointed out to him that what the Ambassadors decided was that the evacuation should take place within one month of the termination of the labours of the frontier commission. It was unnecessary again to go into the question as to who was to blame for the fact that the commission started a month later than had been arranged. It was anyhow certain that their labours had not terminated on the 30th November, and that some time must even now elapse before they were completed. Therefore it was altogether incorrect to say that it would be contrary to the Ambassadors' decision if evacuation were to take place later than the 31st December.

Sir E. Crowe made it clear, however, that his observations were quite personal, and said that he would submit Herr von Kühlmann's communication to me and that I would of course bear it in mind in dealing with Count Mensdorff's declaration.

I am, &c.,
E. Grey

Sir Edward Grey to the German Chargé d'Affaires
Foreign Office, December 15, 1913

SIR EDWARD GREY presents his compliments to the German Chargé d'Affaires, and with reference to Herr von Kühlmann's memorandum of the 6th November respecting the project of the National Bank of Albania, has the honour to state that this subject has received his careful consideration.

As Herr von Kühlmann is aware, it has been Sir E. Grey's view that the so-called Provisional Government at Vallona was not competent to grant definite concessions engaging the economic future of the entire country, of which it controls only a small part. That body, as its self-chosen title indicates is in any case not the definitive Government of Albania, a country whose separate existence is due to the Six Great Powers, and which was at the time when the concession in question was granted, subject to the control of an International Commission already designated and on its way to take up its duties. The Provisional Government of Vallona must have been well aware, moreover, that, in alloting unauthorised concessions, it was acting against the wishes of a large majority of the population. Much opposition to the Provisional Government has, in fact, been created by this very action.

It was in view of these considerations that Sir E. Grey had sent to the British delegate on the International Commission the instructions of which Herr von Kühlmann was informed in Sir E. Grey's memorandum of the 20th November.

Sir E. Grey has seen no cause to modify this view on perusal of the terms of the draft concession, which in its present form appears to him a decidedly one-sided and onerous proposal for the conceding State.

After due consideration of this document he has informed Mr. Lamb that His Majesty's Government remain of the opinion that no concession granted by the Provisional Government can be considered valid unless and until it has been examined and approved by the Commission of Control. Such examination can only be conducted on the principle of considering what is most advantageous for the new Albanian State. If, in the light of this principle, Mr. Lamb considers that the proposed bank should be internationalised, he is authorised to support a proposal to that effect.

The specific points set forth in Herr von Kühlmann's memorandum of the 6th November appear to Sir E. Grey to be subsidiary to the main question. As under the draft concession exclusive rights are granted for the whole of Albania, there would be no necessity, if its validity were recognised, to apply for special authority to extend its operation to Scutari.

In regard to Herr von Kühlmann's allusion to the open door, Sir E. Grey is not prepared to accept the statement that the National Bank is the only existing financial institution in Albania, firstly, because that institution is not yet in legal existence, and secondly because he understands that the branch of the Imperial Ottoman Bank at Scutari is still open.

The assumption of the German expert bankers, to whom Herr von Kühlmann refers, that no other banks will be inclined to enter the field may be said to depend for its validity largely upon the question whether the present draft concession is or is not confirmed, since Article 11 of that concession established in favour of the concessionnaire group a practical monopoly in regard to all financial and industrial enterprise in Albania.

Sir Edward Grey to Sir F. Bertie
Foreign Office, December 24, 1913

Sir,

THE Italian Ambassador read to Sir E. Crowe on the 18th December a long telegram from his Government urging His Majesty's Government to agree in principle and at once to a condition put forward by the Prince of Wied to Italy and Austria as a preliminary to his acceptance of the rulership of Albania. This condition was the guarantee of a substantial loan to Albania by the Powers, without which no proper government of the country could possibly be organised. His Excellency was instructed to say that if this proposal was not accepted—and that in reasonable time—Austria and Italy would feel constrained to proceed in the matter jointly without the other Powers.

Sir E. Crowe said that there was no doubt much to be said for an immediate loan guaranteed by the Powers, a procedure which had been adopted in the case of Crete. If rather more definite proposals were properly put before His Majesty's Government, Sir E. Crowe had no doubt they would give them their best consideration.

Sir E. Crowe pointed out, however, that it was a somewhat curious procedure on the part of the Prince to address Austria and Italy alone in making a demand which all the Powers were expected to meet, and which clearly required their assent and active co-operation. Sir E Crowe added that His Majesty's Ambassador at Berlin had already been instructed to suggest to the Prince that, when negotiating respecting the conditions on which would depend his acceptance of the offer made by the Powers jointly, it would seem only right and correct that His Highness should himself lay his conditions before all the Powers, instead of asking Austria and Italy alone.

You should enquire of the Government to which you are accredited how this proposal is viewed by them.

I am, &c.,
E. Grey

Sir Edward Grey to Sir E. Goschen
Foreign Office, December 24, 1913

It is true that six weeks ago the Roumanian Minister for Foreign Affairs told His Majesty's Minister at Bucharest, in very vague and general terms, of certain conditions on which Prince of Wied would accept Albanian throne, but His Majesty's Government clearly could not be expected to recognise Roumanian Government on that account as official channel of Prince's wishes.

Italian Ambassador has now communicated to me in greater detail proposals for a loan, stating that these proposals were put forward on behalf of the Prince of Wied. The British Government cannot, however, accept the position that, in communications between them and the Prince, the Italian or any other Government should serve as an intermediary. We shall therefore discuss any proposals made through Italian Government as being put forward by that Government on its own responsibility.

The Six Great Powers have done themselves the honour to make a formal offer of the Throne of Albania to the Prince of Wied, and his reply and any conditions he may wish to attach to acceptance should be communicated direct by him to those Powers.

It appears to His Majesty's Government all the more necessary to emphasise this point of view, as they understand the Austro-Hungarian and the Italian Governments wish to make their participation in proposed loan depend, among other things, on the recognition or confirmation of a concession which Ismail Kemal has been induced to grant to an Austro-Italian group for a banking monopoly in Albania. The terms of that concession are now under discussion in the Commission of Control, where it has been subject to criticism as being adapted to benefit concessionnaires at the expense of the Albanian State, and likely to create a kind of Austro-Italian mortgage over the country.

This being a matter in the settlement of which all the Powers represented in the Commission of Control have a right to be heard, it would not, in the opinion of His Majesty's Government, be proper to make it the subject of a bargain between the Prince and one or two of the Powers in connection with a loan which they are all asked to guarantee jointly.

I do not want to get into a separate discussion with the Prince of Wied, and shall therefore communicate these views to the Italian Government when necessary, but if Prince of Wied approaches you again you can inform him of substance of first paragraph of this telegram. You should explain our whole view to the German Government when there is a suitable opportunity.

Sir Edward Grey to Sir F. Bertie
Foreign Office, January 6, 1914

Sir,

M. CAMBON came to see me to-day on his return from Paris.

I told him the reply from the Triple Alliance about the southern frontier of Albania. A further reply was expected shortly about the Ægean islands, and there were indications that this reply would be favourable as regards the islands in Greek occupation, but would perhaps not be so satisfactory with regard to the islands in Italian occupation. As to these latter islands, it was true that we could not at once have a date fixed for the Italian withdrawal, so as to connect it with the negotiations as to the southern frontier of Albania, but I considered that we could not make a peremptory communication in Athens, insisting upon the acceptance by Greece of the Southern Albanian frontier, and her evacuation of territory to the north of it, without also making a communication to her about the islands in her occupation which would be more or less satisfactory. If I was pressed for a reply to the communication that the Triple Alliance had now made about the southern frontier of Albania I would reply in this sense.

M. Cambon said that this was entirely the view of his Government, who thought that the question of the southern frontier of Albania must be connected with a settlement of the Ægean islands question satisfactory to Greece. He heard that the authorities in Vienna were much preoccupied about the state of things in Southern Albania, where there were said to be 60,000 or 70,000 armed Greeks. The Prince of Wied had suspended his acceptance of the post of Prince of Albania until the country had been pacified and a loan guaranteed. Greece might very well ask, in connection with the withdrawal of her troops, what the

Powers were going to do to prevent anarchy in the district evacuated by her.

I added to this that I heard it was physically impossible for the Greek troops to be withdrawn from some districts in the middle of the winter. I thought, however, that these were difficulties with regard to which Italy and Austria might be asked to make suggestions.

M. Cambon said that Italy was now going to claim some compensation for all her expenses in the islands in her occupation. Italy wished this to take the form of a concession in the region of Adalia.

On this I said that, as he knew, I could not agree to admit any sphere of interest, but, as regards this particular concession, I opposed it only in the interests of the Smyrna-Aidin Railway Company. As we ourselves were not going to apply for new railway concessions in that part of Asia Minor, which was a field almost entirely covered now by French and German railway concessions, I should disinterest myself in the negotiations in Constantinople for the Italian concession, if the Italians succeeded in satisfying the Smyrna-Aidin Railway Company.

I am, &c.,
E. Grey

Sir Edward Grey to Consul-General Lamb
Foreign Office, January 6, 1914

I am authorising His Majesty's Minister at The Hague to join his colleagues in making suggested communication to Netherlands Government.

As regards date for evacuation of Southern Albania, 18th January is contemplated, but proposed joint communication by the six Powers to press this date upon Greece can only be made when they have come to an agreement respecting the fate of the islands in Greek occupation, and a reply from the Powers of the Triple Alliance about the islands is expected shortly, but has not yet been received.

Consul-General Lamb to Sir Edward Grey
Vallona, January 6, 1914

ANXIETY is being caused by Young Turk intrigues alluded to in my despatch No. 1 of the 2nd January. Armed bands are believed to be on the way from Constantinople.
Essad Pasha having ostensibly rejected Young Turk proposals, landings will be probably attempted here and at Medua. At present Ismail Kemal is believed to be in connivance, but Essad may very probably be awaiting a propitious moment to utilise this as a pretext for resuming his interrupted move against the Government of Vallona. In any case situation is perplexing, and may become critical.

Sir Edward Grey to Sir F. Bertie
Foreign Office, January 12, 1914

Sir,

I TRANSMIT herewith to your Excellency a copy of a despatch from His Majesty's Ambassador at Berlin, enclosing a letter from Herr von Jagow which covers copy of a letter from Prince William of Wied, stating the conditions on which His Serene Highness would be prepared to accept the Throne of Albania.

The question whether His Majesty's Government should join in guaranteeing a loan to Albania involves grave parliamentary considerations, and I have referred the matter to the Cabinet. Meanwhile, however, since the communication in question has been received from the Prince, it appears to me advisable that the French, Russian, and British Governments should consider what reply should be returned thereto, on the supposition that a loan will be sanctioned.

In regard to the seven points formulated by the Prince, the first seems superfluous, since the offer of the Throne of Albania conveyed to him by the Powers must necessarily also cover their "approval" of his candidature. If, however, the Prince desires a second approval, the Powers could of course meet his wishes.

As to the second point, it is not, in my opinion, for the Powers to organise Albanian deputations. The throne is offered by the Powers, and the Prince must do what he thinks fit to satisfy himself as to the feeling of the Albanian people.

On the third point I would observe that there seems to me no reason whatever why the Powers should give a special guarantee for the good behaviour of Essad Pasha, nor are they in a position to give such a guarantee if they would.

Passing to the fourth point, it is a new condition that the loan must necessarily be issued on a 4 per cent basis. It appears to me doubtful whether the Powers can pledge themselves on this point. All the details of the loan must depend, among other considerations, on the state of the money market at the time of issue.

As to the fifth point, I doubt whether His Serene Highness is wise to stipulate at once for a definite civil list. The amount thereof will have to bear some proportion to the national income, which is at present an unknown factor.

The sixth and seventh points of the Prince's conditions seem to me to be reasonable.

Your Excellency should communicate the foregoing views to the Government to which you are accredited, and say that, subject to their concurrence, I would propose to reply to the seven points in this sense.

I would also suggest that something definite should be said as to the importance of not prejudging the question of the seat of the proposed Central Government. The Prince would, in my opinion, be well advised to avoid committing himself on this point before he has had an opportunity of judging the situation for himself on the spot; and, from this point of view, he would do well to proceed to the present seat of the Commission of Control, and not to Durazzo. His Serene Highness may possibly convince himself that neither Vallona nor Durazzo, but Scutari, would be the most suitable selection for his capital.

I am, &c.,
E. Grey

Consul-General Lamb to Sir Edward Grey
Vallona, January 21, 1914

    Mutessarif of Berat reports that, on the withdrawal of Greek regular troops, several of these villages were occupied by bands which began to persecute Mussulman population, part of whom took refuge on this side. Exasperated by this, Albanian volunteers crossed the border and occupied village of Lavdari. Local authorities ask whether evacuation de facto without any notification justifies them in advancing to protect lives and property. I am inclined to think it does, but question is delicate in view of smallness of our force.

Sir Edward Grey to Sir F. Elliot
Foreign Office, January 21, 1914

Sir,

M VENIZELOS came to see me this morning.

He said that he had discussed in Rome a certain exchange as regards details of the frontier of Southern Albania. He proposed, when the Powers communicated their decision about the frontier, to make it quite clear that he would accept this decision as it stood, but also to suggest the alteration that he had discussed in Rome.

I said that, having been the President of the meetings of Ambassadors, I could not propose any alteration of the decisions come to by the meetings, but I would not object to any alteration of the frontier of the south of Albania to which M. Venizelos could secure the assent of Austria and Italy.

M. Venizelos said that he would like to have the communication of the Powers about the southern frontier and the Ægean islands as soon as possible; and in accepting it he would like to state, not as a condition of Greek acceptance, but as a request to the Powers, that liberty of religion and schools should be granted to the Christian element in Epirus.

M. Venizelos said that he hoped it would be agreed that the Greek evacuation should be gradual.

I said that the Italians had complained bitterly of the proceedings of the Greek authorities. For instance, during the last day or two the Italian Ambassador had complained to me of the severe measures of disarmament taken against Mussulmans at Delvino. It was most important that the Greek authorities should avoid all acts of provocation which aroused Italian susceptibilities.

M. Venizelos then went on to discuss the question of a guarantee by the Powers of the Greek possession of the Ægean

Islands. If the islands were to be neutralised, Greece would be placed at some disadvantage in defending them; she could not fortify them or make preparations in advance for their defence. If, therefore, the Powers imposed the condition of neutralisation, it would be only fair that they should guarantee to Greece their peaceful possession. He had spoken of this to M. Tittoni, the Italian Ambassador in Paris. The latter had said that he thought his Government would consider this reasonable, and he had suggested that I might propose it.

I told M. Venizelos that I could not make this proposal. It would be for Greece to raise the question of a guarantee in her reply to the communication of the Powers. I would raise no objection on my part to her doing this, but I thought that it would be well for M. Venizelos to feel the ground in Berlin. If Greece asked for a guarantee, and the Powers did not agree to give it, the fact would be emphasised that no guarantee existed. If, however, he found that the German Government saw no objection to a guarantee, then I thought it probable that the Powers would agree to it, and Greece might ask for it in her reply to the communication that she would receive from all the Powers. I pointed out that, if there was to be a guarantee, it would have to be one by all the Powers. If France and we alone were to give a guarantee, or if some of the Powers gave a guarantee while other Powers abstained, there would be a division of the Powers into two parties, one for Turkey and one for Greece, and things would be thrown into confusion.

I am, &c.,
E. Grey

Sir Edward Grey to M. Cambon
Foreign Office, February 3, 1914

SIR E. GREY presents his compliments to the French Ambassador, and has the honour to state that His Majesty's Government have given careful consideration to the question of the establishment of neutral zones in the North Albanian-Servian frontier region.

Sir E. Grey recognises that until a decision has been reached as to the final attribution of the kaza of Gora and as to the line to be followed north of Dibra, there would be undoubted advantages in the creation of such zones, which would prevent the occurrence of frontier incidents and disputes, and would be a check on either Albanians or Servians, where they were in superior force, terrorising the weaker party. There are, however, difficulties of a practical nature in the way of such an arrangement. The chief of these difficulties arises from the necessity of securing the observance of the neutrality of the zones once it has been formally proclaimed by the Powers. In practice this could only be done effectively either by despatching troops of the Great Powers to occupy the zones or by sending consular officers to Dibra and Prisrend with instructions to see that the neutrality of the zone was maintained. Either of these courses appear to His Majesty's Government to be open to the grave objection that they would involve the Powers in serious embarrassments altogether incommensurate with the advantages to be reaped, and they consider it on all grounds more advisable to leave the situation as it is until the Delimitation Commission resumes its work in the spring.

Sir E. Grey would take this opportunity to observe that, in the opinion of the British delegate on the Delimitation Commission, the attribution of the kaza of Gora should, in view of the difficulty of basing a decision upon the wording of the resolution passed at the Ambassadors' meeting on the 14th April last, be made to depend on the result of a local enquiry into the religion and nationality of its inhabitants. In this view Sir E. Grey concurs.

The British delegate has raised a further point as to the meeting place of the commission when it reassembles in April next. As at present arranged, Sir E. Grey understands that it will reassemble at Scutari, and thence work eastward along the Montenegrin frontier, thus, in all probability, not reaching Prisrend till the end of May, or Dibra before the end of June. Colonel Granet suggests that it might perhaps be better for the commission to complete its work in the Dibra and Prisrend areas before beginning work on the western extremity of the frontier line, and that, in this case, Bari or Brindisi would be suitable as the meeting place.

Sir E. Grey is prepared to leave the decision on this point to the commission, who should be guided by local information as the time for reassembly approaches. If there were signs of the necessity for their presence between Ljuma and Prisrend, the delegates might meet at Bari or Brindisi and go to Dibra. Otherwise they might meet at Scutari as arranged.

Consul-General Lamb to Sir Edward Grey
Vallona, February 6, 1914

Sir,

IN continuation of the despatch No. 26 addressed to you yesterday by Mr. Harris, I have the honour to inform you that, according to reports received here from both private and official sources, the Greek attacks upon the Albanian villages on both sides of the border line are still continuing.

On Sunday, the 2nd instant, a Greek detachment approaching the large Mussulman village of Bolena proceeded to arrest a shepherd whom they encountered on its outskirts. The latter, having attempted to resist, was shot down. Three other shepherds who were grazing their flocks somewhat nearer to the village, and who were witnesses of the murder, seem to have fired on the Greeks (whether before or after they had themselves been fired on is not quite clear). Two of them were killed and the other wounded by the Greeks, who are now reported to have entirely destroyed the village by fire. […]

Sir G. Buchanan to Sir Edward Grey
St. Petersburgh, February 9, 1914

Minister for Foreign Affairs had not heard that French Government were proposing to reduce the amount below 75,000,000 fr. He would agree to this figure if accepted by France and England.

He thinks that all the Powers should be admitted to bank on an equal footing, and considers proposal to give Austria and Italy predominant position in it as unacceptable, and as contrary to the spirit of London protocol.

He has no definite views on subject of advance, and does not mind whether it is fixed at 20,000,000 or 30,000,000 fr.

He insists on proceeds of loan being handed over to International Commission, and on its expenditure being controlled by them. He is much annoyed at hearing that Austria and Italy have made the Prince an advance of 10,000,000 fr. on future loan. He suggested that we should consult French Government as to what we should do in consequence, as we cannot pass over such an incorrect proceeding in silence. At the same time he does not wish to take any action which might be used as a pretext by those two Powers for acting separately from the rest or acquiring a free hand in financing Albania.

Sir Edward Grey to Sir F. Bertie
Foreign Office, February 9, 1914

Sir,

WITH reference to your despatch No. 40 of the 22nd ultimo, I transmit herewith to your Excellency a copy of a telegram from His Majesty's Ambassador at St. Petersburgh containing the views of the Russian Government on some of the points raised by the Prince of Wied as conditions to his acceptance of the Throne of Albania.

Your Excellency will observe that the views of the Russian Government are far from fully expressed. They appear to be at one with His Majesty's and the French Governments in deprecating an attempt to fix in advance the rate of interest of the loan, but there is otherwise a considerable lack of precision in the Russian reply; no allusion is made to the amount of the loan nor to the question of the internationalisation of the Albanian Bank.

On this latter point further proposals, as it seems from Sir R. Rodd's telegrams Nos. 19 and 22 of the 30th January and the 3rd February respectively, may be expected from the Italian Government. I propose to await the receipt of these proposals in fuller detail, but it appears doubtful whether they will be acceptable.

In such an event it will be well for Great Britain, France, and Russia to be in full agreement respecting the line they intend to adopt in Albania generally, in regard to the question of the loan and the bank in particular, and I have accordingly to request that your Excellency will ascertain the views of the Minister for Foreign Affairs on the Russian reply and the points in question.

I am, &c.,
E. Grey

Sir Edward Grey to Sir M. de Bunsen
Foreign Office, February 10, 1914

Sir,

COUNT MENSDORFF informed me to-day that the Austrian Government were sending the reply, of which a copy is enclosed herein, to the French Government about the Albanian Bank.

Count Berchtold hoped that I would be able to accept the view contained in this reply.

I said that I did not wish to precipitate an unfavourable answer, and I would wait to hear what the French Government had to say; but I did not think that it would be fair to withhold from Count Mensdorff the fact that our view had been that there should be equal participation. If the French Government adhered to this view, we could not depart from it. Count Mensdorff instanced the precedents of the Morocco Bank and the Commission of the Debt in Constantinople as cases in which the Powers with special interests had special positions. On this I said that the special positions of France and Spain in Morocco had been recognised by agreements that preceded the establishment of the Morocco Bank. The Commission of the Debt in Constantinople had originally been arranged as it was, because at the time the greater part of the Debt was held by France and England. But internationalisation was the foundation on which the Albanian State was built; there was no privileged position on the Commission of Control, and to recognise a privileged position in connection with the State Bank would be a new departure.

Count Mensdorff urged that the State Bank was an economic affair. The concession had been obtained by the Austrian and Italian Banks, and it was natural that they should have a privileged position.

I observed that the concession had been obtained from Ismail Kemal, whose Government had been very partial and provisional, so much so that the obtaining of a concession for a permanent monopoly of this sort from such a Government was rather stealing a march upon other Powers.

Count Mensdorff said that it was necessary to make some progress, and that unless the Austrian and Italian Banks had acted, we should not now be able to discuss financial questions at all.

In reply to a remark of mine that I doubted whether the State Bank had been essential for Albania when the concession was granted, he assured me that the bank had been very useful.

I pointed out to Count Mensdorff, in answer to further pressure from him to accept the Austrian point of view about the internationalisation of the bank, that I should have difficulty in getting Parliament to agree to take an equal share of international liability with regard to the loan for Albania while having only an unequal share in the bank.

Count Mensdorff suggested that perhaps this might be met by the taking of a larger share of financial liability by Austria and Italy, but we did not pursue this suggestion.

I am, &c.,
E. Grey

Enclosure in No. 157.
Note communicated to French Government by Austrian Government.

THE point of view of the Austro-Hungarian Government is that, as during the conferences on the subject of the Albanian Statute, the Ambassadors reunion in London arrived at no decision concerning a future State Bank, the financial institutes of every country are at liberty to apply for the concession.

Taking their eminently important economic interests into consideration, Austria-Hungary and Italy have supported the steps taken by their banks in this respect at the Albanian Provisional Government, and are of opinion that the concession granted them by the Provisional Government is quite free of objection ("einwandfrei") and legal.

Nevertheless, to meet as far as possible the desire pronounced by France and the other Entente Powers, and to enable the Powers to work together in the interest of the new Albanian State created by the will of Europe, the Austro-Hungarian Monarchy and Italy are ready to enter into a compromise between their aforesaid own and the French point of view, which desires to internationalise the bank with an equal participation of all the Powers.

The Austro-Hungarian Government consents, therefore, to the principle of internationalisation, on the condition that a special position should be secured for Austria-Hungary and Italy in the State Bank, on account of their eminently superior interests in Albania created by their geographical position. (1) That a larger participation in the capital should be granted to the Austro-Hungarian and Italian concerns, i.e., 30 per cent. to each of them, and 10 per cent. to each of the other four Powers; (2) representation on the broad equivalent to the above-mentioned participation and the alternative chairmanship; (3) the sole direction of all the banking transactions and of the personnel.

Concerning the French proposal on the subject of the sphere of action of the International Commission of Control, the Austro-Hungarian Government is of opinion that this has been settled by the Ambassadors' Conference. Through the momentary exceptional situation in Albania this sphere has been temporarily enlarged, but it does not appear admissible that this extension should assume a permanent character. The installation of the Prince brings it to its natural end. The Austro-Hungarian Government had also only given their consent to this provisional extension on the condition that it should be temporary.

Sir M. de Bunsen to Sir Edward Grey
Vienna, February 16, 1914

Sir,

THE Prince of Wied arrived in Vienna from Rome early in the morning of the 13th February, and left again for Berlin the following evening. For some time past he has been strongly urged in the Vienna press to delay no longer his acceptance of the Throne of Albania and his installation in that country as its Sovereign. The money question has been represented as a very secondary one, and his Highness was repeatedly assured that, if only he would proceed to his principality, means would be found to supply him with the necessary funds. His presence at Durazzo was, indeed, all that was required to put an end to the dissensions between the various self-constituted Albanian authorities and to restore peace to the country.

Yielding to these appeals and similar ones from other quarters, His Serene Highness seems to have made up his mind to lose no more time in thinking the matter over. The financial difficulty was temporarily met by the promise of an Austro-Italian advance of 400,000 l. An Albanian deputation, led by Essad Pasha himself, was formed to proceed to Neuwied and invite the Prince on behalf of the Albanian people to accept the throne. The Prince, without waiting for the fulfilment of all the conditions on which he had at first insisted, started on his preliminary visits to Rome and Vienna. He has thus marked his sense of the special interest, over and above that of the other controlling Powers, which is taken by Italy and Austria-Hungary in the maintenance of an Albanian State as a buffer against the advance of Slavism to the Adriatic Sea.

The Prince was awaited at the Vienna station by representatives of the Albanian colony in this country, headed by the first dragoman of the newly constituted Austro-Hungarian Legation at Durazzo. Captain Heaton Armstrong, described as the Prince's private secretary, was also on the platform, with Colonel Mietzl, formerly of the North Albanian Frontier Commission, who had been appointed by the Emperor to be in attendance on the Prince during his stay in Vienna.

The Prince was greeted on arrival with Albanian cheers, which the newspapers have translated as "Long live the King of Albania!" His Serene Highness was accompanied by Herr Buchberger, an Austro-Hungarian consular officer, and by Signor Castoldi, both these gentlemen being described as members of his personal Cabinet. He proceeded in a Court carriage to the Imperial Hotel, where rooms had been reserved for him as the guest of the Emperor.

A lunch was given in his honour by Count Berchtold, Minister for Foreign Affairs, the German and Italian Ambassadors being also present, as well as the Prime Minister, Count Stuergkh, and several other Austrian Ministers.

His Serene Highness dined with the Emperor, meeting again the German Ambassador as well as Count Berchtold and a number of Court officials, but not this time the Italian Ambassador […].

Sir Edward Grey to Sir F. Bertie
Foreign Office, February 18, 1914

Sir,
    M. CAMBON told me to-day that M. Doumergue, having received the Austrian and Italian suggestion with regard to the loan to Albania of 60 per cent. participation for themselves and 40 per cent. for the other four Powers, reserving to Austria and Italy the control and management of the National Bank of Albania, still considered that there ought to be equal participation by the Powers. But he was anxious not to assume an obstructive attitude, and he was trying to find some way in which some satisfaction could be given to Austria and Italy. It was something gained that the principle of internationalisation was recognised. He thought it possible that some impartial English manager might be selected for the bank. As regards the powers of the Commission of Control, M. Doumergue agreed that, after the arrival of the Prince of Wied, the exceptional powers that the Commission had assumed when Ismail Kemal and Essad Pasha resigned would cease. On these and other questions connected with Albania M. Sazonof was anxious that agreement should be come to in London between the French and Russian Ambassadors and myself. M. Cambon therefore asked if he could see me with Count Benckendorff to-morrow.
    I arranged to do this.

I am, &c.,
E. Grey

Sir Edward Grey to Sir E. Goschen
Foreign Office, February 18, 1914

Sir,

THE Prince of Wied came to see me to-day.

I said that I was sure that, on the part of all the Powers, there was the greatest goodwill to him personally.

In the course of conversation, I took an opportunity of telling him that we had informed the Austro-Hungarian and Italian Governments that, in our opinion, the advance made by them, which was to be repaid out of a loan guaranteed by all the Powers, should be expended by arrangement with the International Commission of Control.

I also said that there were two main points at present being discussed between the Powers.

One of these was equal participation in the National Bank of Albania. I explained how, when I went to Parliament to get its consent to our joining the guarantee of the loan for Albania, I should be asked what British interest was involved which justified the assumption by the British Government of this financial liability. I should reply that it was an international obligation, because we were one of the founders of the State of Albania. But if we were not to have equal participation in the Albanian Bank, Parliament would ask why we should assume equal participation in the financial liability.

The second point was that the expenditure of all advances made to Albania, such as the existing one from Austria and Italy, should be controlled by the International Commission.

I went on to say that, in order that the discussion of these troublesome financial questions should be as little disagreeable as possible to the Prince of Wied, the discussion was being carried on between the Governments.

The Prince of Wied expressed great satisfaction and pleasure at the way in which he had been received by the King to-day.

He told me that he was going to Paris at once, and regretted that the length of time it would take to go to St. Petersburgh and back made it impossible for him to go there at the present moment, as he was to receive the Albanian deputation soon.

I said that, though there were many difficulties in connection with Albania, every thing that we heard from unofficial Englishmen who travelled there was in favour of the people. Under the Turkish rule the people had had no chance to develop their country, but I hoped that an independent State and the qualities of the people would enable it to be developed now. In any case, I understood that the people were attractive and the country picturesque.

I am, &c.,
E. Grey

Sir Edward Grey to Sir F. Bertie
Foreign Office, February 19, 1914

Sir,

M. CAMBON and Count Benckendorff came together to see me this morning.

M. Cambon said that he assumed that we all adhered to the view that there must be equal participation in the National Bank of Albania, and also that the expenditure of advances made to Albania should be controlled by the International Commission. After the arrival in Albania of the Prince of Wied, the Commission would retain the powers that it had originally, but it would give up the executive power that it had assumed since the resignation of Ismail Kemal and Essad.

I agreed to these propositions, saying that I thought the proper course would be for the Prince of Wied to consult with the International Commission as to the formation of an "autorité indigène," which would be the executive, the Commission of Control retaining the powers that had been assigned to it at the reunions in London. Without referring to the text of the resolution, I could not say exactly what these powers were.

Finally, I observed to M. Cambon that, as he was going to Paris for a few days, it might be well for him to discuss there with M. Doumergue what we were to do if Italy and Austria refused to agree to equal participation in the Bank of Albania and control of expenditure by the International Commission, and continued to advance money to Albania, perhaps making themselves the whole loan required by Albania. We need not discuss this to-day, but if the situation arose we should have to consider whether we should withdraw from Albania, or what our attitude should be.

M. Cambon and Count Benckendorff agreed that this was a question to be considered.

M. Cambon observed that there would be one lever to influence Italy, because Italy was very anxious not to be left alone with Austria in the Albanian question.

I am, &c.,
E. Grey

Sir Edward Grey to Sir M. de Bunsen
Foreign Office, February 19, 1914

Sir,

COUNT MENSDORFF informed me to-day, in reply to an observation that I had made some days ago, that, as the advance now made by Austria and Italy was to be repaid out of the loan to be guaranteed by the Powers, the expenditure of the advance should be under the control of the International Commission, that Count Berchtold had instructed him to tell me that Austria would agree to the expenditure of the advance being controlled in this way, if the Powers would agree that it should be repaid out of the loan. He thought, however, that an exception to this control should be that 80,000 l. of the advance should be placed at the disposal of the Prince of Wied for his personal use.

I said that I thought this might be agreed to. Even the 80,000 l. to be assigned to the Prince of Wied could be made the subject of a resolution by the Commission, that it should be paid to his civil list. But, of course, the Powers could promise that the advance should be repaid out of the loan to be guaranteed by them only when they were all prepared to join in the guarantee of the loan, and this, as far as some of us were concerned, depended upon equal participation in the National Bank of Albania.

Count Mensdorff again explained the necessity for Austria and Italy to have a special participation in the bank, and maintained that, being an economic thing, it did not give them a privileged political position.

I did not pursue the discussion, beyond expressing to Count Mensdorff the opinion that there ought to be equal participation in the bank, and that the expenditure of advances should be controlled by the International Commission. I added that the executive powers assumed by the Commission after the resignation of Ismail Kemal and Essad might cease when the Prince of Wied arrived in Albania. I thought the proper course would be that the Prince should, in consultation with the Commission, form a native Government, which would be the executive, and the Commission of Control would then exercise only such powers as had been assigned to it by the resolution of the reunion of Ambassadors in London last year.

I am, &c.,
E. Grey

Sir Edward Grey to Sir E. Goschen
Foreign Office, February 19, 1914

Sir,

    I TOLD the German Ambassador to-day the substance of my conversation with the Prince of Wied yesterday.

    I said that he had made a most favourable impression, and appeared to be one of the most amiable of men. As far as I could gather he had made this impression on everyone. I thought that it was an excellent thing that he had come here, and also that he was visiting Paris.

    The Prince had expressed himself with the greatest pleasure and satisfaction respecting his reception by the King.

I am, &c.,
E. Grey

Sir Edward Grey to Sir F. Bertie
Foreign Office, March 4, 1914

Sir,

THE French and Russian Ambassadors came to see me to-day, and, in the course of conversation, Count Benckendorff gave me the two memoranda of which copies are enclosed herein.

M. Cambon read to us the answer that M. Doumergue had given to the Austrian and Italian proposal of a 60 per cent participation for themselves, and other privileged conditions, in the Albanian National Bank. M. Doumergue had declined to accept these conditions, but had said that, outside these conditions, he was willing to examine what means could be found of satisfying Austrian and Italian interests as regards the bank. M. Cambon said that he had no idea what means could be found.

We then discussed the presidency of the bank.

They thought that Austria and Italy would object to each of the Powers having the presidency in turn for a year, but that the presidency of an Englishman might be accepted.

I said that I doubted whether it would be accepted, and we did not desire it. I could not propose it; but, of course, if the five Powers asked us if we could find some one of financial experience who would take the presidency of the bank, we would try to do so.

I added that I agreed with M. Doumergue's reply to Austria and Italy, and had no objection to raise to his proposal to find some means of satisfying Austrian and Italian interests, but I should like to know what he had in his mind.

I am, &c.,
E. Grey

Consul-General Lamb to Sir Edward Grey
Vallona, April 11, 1914

Sir,

I HAVE the honour to enclose herewith an abstract from a letter which I have received from Colonel Phillips concerning the state of affairs in the district of Scutari.

Colonel Phillips appears to anticipate more or less serious trouble early in May on both the Montenegrin and the Servian frontiers, and I am inclined to share his apprehension. The failure of the Powers to enforce their decisions in regard to Epirus against Greece can hardly fail to encourage Servia and Montenegro to increase their pretensions.

Colonel Phillips is also in agreement with myself in regard to the unfortunate effect of the Prince's action in allowing Essad Pasha to again concentrate all the power into his own hands.

As regards the question of refugees, I gather from a telegram which I received from Colonel Phillips yesterday that there is already a fresh influx into Scutari from the district south-east of Djakova, a fact which seems to justify the fear expressed in my telegram No. 66 of the 4th instant, that the Serbs were contemplating renewed "repressive action" in those regions.

I have, &c.,
Harry H. Lamb

Enclosure in No. 21
Abstract of Letter received from Colonel Phillips, dated Scutari, April 2, 1914

THE definite policy of Montenegro now seems to be to seize hold of every small incident, such as thefts or common assaults by Albanians on Montenegrins, to serve not only as an excuse for their proposed occupation of Hotti and Gruda, but also as a pretext for pushing on into Kastrati and Stoiya up as far as Vraka, in case the Klementi, Shkrielli, and Kastrati should assist Hotti and Gruda, as they undoubtedly will do, in their resistance. The Montenegrins are taking exactly the same line on the Obotti frontier also, doing everything they can to irritate the Albanians under cover of counter-accusations from their side. This question, as a whole, will be upon us, I suppose, in about six weeks.

The feeling against the new Cabinet is steadily increasing, and the hatred against Essad, I am convinced, is genuine and deep. Scutari will have none of him, and that, in my opinion, is the reason why you will have so much difficulty in choosing a Governor for Scutari. No nominee of Essad will stand a chance, and Essad, I imagine, will not allow anyone to be appointed who is not under his direct influence. There are even many rumours here of a combined rising against his rule. If Bib Doda definitely refuses the place offered him in the Cabinet and comes up to Scutari, he will find a powerful following ready to declare against Essad and the Turkish tendency. The Malissores, if not engaged in fighting Montenegro, will rally to him, with the exception of a few whom Essad subsidises. Krasnitchi, Gashi, and Puka would undoubtedly follow Bib, joining hands with Dibra and Matia.

Can you tell me what action I ought to take, as commander of the international troops, if after the establishment of a civil Government, the Montenegrins penetrate into Albania? It appears to me an interesting point

I suppose you have heard of the threatened movement of Albanians against Servia in May? I sincerely trust that nothing will come of it, for I have had enough of refugees. At present there seems to be every likelihood of a large number coming in from Hotti and Gruda before very long [...].

Sir Edward Grey to Sir F. Bertie
Foreign Office, May 5, 1914

Sir,

  THE French and Russian Ambassadors spoke to me to-day of the memorandum given by the Servian Minister as to a strategic frontier line in the neighbourhood of Prizrend and Dibra. The line at present went so close to these two places that the Albanians could positively fire into these towns from the heights near. It was only reasonable that the Servians should have the protection for which they asked.

  I said that my recollection was that, according to independent information, the violations of the frontier by Albanians, of which the Servians had complained, had arisen from the fact that, when the Servians evacuated Albanian territory in accordance with the decision of the Powers, they took with them the cattle belonging to the Albanians, and the Albanians had come over in pursuit of their cattle. There had been further trouble because the Albanians were denied access to places which had been allocated to Servia, but which were the natural markets for the Albanians to secure supplies. It seemed to me, primâ facie, quite reasonable that the Albanians should not have the heights that commanded Prizrend and Dibra, but, if this point was conceded, there ought to be a clear understanding that the Servians did admit the Albanians to the markets necessary to them for securing supplies.

I am, &c.,
E. Grey

Sir Edward Grey to Sir F. Bertie
Foreign Office, May 30, 1914

Sir,

I HAVE to request your Excellency to inform the French Government that His Majesty's Government have only recently received from the British delegate on the International Commission of Control the draft Organic Statute of Albania, M. Fromageot's criticism of which, no doubt based on an earlier version of the draft, was communicated to me by the French Ambassador at this Court on the 10th February last.

His Majesty's Government are disposed to agree generally with the views provisionally expressed by M. Fromageot, and would be glad to consider any suggestions which, on further examination of the draft as now finally submitted to the six Powers, the French Government may wish to make for giving practical effect to those views.

I understand that the Russian Government are also in communication with the French Government, respecting the draft statute, into which they propose to insert a clause dealing with the question of access by railway to the Adriatic which, under the terms of the resolution passed at the Ambassadors' conferences in London, is to be guaranteed to Servia. I have, in conversation with the Russian Ambassador at this Court, expressed my readiness to assent to such an addition, and I have no doubt that the French Government will be prepared to consider the suggestion favourably when preparing the amendments to be introduced into the draft statutes.

I am, &c.,
E. Grey

Mr. Lamb to Sir Edward Grey
Durazzo, May 31, 1914

Sir,

ALTHOUGH a considerable amount of mystery still surrounds the causes and circumstances of Essad Pasha's arrest, yet all that I have been able to gather on the subject from various sources seems to leave no doubt that the responsibility for the manner in which it was effected lay with the Austrians and Major Sluyss, the Dutch officer then in command of the town. An attempt to transfer this command to another officer on the previous afternoon had led to a violent altercation between the Austrian Minister, M. de Lowenthal, and Mufid Bey, the Minister who stood in closest relations with Essad.

There remains much doubt as to the extent to which the Prince himself was cognisant of what was being done in his name. Some persons, generally well informed, have assured me that no order for Essad's arrest was ever given by the Prince at all, but that it was the result of a plot between the Austrians and the Dutch, fostered by the Princess, who was frantically jealous of Essad's influence and power, and that the Prince was only moved to accept responsibility for the deed after it had been done. However that may be, it seems established that His Highness had not authorised the use of the guns. Both the Austrian officer who had directed their fire and Major Sluyss under whose orders he acted, found it necessary to leave Durazzo within the next few days. General de Weer and Commandant Thomson, the chiefs of the Dutch mission, were both absent at the time, the former at Tepelen and the latter at Vallona, where he had been ordered to remain in spite of his own request to be allowed to come to Durazzo on urgent business […]

Sir Edward Grey to Mr. Lamb
Foreign Office, May 31, 1914

Arrangement between the Epirotes and the Commission of Control.

Greek Government strongly urge that the agreement provisionally arrived at with the Epirotes should be formally approved and guaranteed by the six Powers. They assure His Majesty's Government that if this were done, and the agreement loyally adhered to by Albanian Government, the Epirotes could be relied upon to respect it faithfully and remain quiet.

I should be glad to have your views and advice.

Mr. Lamb to Sir Edward Grey
Durazzo, May 31, 1914

THE insurrectionary movement is gaining ground. Pekene has hoisted the Ottoman flag and Croya is threatened.

Failing European intervention, the new Ministry seems to be decided to attack the insurgents with a force of 5,000 Mirdites collected at Alessio.

I regard danger of civil and religious war with the greatest apprehension, but I see no other solution of the problem.

Sir Edward Grey to Sir R. Rodd
Foreign Office, June 1, 1914

    ITALIAN Ambassador here has repeatedly urged me to consent to associating His Majesty's Government in the despatch of an international contingent from Scutari to Durazzo. I would not, of course, raise any objection to any steps which other Governments may consider it desirable to take in the matter, but I could not sanction the despatch of a British contingent without consulting the Cabinet, who have only authorised the presence of British troops at Scutari. Other and further measures were not contemplated when these troops went to Albania, and I do not feel disposed at present to recommend that the sphere of their activities should be enlarged.

    If a crisis at Durazzo required some special measure of a temporary nature for the protection of the person of the Prince, we should send a ship if all the other Powers did so, but I do not consider that His Majesty's Government would or should themselves engage in a military occupation of Albania, of which the sending of British troops to Durazzo would be the first step.

Sir Edward Grey to Sir R Rodd
Foreign Office, June 4, 1914

YOUR telegram No. 88 of 2nd June.

If any communique is made it must be to the effect that His Majesty's Government, while not raising objection to any other Powers sending troops to Durazzo, do not propose themselves to take part in a military occupation of parts of Albania other than Scutari, but, if all the Powers who have ships in the Mediterranean decide to send ships to Durazzo, His Majesty's Government will send a ship to co-operate in protecting the person of the Prince.

Sir Edward Grey to Sir G. Buchanan
Foreign Office, June 4, 1914

Sir,

M. DE ETTER, in the course of his conversation with me to-day, remarked on the danger that would arise if Servia took matters into her own hands about Albania. He heard that she had threatened that she could not keep quiet if one or two Powers acted alone in Albania. He also asked me how I thought that Austria and Italy would get on if they were left alone in Albania.

I said that I thought they would get on badly. With regard to Servia, I thought that she ought to be told that, so long as the boundaries of Albania that had been settled internationally were observed, she had no occasion for interfering, whether it was one or two Powers or all the Powers who took action in Albania itself. Of course, if the Albanian frontiers were not observed, Servia would have to take measures in her own territory to protect herself; but I could not see that she had a case for taking action because of what went on internally in Albania, so long as the frontiers were not violated.

I am, &c.,
E. Grey

Sir Edward Grey to Sir R. Rodd
Foreign Office, June 4, 1914

Sir,

THE Italian Ambassador came to see me to-day about Albania, and prefaced his remarks by saying, with reference to our disinclination to send troops to Durazzo, that there had been in the past many things in connection with Albania which were obvious, but that it was not too late to amend. It was evident that he meant that things had been done by Austria and Italy which would naturally account for our disinclination to participate in Albanian responsibilities, but that, if we would continue our participation, we should have less cause for complaint in future.

The Ambassador went on to say, on the instructions of the Marquis di San Giuliano, that the Italian Government had endeavoured to keep between the two limits of the intervention of Europe and the activity of the two Adriatic Powers. Italy had always desired real internationalisation, and all that had happened had been a compromise between her views and those of the Austrian Government. They felt now that the Prince of Wied ought to be kept in Albania, and that the arrangements come to by the International Commission and M. Zographos about Epirus should be agreed to.

Finally, the Marquis di San Giuliano made an appeal to us to make proposals as to what we should be prepared to do in Albania, and to stipulate the conditions on which our proposals would be based. The Marquis di San Giuliano would do his best to get Austria to accept any reasonable conditions that we proposed.

I said that public opinion here would not be favourable to undertaking responsibility for Albania. For us to make proposals and stipulate conditions would be to propose a policy, and I could not undertake this responsibility. The sending of troops to Durazzo we regarded as the beginning of a military occupation of Albania. We knew by experience that to send a few troops meant being confronted with a demand to send more troops, and one thing led to another. I doubted whether, even if I recommended it to the Cabinet, they would agree to send British troops to Durazzo, and I was not disposed to recommend it. On the other hand, I felt that we had some responsibility to the Prince. One suggestion had been that we should send troops solely to protect the person of the Prince. We felt that this could be done as effectively by sending ships, and this course would be more convenient, as it was much easier to withdraw ships than troops. I had therefore telegraphed this morning to say that we would send a ship for the protection of the person of the Prince at Durazzo if all the other Powers who had ships in the Mediterranean were prepared to send one. By this I meant that, though we should be glad if Russia sent a ship, yet, as Russia had not joined in the naval demonstration or the occupation of Scutari, we should not make the abstention of Russia from sending a ship to Durazzo a reason for abstaining ourselves. In conclusion, I said that a condominium of six Powers was most difficult under the most favourable conditions; but if even one of the Powers worked against it, it becomes impossible; and I instanced the proceedings in connection with the Albanian Bank.

The Ambassador admitted my objections as regards the bank, but said that Italy could not always object to everything that Austria wished. He took a gloomy view of what might happen in Albania. He doubted if Italian public opinion would allow Italy to send troops to co-operate with Austrian troops alone; and, even if there were action by the two Powers alone, Servia had already intimated that, if action were taken by one or two Powers without the others, she would feel obliged to do something, and this might precipitate a European war.

I said that M. Grouich had said something of this sort in Belgrade, but I did not see that Servia had any concern in the matter, so long as the boundary of Albania, as laid down by international decision, was respected.

I am, &c.,
E. Grey

Sir Edward Grey to Sir R. Rodd
Foreign Office, June 5, 1914

Sir,

    WITH reference to my immediately preceding despatch of to-day, the Italian Ambassador called again on the 29th ultimo and read to Sir Arthur Nicolson a telegram from the Italian Minister at Durazzo describing the situation there in the blackest colours. The insurgents at Tirana, with 100 neighbouring villages, had, he said, proclaimed the Sultan and hoisted the "Koranic flag"; the position of the Prince was slated to be almost untenable; and the only hope of saving the situation was the despatch of international troops. Germany, however, had said that she would not move troops in view of the fact that His Majesty's Government abstained from doing so, and France declined unless all the Powers agreed to join.

    The Marquis di San Giuliano desired that the above should be communicated to His Majesty's Government. Sir Arthur Nicolson undertook to do so, but said that it was clear that so serious a step as sending soldiers to Durazzo could only be taken with the consent of the Cabinet. He added that, if the reports were not exaggerated as to the seriousness of the situation, it was clear to him that a mere military demonstration of 400 or 500 men at Durazzo would have no effect; while he could hardly imagine the British public seeing favourably a British contingent despatched to take hostile action against the tribes of Albania.

I am, &c.,
E. Grey

Sir Edward Grey to Sir R. Rodd
Foreign Office, June 5, 1914

Sir,

THE Italian Ambassador called on the 27th ultimo and read to Sir A. Nicolson a telegram from the Marquis di San Giuliano strongly urging, in view of the grave situation still existing at Durazzo, that an international contingent should be sent there from Scutari, and adding that the "insurgents" themselves desired it. He used the old arguments, and added, "as from himself," that His Majesty's Government might "lay down their conditions."

Sir A. Nicolson said that he could do no more than transmit to me the message from the Italian Minister for Foreign Affairs, and that his Excellency must remember that I was not able to come to any decision without consulting the Cabinet.

I am, &c.,
E. Grey

Sir Edward Grey to Sir F. Bertie
Foreign Office, June 10, 1914

Sir,

THE French Ambassador informed Sir A. Nicolson on the 27th ultimo that the Italian Ambassador had again appealed to him in regard to the despatch of international contingents from Scutari to Durazzo, and had added, "and you can lay down your conditions." This remark has given M. Cambon the idea that perhaps small detachments of, say, fifty men each could be sent on condition that the Italian and Austro-Hungarian Governments agreed to accord a thoroughly international character to the Albanian State Bank, and he thought the Italian Government should consequently endeavour to secure Austria's consent. M. Cambon, who evidently regarded this idea with much favour, was suggesting it to his Government. He pointed out that the Italian Government were anxious for the despatch of international detachments on the ground that the international character of the new State ought to be maintained.

Sir A. Nicolson made no comment on M. Cambon's proposal, but limited himself to observing that it seemed to him that the international character of Albania was sufficiently emphasised by the presence at Durazzo of the International Commission of Control.

I am, &c.,
E. Grey

Sir Edward Grey to Colonel Granet
Foreign Office, June 10, 1914.

    Question of whether "territoire de Goussigné" means "kaza" does not seem to arise, as Ambassadors' Conference did not assign "territoire" to Montenegro, but only the towns of Gustinje and Plava "avec leurs dépendances," which are described as bounded by the main mountain chain and the watershed between the Lim and the Drin. On the assumption that mountain of Kom is limit of Clementi country, the above line, starting from Kom, would presumably leave Vermoc in Albanian territory.

    You may put this reasoning before your French and Russian colleagues, and endeavour to secure a solution which will find general acceptance. Should, however, the result be to give Vermoc to Montenegro, you should insist on guarantees for Albanian inhabitants, as suggested in your telegram.

Sir Edward Grey to Sir F. Bertie
Foreign Office, June 15, 1914

Sir,

THE French and Russian Ambassadors came to see me together to-day.

I gave them a paraphrase of the telegram sent to Colonel Granet on the 11th May last about the frontier in the neighbourhood of Dibra and Prisrend.

M. Cambon showed me a map on which were marked the concessions that the French thought necessary for strategic reasons in the neighbourhood of Dibra and Prisrend. He said that it appeared that the district of Luma, which we had agreed at the Conference in London should go to Albania, was further west than had been supposed.

I said that I would inform Colonel Granet, with reference to my telegram to him of the 11th May, that I had been shown on the map the concessions to Servia which the French Government thought justifiable, and I would instruct him to discuss them on the map with his French and Russian colleagues, and tell me what he thought of them on the merits.

I am, &c.,
E. Grey

Sir Edward Grey to Sir E. Goschen
Foreign Office, June 15, 1914

Sir,

In speaking to-day with the German Ambassador of Albania generally, I said that possibly, if the Prince of Wied moved to Scutari, it might give him a position of more advantage, but I believed that Austria objected to this, and I did not intend to propose anything to which any Power objected.

The Ambassador said that he thought it would look rather like a flight if the Prince went to Scutari now.

I said that it might perhaps be a half-way house between staying in Durazzo and leaving Albania altogether.

I am, &c.,
E. Grey

Sir Edward Grey to Mr. Lamb
Foreign Office, June 25, 1914

AUSTRIAN and Italian Governments consider that the Powers should put Prince of Albania into a position to maintain and defend himself, and have accordingly proposed that Colonel Phillips should be authorised to form a military force recruited from Albanians. Officers of the international detachments at Scutari to be lent gratuitously by the Powers as instructors.

The force to be composed of 5 battalions of 500 men, 5 machine-gun detachments of 20 men each, and 4 mountain batteries of 100 men, constituting an effective total of 3,000 men. One officer of each international detachment at Scutari to instruct one battalion and one machine-gun party, while the Austrian and Italian detachments will also each provide instructors for two of the mountain batteries, unless the Powers wish to share this instruction proportionately.

Recruiting and composition of the battalions to be without distinction of race or religion.

Choice of officers and Albanian under-officers for the new force to be exclusively reserved for the Prince.

The two Governments consider that a force so organised should be sufficiently trained in eight or ten weeks to take the field and secure the Prince's position in the seaports and suppress risings of small importance.

Expenses of instruction and equipment, except expenses of the foreign instructors, to be at the cost of the Albanian Government, under control of the International Commission.

I understand that it is not proposed that the British and foreign officers shall leave Scutari with this force, when trained; their function will be that of instructors at Scutari only, and I see no primâ facie objection to this, but I cannot acquiesce in imposing a duty upon Colonel Phillips without first knowing whether he considers it reasonable or practicable.

Please telegraph your opinion of this proposal, and whether you consider it is practicable.

Colonel Phillips has been informed.

Sir Edward Grey to Sir M. de Bunsen
Foreign Office, June 26, 1914

Sir,

I HAVE to inform your Excellency that the Austro-Hungarian Ambassador called at this Office on the morning of the 19th instant to ask whether any decision had been arrived at in regard to the Austrian proposal that the British admiral should be authorised, if the necessities of the case called for it, to open fire on the insurgents should the latter advance on Durazzo. His Excellency was informed that the orders sent to Rear-Admiral Troubridge, were that he was not to take action of any kind without express authority from His Majesty's Government. Count Mensdorff said that perhaps in certain circumstances His Majesty's Government would authorise fire being opened on the insurgents, but he was told that there was no likelihood of His Majesty's Government giving such authority.

As your Excellency is aware, the Austrian proposal is in point of fact met by the instructions which have now been sent to the British admiral at Durazzo that a force may be landed temporarily to rescue the Prince and his family and the International Commission, especially Mr. Lamb and his staff, and to secure their being safely conveyed on board ship, but must not be landed to give permanent protection on shore.

It must be remembered that His Majesty's Government were no party to the arrest and deportation of Essad Pasha, which seems to have started the general disturbance, and cannot be expected to make war on the insurgents.

I am, &c.,
E. Grey

Sir Edward Grey to Mr. Chilton
Foreign Office, July 22, 1914

Sir,

THE Netherlands Minister spoke to me to-day with anxiety about the Dutch officers in Albania. He did so without instructions, but it was evident that his Government were considering the question of whether they should not be advised to resign and withdraw. He also asked me about the sending of Roumanian troops, and the situation generally.

I told him how matters stood with regard to Roumanian troops, and the possible instruction of an Albanian force at Scutari. I admitted that things in Albania were very unsatisfactory, and I said that I was sure the Powers of Europe would not wish them to be made still worse by the withdrawal of the Dutch officers.

I am, &c.,
E. Grey

Mr. Chilton to Sir Edward Grey
The Hague, July 22, 1914

Sir,

THE Minister for Foreign Affairs sent for me to-day as he wished to talk to me about the position of the Dutch officers in Albania.

M. Loudon said he had spoken to several of the officers who had been home on leave, including Colonel de Veer, and that they were all of the opinion that it was impossible for them to fulfil the object of their mission in Albania, viz., the organisation of a gendarmerie, if the present state of affairs continued. His Excellency said that not one of these officers had for one moment suggested the idea of abandoning their work and coming home nor did he himself wish to suggest that they should return. They had been seconded from the army for a certain time and that was their own affair.

What his Excellency wanted to impress upon me was the uselessness of their remaining in Albania accomplishing nothing and with, he thought, very little hope of being able to accomplish anything unless things took a turn for the better. If the Prince of Albania were able to suppress the insurgents, the Dutch officers might get a chance, but if His Highness was obliged to leave the country, Essad Pasha might return, and Essad did not like the Dutch officers and would not make their work easy for them.

M. Loudon told me that one of the Dutch officers, who had been in Albania, had said to him that if only the Great Powers would land 2,000 men to help them something might be done.

His Excellency added that his Government had given their permission for the officers to go to Albania, and they were not going to ask for their recall, but he begged me to ask you whether the members of the Commission of Control could not be given a hint to suggest to the Albanian Government that the Dutch officers should be sent home if it were found impossible for them to carry out their work.

His Excellency said that he had talked to the Austrian and Italian Ministers in the same sense, and that he was going to see the French and German Ministers and the Russian Chargé d'Affaires to-day.

The two officers who had been taken prisoners and were being kept as hostages were being well-treated [...]

Sir Edward Grey to Mr. Lamb
Foreign Office, July 28, 1914

Sir,

TURKHAN PASHA called and saw Sir A. Nicolson on the 17th instant. He showed him a telegram from Durazzo recounting all that was passing in Epirus and calling upon the Powers to intervene at Athens. Sir A. Nicolson told him that the Greek Government absolutely denied all connivance at the movement, and that His Majesty's Government believed in M Venizelos's good faith. Turkhan Pasha evidently thought them very naïve. He said that M. Venizelos had been an employé under him when he was Governor-General in Crete, and that though he recognised his ability he did not trust him any more than he trusted any other Greek; and he had occasion to know the Greeks because he had been educated in Greek schools. He considered it ridiculous to assert that a few Greek deserters alone were taking part in the advance in Epirus, with all its attendant excesses. Guns and thousands of men did not desert, and it was clear that it was a regular Greek force which was engaged. If M. Venizelos were really sincere he could easily stop the movement. Turkhan Pasha warned Sir A. Nicolson that what was passing in Epirus would have most serious consequences, not only in Albania but throughout the Balkans, as it could not be imagined that Servia would remain quiescent. She would also endeavour to get her pickings out of Albania, and then Bulgaria would move. The solution of the question lay in London.

Sir A. Nicolson denied this. He said that Turkhan Pasha should speak at Vienna and Rome where he would find the original creators of Albania. His Majesty's Government would not send British troops into Albania, but they were ready to agree to a force being trained at Scutari; they would not object to foreign troops being employed if the Powers wished to do so; they would be ready to undertake their share of a guarantee of a loan if the difficulties as to the bank were arranged between Paris and Vienna. In short, His Majesty's Government placed no obstacles in the way of any measures in the interest of Albania on which the Powers might agree, but the initiative did not rest with them. Turkhan Pasha seemed depressed. He said he was leaving London at once.

I am, &c.,
E. Grey

Resolution of the London Conference on the Independence of Albania

The Ambassadors of the Great Powers meeting in London had initially decided that Albania would be recognized as an autonomous state under the sovereignty of the sultan. After much discussion, however, they reached a formal decision that Albania, though deprived of almost half of its ethnic territory (esp. Kosovo), would be a sovereign state Independent of the Ottoman Empire. This decision, reached at the fifty-fourth meeting of the conference on 29 July 1913, was formulated briefly in the following eleven points and provided the basis for the international recognition for Albanian independence:

1. Albania is constituted as an autonomous, sovereign and hereditary principality by right of primogeniture, guaranteed by the six Powers. The sovereign will be designated by the six Powers.
2. Any form of suzerainty between Turkey and Albania is excluded.
3. Albania is neutral; its neutrality is guaranteed by the six Powers.
4. The control of the civil administration and finances of Albania is to be given over to an International Commission composed of the delegates of the six Powers and one delegate from Albania.
5. The powers of this commission will last for ten years and may be extended if necessary.
6. The commission will be charged with preparing a draft for the detailed organisation of all branches of the

administration of Albania. Within six months, it will present to the Powers a report on the results of its work and its decisions on the administrative and financial organization of the country.

7. The sovereign is to be nominated within six months. Until his designation and until the formation of a definitive national government, the activities of the existing local authorities and the gendarmerie will be controlled by the International Commission.

8. Public order and security will be assured by the international organisation of a gendarmerie. This organisation will be in the hands of foreign officers who will exercise effective command in the gendarmerie.

9. These officers will be selected from the Swedish army.

10. The mission of the foreign officers and instructors will not interfere with the unity of service, or with the employment of native commissioned and non-commissioned officers and gendarmes.

11. The salaries of these officers may be ensured from the revenue of the country as guaranteed by the Powers.

[Translated from the French by Robert Elsie.]

Biographical Notes

AEHRENTHAL, Count. *See* LEXA VON AEHRENTHAL
AKERS-DOUGLAS, Aretas (1876-1947). British diplomat posted to Montenegro (1911-1914).
BARCLAY, Colville, Sir (1869-1929). British diplomat posted to Serbia (ca. 1913).
BAX-IRONSIDE, Henry, Sir (1859-1929). British diplomat and ambassador to Bulgaria (1911-1915).
BENCKENDORFF, Alexander Konstantinovich, Count (1849-1917). Russian diplomat and ambassador to Great Britain (1903-1917).
BERCHTOLD, Leopold, Count (1863-1942). Austro-Hungarian diplomat. He was ambassador to Russia (1906-1911) and later Austro-Hungarian foreign minister (1912-1915).
BERTIE, Francis, Sir (1844-1919). British ambassador to France (1905-1918).
BETHMANN-HOLLWEG, Theobald von (1856-1921). Chancellor of the German Empire (1909-1917).
BUCHANAN, George William, Sir (1854-1924). British diplomat and ambassador to Russia (1910-1917).
BUCHBERGER, Carl (1887-1974). Austrian diplomat who served Prince Wilhelm zu Wied in Albania in 1914.
BURNEY, Cecil, Admiral (1858-1929). British military figure who commanded the international forces that occupied Shkodra in 1913.
CAMBON, Paul (1843-1924). French diplomat and ambassador to Great Britain (1898-1920).
CARNEGIE, Andrew (1835-1919). Scottish-American industrialist and philanthropist.
CARTWRIGHT, Fairfax Leighton, Sir (1857-1928). British ambassador to Austria-Hungary (1908-1913).

CASTOLDI, Fortunato, Captain (1876-1961). Italian diplomat who served Prince Wilhelm zu Wied in Albania in 1914.

CRACKANTHORPE, Dayrell E. M. (ca. 1871-1950). British diplomat. He was chargé d'affaires at the British legation in Belgrade on the eve of the First World War. He later served as British Ambassador to Serbia.

CROWE, Eyre, Sir (1864-1925). British diplomat who was considered the leading expert on Germany at the British Foreign Ministry.

DANEFF, Dr. *See* DANEV, Stojan.

DANEV, Stojan (1858-1949). Bulgarian political figure and prime minister (June-July 1913). He was the Bulgarian representative at the London Conference.

DE BUNSEN, Maurice, Sir (1852-1932). British diplomat and ambassador to Austria (1913-1914).

DE ETTER, Nikolai S. (1865-1935). Russian diplomat and counsellor at the Russian Embassy in London (1905-1915).

DE FLEURIAU, Aimé-Joseph (1870-1938). French diplomat and ambassador to Great Britain (1824-1933).

DE GIERS, *See* VON GIERS, Mikhail Nikolayevich.

DE SALIS, John Francis Charles, Count (1864-1939). British diplomat and ambassador to Montenegro (1911-1916).

DE VEER, Willem, Colonel (1857-1931). Dutch military figure and head of the Dutch military mission in Albania (1913-1914)

DERING, Herbert Guy, Sir (1867-1933). British diplomat and counsellor at the British Embassy in Rome (1911-1915).

DOUGHTY-WYLIE, Charles, Colonel (1868-1915). British military figure and diplomat. During the Balkan Wars he led a Red Cross unit in the Turkish army.

DOUMERGUE, Gaston (1863-1937). French political figure and foreign minister (1913-1914).

ELLIOT, Francis, Sir (1851-1940). British diplomat and ambassador to Greece (1903-1917).

ESSAD PASHA. *See* TOPTANI, Essad Pasha.

FERID PASHA (1853-1923). Ottoman diplomat and political figure of Albanian origin.

FROMAGEOT, Henri (1864-1949). French diplomat, lawyer and judge.

GAUTSCH VON FRANKENTHURM, Paul, Baron (1851-1918). Austrian political figure and prime minister of Cisleithania (1911).

GENNADIUS, Ioannes (1844-1932). Greek diplomat and ambassador to Great Britain (1910-1918).

GESHOV, Ivan Evstratiev (1849-1924). Bulgarian political figure and prime minister (1911-1913).

GOSCHEN, William Edward, Sir (1847-1924). British diplomat. He served as ambassador to Austria-Hungary (1905-1908) and to Germany (1908-1914).

GRANET, Edward John, Colonel (1858-1918). British military attaché in Rome (1911-1915).

GREY, Edward, Sir (1862-1933). British political figure. He served as foreign secretary from 1905 to 1916.

GROUITCH, Slavko. *See* GRUJIĆ, Slavko.

GRUJIĆ, Slavko (1871-1937). Serbian diplomat. He served as chargé d'affaires and head of the Serbian legation in Great Britain (1908-1914).

GUESHOFF. *See* GESHOV, Ivan Evstratiev.

HEATON-ARMSTRONG, Duncan, Captain (1886-1969). Irish-Austrian military figure. He served as the private secretary to Prince Wilhelm zu Wied in Albania in 1914.

IMPERIALI, Guglielmo, Marquis (1858-1944). Italian diplomat and ambassador to Great Britain (1910-1920).

ISWOLSKY. *See* IZVOLSKY, Alexander.

IZVOLSKY, Alexander (1856-1919). Russian diplomat. He served as foreign minister (1906-1910) and ambassador to France (1910-1917).

KEMAL, Ismail. *See* VLORA, Ismail Qemal bey,

KHEMAL, Ismael. *See* VLORA, Ismail Qemal bey,

KRAJEWSKI, Léon Alphonse Thadée (1863-1931). French diplomat and member of the International Control Commission in Albania in 1913.

LAMB, Harry Harling, Sir (1857-1948). British diplomat. He served as British consul-general in Salonika (1907-1913) and thereafter consul-general in Vlora and the British member of the International Control Commission in Albania in 1913.
LEONI, Alessandro (1852-1918). Italian diplomat and member of the International Control Commission in Albania in 1913.
LEXA VON AEHRENTHAL, Alois, Count (1854-1912). Austrian foreign minister (1906-1912).
LIBOHOVA, Mufid Bey (1876-1927). Albanian political figure, He served as minister of the interior in the first provisional government of Ismail Qemal bey Vlora in November 1912, then as foreign minister and briefly as prime minister (1913-1914). He was the Albanian member of the International Control Commission in Albania in 1913.
LICHNOWSKY, Karl Max, Prince (1860-1928). German diplomat and ambassador to Great Britain (1912-1914).
LOUDON, John (1866-1955). Dutch diplomat and foreign minister (1913-1918).
LÖWENTHAL VON LINAU, Heinrich, Ritter (1870-1915). Austro-Hungarian envoy to the court of Prince Wilhelm zu Wied.
MENSDORFF-POUILLY-DIETRICHSTEIN, Albert Viktor Julius, Count (1861-1945). Austro-Hungarian diplomat and ambassador to Great Britain (1904-1914).
MIETZL VON STENDE, August (1869-1918). Austro-Hungarian military figure. He served as a member of the northern Albanian border commission in 1913.
MIŞU, Nicolae (1858-1924). Romanian diplomat and ambassador to Great Britain (1912-1919?).
MUFID BEY. *See* LIBOHOVA, Mufid Bey.
NAZIM PASHA (1848-1913). Ottoman military figure. He was chief of staff of the Ottoman military during the First Balkan War.
NERATOV, Anatolii Anatolyevich. Deputy and acting foreign minister of Russia (ca. 1911-1913).

NICHOLAS, King of Montenegro (1841-1921). Sovereign prince of Montenegro (1860-1910) and king of Montenegro (1910-1918).

NICOLSON, Arthur, Sir (1849-1928). British diplomat and ambassador to Russia (1906-1910) and thereafter permanent under-secretary for foreign affairs (1910-1916).

O'BEIRNE, Hugh James (1866-1916). British diplomat. He served as counsellor and later minister at the British Embassy in Russia (1906-1915).

PAGET, Ralph, Sir (1864-1940). British diplomat and ambassador to Serbia (1910-1913).

PASHITCH, PACHICH, PASITCH, PASSICH. *See* PAŠIĆ, Nikola.

PAŠIĆ, Nikola (1845-1926). Serbian political figure and prime minister (1909-1911, 1912-1918).

PËRMETI, Turhan Pasha (1839-1927). Albanian political figure. Under Prince Wilhelm zu Wied, he served as prime minister of Albania from March to August 1914.

PETRIAEF, Aleksandr Mihajlovič (1875-1933). Russian diplomat and member of the International Control Commission in Albania in 1913.

PETROVIĆ Aristoteles (1868-19??). Austro-Hungarian consul in Vlora and member of the International Control Commission in Albania in 1913.

PETROVITCH, Aristoteles. *See* PETROVIĆ Aristoteles.

PHILLIPS, George Fraser, Colonel (1863-1921). British military figure. He was head of the International Administration in Shkodra from October 1913 to the withdrawal of the forces in 1914.

PICHON, Stéphen (1857-1933). French diplomat and foreign minister (1906-1911, 1913)

POINCARÉ, Raymond (1860-1934). French political figure. He served as prime minister and foreign minister (1912-1913) and as the president of France (1913-1920).

POPOVIĆ, Evgenije (1842-1931). Montenegrin political figure. He served as consul general in Rome (1900-1917).

POPOVITCH. *See* POPOVIĆ, Evgenije.

RODD, Rennell, Sir (1858-1941). British diplomat and ambassador to Italy (1908-1919).

RUSSELL, Odo William Theophilus (1870-1951). British diplomat and counsellor at the British Embassy in Austria-Hungary (1909-1915).

SAN GIULIANO, Marquis di. Antonino Paternò-Castello (1852-1914). Italian foreign minister (1905-1906, 1019-1914).

SAZONOF, SAZONOFF, SAZONOW. *See* SAZONOV, Sergey.

SAZONOV, Sergey (1860-1927). Russian diplomat and foreign minister (1910-1916).

SKOULOUDIS, Stephanos (1838-1928). Greek diplomat. He served as the Greek representative at the London Conference in 1913.

THOMSON, Lodewijk, Major (1869-1914). Dutch military figure and second-in-command of the Dutch Military Mission in Albania (1913-1914). He was the principal military advisor to Prince Wilhelm zu Wied.

THURN UND VALSÁSSINA-COMO-VERCELLI, Duglas, Graf von (1864-1939). Austro-Hungarian diplomat and ambassador to Russia (1911-1913)

TITTONI, Tommaso (1855-1931). Italian diplomat He served as foreign minister (1903-1909) and ambassador to France (1910-1916).

TOPTANI, Essad Pasha (1863-1920). Albanian political figure. He set up a government administration of his own in Durrës (October 1913-January 1914) and later served as minister of war and minister of the interior under Prince Wihelm zu Wied (March-May 1914).

TURKHAN PASHA. *See* PËRMETI, Turhan Pasha.

VENIZELOS, Eleftherios (1864-1936). Greek political figure and prime minister (1910-1920).

VLORA, Ekrem Bey (188-1964). Albanian political figure. He served in 1912 as a senator under Ismail Qemal bey Vlora, his father's cousin.

VLORA, Ismail Qemal Bey (1844-1919). Albanian political figure. He declared Albanian independence in Vlora on 28 November 1912 but resigned in January 1914, transferring his authority to the International Control Commission.

VOJNOVIĆ, Lujo (1864-1951). Montenegrin diplomat. He served as a delegate to the London Conference (1913).

VOINOVITCH, Count. *See* VOJNOVIĆ, Lujo.

VON GIERS, Mikhail Nikolayevich. Russian diplomat and ambassador to the Ottoman Empire (-1914).

VON JAGOW, Gottlieb (1863-1935). German diplomat. He served as ambassador to Italy (1909-1913) and foreign minister (1913-1916).

VON KIDERLEN-WAECHTER, Alfred (1852-1912). German diplomat and Secretary of State at the German Foreign Ministry (1910-).

VON KÜHLMANN, Richard (1873-1948). German diplomat and counsellor at the German Embassy in London (1908-1914).

WIED, Wilhelm, Prinz zu (1876-1945). German prince and monarch of Albania (March-September 1914).

WINCKEL, Julius, Dr (1857-1941). German diplomat. He served as the German consul-general in Albania and the German member of the International Control Commission in Albania in 1913.

Books Published in the Series "Albanian Studies," Edited by Robert Elsie (available on www.amazon.com)

Volume 1
Tajar Zavalani, *History of Albania*. Albanian Studies, Vol. 1. London: Centre for Albanian Studies, 2015. ISBN 978-1507595671. 356 pp.

Volume 2
Robert Elsie, *Albanian Folktales and Legends*. Albanian Studies, Vol. 2. London: Centre for Albanian Studies, 2015. ISBN 978-1507631300. 188 pp.

Volume 3
Robert Elsie, *The Albanian Treason Trial (1945)*. Albanian Studies, Vol. 3. London: Centre for Albanian Studies, 2015. ISBN 978-1507709511. 347 pp.

Volume 4
Robert Elsie, *Gathering Clouds: The Roots of Ethnic Cleansing in Kosovo and Macedonia – Early Twentieth-Century Documents*. Second expanded edition. Albanian Studies, Vol. 4. London: Centre for Albanian Studies, 2015. ISBN 978-1507882085. 245 pp.

Volume 5
Robert Elsie, *Tales from Old Shkodra: Early Albanian Short Stories*. Second edition. Albanian Studies, Vol. 5. London: Centre for Albanian Studies, 2015. ISBN 978-1508417224. 178 pp.

Volume 6
Robert Elsie, *Kosovo in a Nutshell: A Brief History and Chronology of Events*. Albanian Studies, Vol. 6. London: Centre for Albanian Studies, 2015. ISBN 978-1508496748. 120 pp.

Volume 7
Robert Elsie, *Albania in a Nutshell: A Brief History and Chronology of Events*. Albanian Studies, Vol. 7. London: Centre for Albanian Studies, 2015. ISBN 978-1508511946. 94 pp.

Volume 8
Migjeni, *Under the Banners of Melancholy. Collected Literary Works*. Translated from the Albanian by Robert Elsie. Albanian Studies, Vol. 8. London: Centre for Albanian Studies, 2015. ISBN 978-1508675990. 160 pp.

Volume 9
Robert Elsie and Bejtullah Destani (ed.). *The Macedonian Question in the Eyes of British Journalists (1899-1919)*. Albanian Studies, Vol. 9. London: Centre for Albanian Studies, 2015. ISBN 978-1508696827. 312 pp.

Volume 10
Berit Backer. *Behind Stone Walls: Changing Household Organisation among the Albanians of Kosovo*. Edited by Robert Elsie and Antonia Young, with an introduction and photographs by Ann Christine Eek. Albanian Studies, Vol. 10. London: Centre for Albanian Studies, 2015. ISBN 978-1508747949. 329 pp.

Volume 11 (in German)
Franz Baron Nopcsa, *Reisen in den Balkan. Die Lebenserinnerungen des Franz Baron Nopcsa*. Eingeleitet, herausgegeben und mit Anhang versehen von Robert Elsie. Albanian Studies, Vol. 11. London: Centre for Albanian Studies, 2015. ISBN 978-1508953050. 638 S.

Volume 12 (in German)
Robert Elsie, *Handbuch zur albanischen Volkskultur: Mythologie, Religion, Volksglauben, Sitten, Gebräuche und kulturelle Besonderheiten*. Albanian Studies, Vol. 12. London: Centre for Albanian Studies, 2015. ISBN 978-1508986300. 484 S.

Volume 13 (in French)
Jean-Claude Faveyrial. *Histoire de l'Albanie*. Edition établie et présentée par Robert Elsie. Albanian Studies, Vol. 13. Londres:

Centre for Albanian Studies, 2015. ISBN 978-1511411301. xxiv + 530 pp.

Volume 14
Margaret Hasluck. *The Hasluck Collection of Albanian Folktales*. Edited by Robert Elsie. Albanian Studies, Vol. 14. London: Centre for Albanian Studies, 2015. ISBN 978-1512002287. 474 pp.

Volume 15
Ali Podrimja. *Who Will Slay the Wolf. Poetry from Kosovo*, edited and translated by Robert Elsie. Albanian Studies, Vol. 15. London: Centre for Albanian Studies, 2015. ISBN 978-1514100301. 163 pp.

Volume 16
Robert Elsie. *Keeping an Eye on the Albanians. Selected Writings in Albanian Studies*. Albanian Studies, Vol. 16. London: Centre for Albanian Studies, 2015. ISBN 978-1514157268. 556 pp.

Volume 17 (in German)
Michael Schmidt-Neke. *Über das Land der Skipetaren: Buchbesprechungen aus 25 Jahren*. Herausgegeben von Robert Elsie. Albanian Studies. Vol. 17. London: Centre for Albanian Studies, 2015. ISBN 978-1514737705. 413 pp.

Volume 18
Robert Elsie. *Classical Albanian Literature: A Reader*. Albanian Studies, Vol. 18. London: Centre for Albanian Studies, 2015. ISBN 978-1515132769. 248 pp.

Volume 19
Edith Durham. *Twenty Years of Balkan Tangle*. Second Edition. Edited by Robert Elsie. Albanian Studies, Vol. 19. London: Centre for Albanian Studies, 2015. ISBN 978-1515310440. 253 pp.

Volume 20
Edith Durham. *High Albania*. New edition, edited and introduced by Robert Elsie. Albanian Studies, Vol. 20. London: Centre for Albanian Studies, 2015. ISBN 978-1516996766. 297 pp.

Volume 21
Edith Durham. *The Burden of the Balkans*. New edition, edited and introduced by Robert Elsie. Albanian Studies, Vol. 21. London: Centre for Albanian Studies, 2015. ISBN 978-1516996827. 255 pp.

Volume 22
Edith Durham. *The Struggle for Scutari (Turk, Slav, and Albanian)*. New edition, edited and introduced by Robert Elsie. Albanian Studies, Vol. 22. London: Centre for Albanian Studies, 2015. ISBN 978-1517209506. 249 pp.

Volume 23
Edith Durham. *Through the Lands of the Serb*. New edition, edited and introduced by Robert Elsie. Albanian Studies, Vol. 23. London: Centre for Albanian Studies, 2015. ISBN 978-1517209643. 241 pp.

Volume 24
Johanna Jutta Neumann. *Escape to Albania: Memoirs of a Jewish Girl from Hamburg*. With an introduction by Michael Schmidt-Neke. Edited by Robert Elsie. Albanian Studies, Vol. 24. London: Centre for Albanian Studies, 2015. ISBN 978-1517749774. 166 pp.

Volume 25 (in German)
Robert Elsie (Hrsg.). *Albanische Volksmärchen*. Albanian Studies, Vol. 25. London: Centre for Albanian Studies, 2016. ISBN 978-1532901959. 390 pp.

Volume 26
Thirty Agas Were Conversing: Albanian Heroic Verse. A bilingual edition translated by Robert Elsie and Janice Mathie-Heck. Albanian Studies, Vol. 25. London: Centre for Albanian Studies, 2016. ISBN 978-1534729841. 320 pp.

Volume 27
The London Conference and the Albanian Question (1912-1914): The Dispatches of Sir Edward Grey. Edited by Bejtullah Destani and Robert Elsie. Albanian Studies, Vol. 27. London: Centre for Albanian Studies, 2016. ISBN 978-1535304726. 361 pp.

Printed in Great Britain
by Amazon